"MEN HAVE BEEN DUPED ABOUT SEX."
—Bernie Zilbergeld

THIS BOOK SHOWS HOW, WHY AND WHAT CAN BE DONE ABOUT IT.

Male Sexuality is a new book by an outstanding clinical psychologist who has specialized for years in sex therapy for men.

Male Sexuality deals with the physical and emotional aspects of sex for men; its aim, the enhancement of male sexuality and the discarding of unrealistic and unworkable sexual attitudes and stereotypes.

Male Sexuality: "If I could have only one book on male sexuality, I'd want this one, and not just because there aren't many in the field. It's the best."

—Ford Lewis, *Sacramento Bee*

MALE SEXUALITY

A Guide to Sexual Fulfillment

BERNIE ZILBERGELD, Ph.D.

With the assistance of John Ullman

BANTAM BOOKS
NEW YORK · TORONTO · LONDON · SYDNEY · AUCKLAND

MALE SEXUALITY:
A GUIDE TO SEXUAL FULFILLMENT
A Bantam Book / published by arrangement with
Little, Brown and Company

PRINTING HISTORY
Little, Brown edition published January 1978
Selection of Playboy Book Club May 1978
Bantam edition / December 1978

Published simultaneously in the United States and Canada

Bantam Books are published by Bantam Books, a division of
Bantam Doubleday Dell Publishing Group, Inc. Its trademark,
consisting of the words "Bantam Books" and the portrayal of a
rooster, is Registered in U.S. Patent and Trademark Office and
in other countries. Marca Registrada. Bantam Books, 666 Fifth
Avenue, New York, New York 10103.

PRINTED IN THE UNITED STATES OF AMERICA

RAI   20   19   18   17   16   15   14

For my father,
who was both father and mother
and gave far more than he knew

Contents

Acknowledgments

This book began as a combined effort by me and John Ullman. We had been working with men at different places in San Francisco—John at Fort Help, I at the Human Sexuality Program, University of California Medical Center, and in private practice—and decided to pool our resources. The book was to have been one of the products of our collaboration. Unfortunately, because of the illness of his wife, John was unable to do as much as he had hoped. As his wife's condition deteriorated, it became clear to both of us that the project could not proceed as anticipated and that I would have to complete it on my own.

The finished work is substantially different from the one John and I envisioned. As new chapters were written and old ones revised, I relied more and more on my own experience and knowledge. Although the final version is my own work, and I assume full responsibility for any errors and stupidities, I want to acknowledge John's contributions. He shared in the original planning of the book, wrote parts of Chapter 9, and contributed some of the material I used in Chapters 1, 5, 7, and 12. He also read my early drafts with care and made many helpful suggestions. I regret that we could not write the book as we had planned and at the same time am grateful for the assistance he gave me.

Many other people gave valuable help.

A few friends and colleagues were there from the beginning, reading the entire manuscript, correcting errors, and giving perspective and support. My thanks to Lonnie Barbach, Jackie Hackel, Bruce Heller, Lillian Rubin, and especially to Carol Rinkleib, as loving a friend and critical an unofficial editor as I could ever ask for.

My thanks to the following people who read portions of the manuscript and/or made suggestions regarding some of the ideas in it: Bob Badame, Harvey Caplan, Bob Geiger, Seymour Freedman, Linda and Bernard Gore, Jose Gutierrez, Linda Janowitz, Sue Knight, Don Linker, Jay Mann, Kate Mollinoff, Ann Spence, Lynn Stanton, Douglas Wallace, and Joyce Welsher.

Everyone in the sex field owes much to three individuals who built the foundation on which the rest of us stand. They fought the battles, cleared the way, and made it easy for those of us who followed. Although I take issue with them in several places, it's an honor to acknowledge my debt to Alfred Kinsey, William Masters, and Virginia Johnson.

I was fortunate in having an excellent agent, editor, and copyeditor. They were all there when I needed them and gave me plenty of help. My thanks to Rhoda Weyr, Bill Phillips, and Mike Mattil.

Last, I owe a special debt to the men and women from whom I learned in therapy, workshops, classes, and talks. Though I was their therapist, teacher, or speaker, I probably learned as much from them as they did from me. In sharing their experiences with me, some of which are recounted in the book, they gave me the understanding and knowledge to better help others.

Bernie Zilbergeld

1

Men and Sex

A common myth in our culture deals with the supposed sexual differences between men and women. According to this bit of fantasy, female sexuality is complex, mysterious, and full of problems, while male sexuality is simple, straightforward, and problem-free.

Part of women's complexity—still following the myth —is due to their equipment. In contrast to men, who have only one sexual organ, women have several; moreover, clitorises and vaginas aren't very visible. Then, too, women have some, well, peculiar attitudes about sex. They seem always to be talking about feelings, tenderness, communication, and relating. What these things have to do with sex is often unclear to men. And women want to go about sex in interesting ways. They don't seem to desire it as much as men and, even when they do, they require endless amounts of gentleness and foreplay, and still take forever to reach orgasm. And they have no end of problems in, and requirements for, sex. They need to feel certain ways to get in the mood; they require stimulation done in a very precise manner; they have pain with intercourse; they have difficulties reaching orgasm or the right kind of orgasm; and when it's all over, it's still not over because then they need cuddling and talking and relating. On the other hand, however, there is the puzzling situation, one which many men have experienced and most others have at least heard about, where a woman gets totally out of control, wanting more sex than any sensible man could supply and acting like a crazed beast, moaning and shrieking through endless orgasms, mocking her man's inability to keep up.

It's clear, then, that women are a bit strange, and it's a good thing there are so many books and articles coming out on female sexuality. Somewhere in one of them must be the answers to what women are about sexually, and how a man can better understand them.

In contrast, the myth goes, men are very simple creatures when it comes to sex. They have no special requirements, they are almost always ready and willing, and their only problem is how to get enough of it. Men's equipment is the essence of simplicity. A man's sexuality is concentrated in one place and there it is, hanging out for all the world to see. What could be mysterious about anything that obvious and what more would anyone need to know about it? A man's sexual tastes are easy, too. He will, as the old maxim has it, take it any way he can get it, but what he really wants to do is stick it in and hump away until he has an orgasm, with as little tenderness, communication, and relating as possible. Of course, given the fact that few women are willing to put up with this kind of behavior anymore, most men are willing to do some foreplay to get their ladies ready and to try to hold off orgasm until their partners have had one of their own.

According to this myth, then, there is quite a lot to be learned about female sexuality—about why women think and act as they do sexually and how their many, mysterious problems in this area can be dealt with— but little or nothing to be learned or said about men and sex. The males, after all, are so simple and quite content as long as they're getting enough.

The myth may appear ridiculous the way we've stated it, and of course it is, but you'd be surprised how many people believe it. It is erroneous in almost every point it makes. Men are neither so simple nor content as we have been led to believe. Moreover, at this point we know much less about male sexuality than about female sexuality.

We started working with men six years ago in two large clinics in San Francisco. At first, we did sex therapy only with couples but soon developed group and individual formats for men without partners and men whose partners refused to participate in treatment. It was not surprising that all the men who came for therapy were dissatisfied with their sex lives. But two factors about them greatly impressed us. By and large, they were normal, healthy men; only a few could be called neurotic or seriously disturbed. It became clear that you didn't have to be psychologically impaired to have sexual difficulties. The other interesting factor was the rigidity with which the men clung to certain rules as to how sex should be and how a man should act in sex. We began to wonder where they had gotten these rules and why they held to them so tenaciously.

Then we also started working with men who had no sexual problems. We gave talks, classes, and workshops on sex, sensuousness, assertiveness, social skills, communication skills, and forming more meaningful relationships. Even though some of these were not intended to deal specifically with sex, sex always came up and we kept hearing the same things again and again. Most men were not satisfied with their sexuality and most wanted to learn more about it. The real shocker, however, was that those without specific sex problems believed in the same set of sexual rules as those with problems, though perhaps not quite as rigidly.

Our observations regarding male discontent and problems were confirmed by the observations and studies of others. Herbert Hendin, for example, in his excellent study of college students, *The Age of Sensation,* noted that sex problems had become one of the main reasons college men came for therapy. And this was the younger generation, thought by so many of us over thirty to be free of sexual troubles. In a survey of over 52,000 people by *Psychology Today,* 55 percent of the men said they were dissatisfied with their sex lives and 39 percent admitted to various problems such as disinterest in sex and premature ejaculation.

We were impressed by both the widespread prevalence of specific sexual problems and the even greater sense of dissatisfaction. All was not as well with men and sex as had been supposed.

If what we are saying is valid, how is it that so many of us believe the opposite, that men are sexually content?

One of the chief reasons is that men have been, and to a large extent still are, extremely secretive about their sexuality. They may joke about sex, talk a lot about this or that woman's characteristics and how they'd like to get her in bed, and make many allusions to their sexual prowess, but, other than these bits of bravado, most men simply don't talk about sex to anyone.

One of the cornerstones of the masculine stereotype in our society is that a man is one who has no doubts, questions, or confusion about sex, and that a real man knows how to have good sex and does so frequently. For a man to ask a question about sex, thereby revealing ignorance, or to express concern, or to admit to a problem is to risk being thought something less than a man.

Almost every man tends to think that all other men are having a better time sexually than he is, with none of the worries or questions that he has (the men in the *Psychology Today* survey guessed that only 1 percent of their peers were virgins, a bad miscalculation since the actual percentage of virgins in that sample was 22). This reinforces his idea that it's best to keep his mouth shut. How would it look, being the only guy on the block who comes too fast or who isn't having much sex or who isn't enjoying it as much as he thinks he should?

So men learn to fake it. They can't fake erections, but we know of more than a few who fake orgasms. But the main things they fake are their feelings. They pretend to be confident when they're not, to know when they don't, to be comfortable when they're uneasy, to be interested when they couldn't care less, and to enjoy when they feel otherwise. The cost of this deception is horrendous. It keeps men from being honest with either men or women, thus preserving the illusion that men have no doubts or questions or concerns about sex, which in turn makes it harder for any other man to voice misgivings or problems.

Another factor that generates a false picture about male sexuality is the sheer quantitative discrepancy between what has been said and written about female sexuality and growing up female on the one hand, and what has come forth about men on the other. A whole literature has appeared on what it's like to be a girl and woman—physically, socially, sexually, and politically—much of which has sensitively portrayed the trials and tribulations, both major and minor, that any growing up and interacting with humans entails. Since much less has been said and written about men, the impression is conveyed that women have many more problems than men and that it must be very easy to be male in this society, especially when it comes to sex.

But, as we have said, men really do have concerns about sex, even though they may try to pretend that this isn't so. What follows is a presentation of the kinds of sexual interests and attitudes expressed by the men we talk to.

Almost all have questions about their sexuality, about how they feel and function, and how they can make sex better for themselves and their partners. They are not content with the knowledge they have acquired; many have questions about what other men are like and whether their own thoughts and behaviors are all right. They wonder about such things as: "Do other men do it like I do?" "Do they also worry if their penises are adequate?" "Does everyone get as nervous as I do when I make it with a new woman?" "Are my fantasies really OK?" "Am I some kind of nut for not wanting sex sometimes or for not liking oral (or anal or group) sex?" They want to know more, to expand and enhance their sexuality, even though they may have only a vague idea of what this might mean.

Other men say they have relatively good sex but wonder if they're missing something. Sex is pleasant, but not quite what it was cracked up to be—the earth doesn't move, bells don't ring, trumpets don't blow—and, when it's over, they still have to walk the dog and pay the bills. Sex just hasn't united them with the cosmos or changed their lives in any way. Is it possible, they ask, that there is some new position, partner, practice, or gimmick that would bring sex up to expectation?

Another attitude is represented by the surprising responses to a question we frequently ask at talks and workshops: "How many men have felt, at least at times, that sex was a burden?" In most instances, at least 30 percent of the men admitted to that feeling, and many times over half of them did. From some of them, as well as from some of the clients we see in sex therapy, come statements that a few years ago were heard only from women: "It feels like work some of the time, like a duty, but I try my best because I want to keep my wife happy." "I often don't enjoy it much but I feel I owe it to her. Besides, if she doesn't get what she wants from me, she might get it somewhere else."

Sex feels more like work than fun to these men. They have so much to do—initiating, getting their partners turned on, orchestrating the whole event, making sure their partners are satisfied, and, finally, finding their own satisfaction. And theirs is the responsibility; they believe they are accountable if their partners don't have orgasms or if the experience is lacking in any way. All the publicity of the last few years about female sexuality, especially about women's "need" for sexual fulfillment and multiple orgasms, has served primarily to increase the dimensions of what these men see as their duty and also to increase their concerns about what might happen if they don't perform well. These men wonder if there are ways of making sex more enjoyable, of making it less work and responsibility and more fun.

And some men have problems that trouble them greatly. The types of problems vary considerably: lack of interest; difficulty getting or maintaining erections; ejaculating faster than they or their partners desire;

inability to get what they want in sex (a much more common problem among men than has been appreciated); and a lack of feeling, although the ability to function may be unimpaired. Older men, and men with serious illnesses or injuries, are often concerned about the effects of aging or physical disability on their sexual expression.

Men who have any of these concerns or problems spend much time and energy worrying about themselves, wondering if there is any help for them or if their manhood, as they are wont to call it, is slipping away. Some give up sex altogether, so greatly do they fear another failure or finding out that things aren't the way they used to be. Others blame the problem on their partners, thus attempting to find release from the fears that haunt them. And still others play musical beds, vainly searching for the magical woman with whom all will be well.

This book is intended for men in all categories—for those who want to learn more about their sexuality, those who want to get more out of sex, those who are looking for ways to integrate sex into their lives in ways consistent with their own values and feelings, and those who want some specific skills for dealing with problems they are experiencing. These categories are not as disparate as they may sound; the principles and methods for dealing with them are quite similar. Change in one area often also means changes in the other areas.

While the book is primarily intended for heterosexual men and employs a heterosexual idiom, much of the material and most of the techniques have been used with equal success by ourselves and others with homosexual men. Gay readers will, of course, have to translate some of our words into language more appropriate to their own situations.

This book is also for women. Many women have told us of their ignorance of male sexuality and their desire to learn more. Because of their candid conversations with other women and the wealth of reading material on female sexuality, they know a lot about women and sex but not nearly as much as they'd like about men's attitudes and experiences with sex.

Even in a book of this length we could not cover everything, so we chose the topics and techniques that we found to be the most interesting and beneficial to the men we have talked to and worked with in enhancing their sexuality and resolving specific problems.

We begin with a discussion of what men learn about sex. Our thesis is that the rules and concepts we learn are destructive and a very inadequate preparation for a satisfying and pleasurable sex life. As incredible as it may sound to you now, we believe that men have been duped about sex. They have accepted unrealistic and, in fact, superhuman standards by which to measure their equipment, performance, and satisfaction, thus ensuring a perpetual no-win situation. Whatever men do, it's somehow not enough, not when compared to the standards they learned. Without a doubt, this learning is the source of most of our sexual discomforts and problems. It prevents us from resolving whatever problems we encounter and also hinders us in our search for sexual expression that is a true reflection of ourselves.

Having a better sex life is in large measure dependent upon your willingness to examine how the male sexual mythology has trapped you. After coming to grips with your learning and expectations, you are in a position to change, and much of the book is devoted to material and techniques that will give you the opportunity to experience different ways of being and behaving sexually.

There are chapters on discovering and asserting your sexual needs and desires; the physical side of sex; touching; masturbation; relaxation and sex; the uses of sex and sex problems (what at first seems like a problem is sometimes a solution to another problem); dealing with partners; and female sexuality. There is also a chapter on sex and aging and another on sex and medical conditions; these chapters are not as specialized as they sound and are intended for all men. The difficulties that older men and disabled men have with sex are really not so different from the difficulties that the rest of us experience. For men with erection problems, there is a three-chapter package, and there is a similar unit for men who want to develop better ejaculatory control. Even if you do not have either of these concerns, you may find it interesting to read the first chapter in each of these units.

Series of exercises are presented in most of the chapters. Readers whose interest is only in obtaining information may be content reading and not doing any of the exercises. Those desiring to make changes in their behavior, however, will want to do the exercises. Behavior change is difficult to accomplish without the development of new skills, and the purpose of the exercises is to help you develop new skills and understanding. And many of them can be fun as well.

The material and exercises are presented in the order that has proved most effective in our experiences working with men. The exercises themselves are arranged so that you always start with ones that are relatively simple and easy to do, gradually working up to ones that are more complex. As we discuss throughout the book, going slowly and being comfortable with what you're doing are essential ingredients for a good sex life.

In a workshop, class, or therapy, the leader or therapist tries to tailor his material to the specific requirements of the individuals involved. This is not easily done in a book, however, since the writer can have only a general idea of who his readers will be. Consequently, a much broader approach must be used so that readers can choose from a variety of sources to fashion their own programs. Some men will want to do most of the exercises, some will do fewer, and others will do only those in one or two chapters. The best guide we can offer is to tell you to do what fits your interests and situation. Some of the exercises and suggestions may strike you as irrelevant to your life or too easy. Start where you like. However—and this is an extremely important qualification—if you have difficulty doing what you choose to do or if you do not obtain the results you desire, the reason is probably that you tried to do too much too soon, a very common tendency among men. Instead of giving up, consider going back and doing the exercises you skipped.

Our approach to helping you enjoy sex more is based on the assumption that you are a unique individual with your own sexual preferences and style. You are the person best qualified to discover what works for you and gives you pleasure. In other words, you need to learn more about your sexual self, a self that in some ways is similar to those of other men but in other ways is different. Such an exploration is not always easy and, in truth, requires both courage and persistence. Despite the lip service given by both professionals and lay people to the idea that people are unique, we all have strong tendencies to want to be precisely like everyone else, particularly in anxiety-laden areas like sex.

There is no right way to have sex. People are too different for there to be one or two or even a dozen right ways. Since people really are different and since no two people function in exactly the same way—regardless of the attempts of our sexual mythology and many sex manuals to convince you of the opposite—a book cannot tell you what you would enjoy or how to turn yourself or your partner on.

What a book can do, and what we attempt to do, is provide a framework within which you can explore what you are about sexually: your own body, patterns, preferences, and turn-ons. Such explorations fare best if they are relaxed experiences, free from demands that you be such and such a way or that you enjoy such and such an activity. Our suggestions and exercises are only opportunities for you to discover something about yourself. We hope you will give some of them a chance to work for you, but we are aware that what you learn from any given exercise may be different from what other men have learned; and that is fine.

Since many of the men we worked with have enjoyed and profited from hearing other men's feelings and experiences, we include numerous examples. Some of them are from men we have seen in therapy, classes, and workshops, and are so identified. Others are from our own lives or from friends or colleagues who did not wish to be identified. We have tried to present sufficient information so that you could develop a feeling for the man and his situation. We hope that some of these examples will be relevant to you and will give you a sense of how other men relate to their sexuality.

Resist the temptation, so common among men, of assuming that something is wrong with you if your experiences or responses are different from what is portrayed in our examples or text. Your feelings and reactions are right for you, and only by acknowledging, exploring, and building upon them will you develop the kind of sexuality that gives you the most pleasure.

2

Learning about Sex

Although many people think of sex as something that is natural or instinctive—just doing what comes naturally—human sexuality is basically a learned phenomenon. Very little of our sexual behavior can properly be called instinctive. There are a few exceptions: newborn males, for example, have erections and obviously they have not had the chance to learn anything. It is easy to assume that since we, like all animals, are programmed to continue our species, intercourse would occur without learning. But the issue is much more complex than this, as we shall soon discuss.

Nature would be content and the human species would survive if some men at some time impregnated some women. This could be accomplished through rape, through sex that involved only penetration and quick ejaculation, with no good feelings between the participants and with neither partner enjoying it at all. The only important thing from nature's point of view is that enough births occur to replenish the lives lost through illness, injury, and old age. The ideas that some ways of having sex are better than others, that certain actions are decent while others are indecent, that some partners and places are appropriate while others are not—all these are products of learning. Nature seems to care not a whit about any of it.

Even lower animals, though they have a much larger component of instinctive programming than humans in sexual and other matters, need to learn about sex. Animals that through accident or human intervention miss their "sex education" have a difficult time of it when they are adults and many never learn to mate. Monkeys who are deprived of certain childhood experiences—touching and being touched by their mothers, playing with and grooming peers, and/or observing adult monkeys engaging in sex—are unable to have sex when they grow up. They may try—the drive seems to be there—but they do it all wrong. Males look puzzled, unsure of what to do. They either physically assault receptive females or clumsily grope them and try to mount in inappropriate ways. The fact that animals whom we think of as more instinctually controlled than ourselves need to learn about sex should alert us to the tremendous importance of learning in our own sexual behavior.

Sex researcher John Gagnon gives this example of the role of learning in human sexuality:

> It is common for heterosexually oriented men to be aroused by seeing women's breasts under clothing, by taking off a brassiere, by touching a woman's breasts. . . . These activities are often accompanied by dramatic psychological and physiological changes in the man, experienced as appropriate to the sexual things he is doing. It is difficult for him as a participant . . . to recall the amount of learning that had to take place for all of these events to make sense as sexual events. There is no automatic connection between touching a woman's breasts and blood flow into the genitals.

The following personal experience may help make the point clearer.

When I went to summer camp, a very naïve thirteen year old, I was quite conscious of being the youngest boy in my cabin. I was intrigued by what most of my roommates were doing at night. It was hard to see but it was obvious that they were doing something to themselves—to their penises, I realized as my observations continued—to the accompaniment of moaning and heavy breathing. I decided that whatever it was, it must be good since all the older boys were doing it, and that it would pay me to find out more about this activity. As soon as everyone else went to their swimming lessons, I headed for the bathroom and got to work.

At first my investigations were a flop. I did just about everything I could think of to my penis—squeezing it, petting it, rubbing it between my hands, pushing it against my thigh, waving it around like a flag—and nothing happened. It hadn't occurred to me that it would help if I had an erection. Then, one day as I was absentmindedly stroking my penis and thinking that I would have to retire from such pursuits unless more rewarding results were forthcoming, I became aware of some pleasurable sensations. I kept stroking, my penis got hard, and the sensations felt better and better. Then I was overcome with feelings I had never before felt and, God help me, white stuff came spurting out the end of my cock. I wasn't sure if I had sprung a leak or what. I was afraid but calmed down when I thought that since it was white it couldn't be blood. I kept on stroking and it hurt. I didn't know if the hurt was connected with the white stuff (had I really injured myself?) or if the event was over and my penis needed a rest. But I decided to stop for the moment. Of course I returned the next day and did it again, thus beginning a daily habit that continued for many years.

As I look back at those days, I can see how much I had to learn. The first ejaculations fired my curiosity—they were certainly interesting—but they didn't feel all that great. I wasn't sure what to make of them. Only gradually did I begin to experience them as extremely pleasurable, perhaps more pleasurable than anything else. The most interesting thing, though, is that for many months after I started masturbating, I never connected what I was doing with girls or what little I knew about sex. Masturbation—"whacking off" is what my roommates called it—was just an enjoyable activity that boys did alone or in darkness. Only after I heard that one could put his penis in a vagina and experience similar sensations did I begin to put together what I was doing with what I might someday do with a girl and start developing sexual fantasies to accompany my solo ministrations.

In all important areas of life we seek information about how we should act. We are acutely sensitive to information regarding roles and behaviors that are applicable to us, and we pick up relevant information in both conscious and unconscious ways.

The boy interested in becoming a doctor may read a book about medicine. He may also get information about doctors in ways that he is not aware of, so that after a while he may start walking or talking or in some manner imitating his doctor or one he has seen on television. Much of what he learns, especially from the media, is misleading, distorted, and inaccurate. He does not have much ability to differentiate between information that is accurate, that which is basically true but exaggerated, and that which is totally false. He may well build up expectations that will cause frustration and disappointment when he encounters the realities of medical practice. If he is to function well and be content with his career, he will have to unlearn or give up the false information he acquired and replace it with more realistic data.

Learning about sex is similar in many ways but also much more difficult. We all want to learn about sex since it seems like such an important part of being masculine and adult but, because of all the double messages we get from our parents and other sources, it is a subject loaded with anxiety. Such anxiety is not conducive to clear thinking, viewing things in perspective, or calmly assessing how what we hear or read fits with our own values and experience. And sex is one of the few areas of life where it is almost impossible to observe accurately how others are doing it. It is of course possible to obtain sexual information—we are deluged with it—but much of this information is absurdly exaggerated and inaccurate and the growing boy has no way of knowing this.

A crucial element that motivated our learning and fueled our anxiety was the necessity of proving that we were men. In our society, as in almost every other society that has ever existed, manhood is a conditional attribute. The possession of a penis is necessary but not sufficient; you still had to prove, and keep on proving, that you were worthy. As Norman Mailer put it: "Nobody was born a man; you earned your manhood provided you were good enough, bold enough."

From countless sources we learned that our masculinity and therefore our self-esteem was always on the line: from Western and gangster movies where men never back away from a fight, even if it means almost certain death; from endless newspaper and magazine articles announcing that so-and-so had "become a man" by enduring some terrible ordeal, leading his team to victory, or performing some other extraordinary task; from the sting, even if experienced only vicariously, of a male being called a "boy," "girl," "fag," or "sissy" for some supposedly unmasculine trait or act.

The badge of manhood can be won only temporarily; it can be questioned or taken away at any time. One job poorly done, one "failure," one sign of weakness—that's all it took to lose our membership in the charmed circle. Many of us can remember how our parents, teachers, coaches, and friends used this knowledge to keep us in line.

Most of us experienced no choice: we had to demonstrate our masculinity no matter how ill-equipped and ill-prepared we felt. In his essay "Being a Boy," Julius Lester captures the agony so many of us felt. Comparing himself to girls, he says:

> There was the life, I thought! No constant pressure to prove oneself. No necessity always to be competing. While I humiliated myself on football and baseball fields, the girls stood on the sidelines laughing at me, because they didn't have to do anything except be girls. The rising of each sun brought me to the starting line of yet another day's Olympic decathlon, with no hope of ever winning even a bronze medal.
>
> Through no fault of my own I reached adolescence. While the pressure to prove myself on the athletic field lessened, the overall situation got worse—because now I had to prove myself with girls. Just how I was supposed to go about doing this was beyond me. . . . Nonetheless, duty called, and with my ninth-grade gym-class jockstrap flapping between my legs, off I went.

Like Lester, we sooner or later realized that sex was one of the most important areas in which to prove ourselves. But where could one go to find out what sex was about?

Our culture does not assist us much in acquiring accurate sexual information. Ten or more years ago, when many of us learned about sex, reliable information was not readily available. Courses on sex, even in medical and graduate schools, were virtually nonexistent, which meant that the professionals we went to for advice often knew little more than we. There were few factually accurate articles in the popular literature. And whom could you talk to? It was widely accepted that nice people didn't talk about such things and, even if you didn't consider yourself nice, it was difficult to admit ignorance or concern.

In recounting his thinking on the days before what was to have been his first sexual experience, Bill Cosby demonstrates the dilemma many of us experienced.

So, man, Saturday comes, and I've been thinkin' all week about this p-u-s-s-y. You know, and I'm tryin' to ask people questions about how they get some p-u-s-s-y. And I don't want guys to know that I don't know nothin' about gettin' no p-u-s-s-y. But how do you find out how to do it without blowin' the fact that you don't know how to do it? So I come up to a guy, and I say, Say, man, have you ever had any p-u-s-s-y? And the guy says, Yeah. And I say, Well, man, what's your favorite way of gettin' it? He says, Well, you know, just the regular way. And I say, Well, do you do it like I do it? And the cat says, How's that? And I say, Well, hey, I heard that there was different ways of doin' it, man. He says, Well, there's a lotta ways of doin' it, you know, but I think that . . . you know, the regular way. . . . I say, Yeah, good ol' regular way . . . good ol' regular way of gettin' that p-u-s-s-y.

As he continues his ruminations on the way to the girl's house, Cosby—all of eleven years old at the time—neatly illustrates the influence of the idea that a man should be able to do it all on his own, even though he hasn't the faintest notion of what sex is about.

> So now, I'm walkin', and I'm trying to figure out how to do it. And when I get there, the most embarrassing thing is gonna be when I have to take my pants down. See, right away, then, I'm buck naked . . . buck naked in front of this girl. Now, what happens then? Do you . . . do you just . . . I don't even know what to do . . . I'm gonna just stand there and she's gonna say, You don't know how to do it. And I'm gonna say, Yes I do, but I forgot. I never thought of her showing me, because I'm a man and I don't want her to show me —I don't want nobody to show me, but I wish somebody would kinda slip me a note. . . . I stopped off at a magazine stand to look and see if there were any sexy magazines about it. I mean if I wasn't going to learn how to do it, I figured there might be some pictures in there of somebody almost getting ready to do it. But I don't find nothin'.

Cosby arrives at the girl's house in a state of near-hysteria and avoids having sex with her. But on the way home he struts like the world's greatest lover. He brags to his friend Rufus about the "goooooooooooood p-u-s-s-y" he had gotten and when Rufus asks how he did it, he answers, "if you don't know how to do it, I ain't gonna tell you how to do it. . . ." And so it goes, with ignorance proliferating at a fantastic pace and everyone thinking that everyone else really knows how to do it.

The anxiety about not knowing, about not being man enough, was so great, as was our need for acceptance from our peers, that we often faked it. Like Cosby, we lied to our friends about how far we had gone with our last date and assumed a mask of confidence and knowledge that had little basis in reality. Better to lie than risk having our fragile egos battered and ridiculed.

I remember trying to smile knowingly whenever my high school friends talked about sex and how much they were getting. I tried to give the impression that

I, too, was getting a lot, even though I was very unclear about what it was I was supposed to have gotten. I felt that I had to fake it, for to have admitted
my ignorance and virginity would have degraded me
in the eyes of those from whom I most wanted and
needed respect. It was obvious that the most adult
and manly thing one could do was get a lot, so I pre-
tended, always fearing that my deception would be
discovered. I was surprised to learn, years later, that
many of my friends had been lying just like me.

The last decade has of course brought a much greater
availability of sexual knowledge and a greater permission to be interested in it. Stopping at a magazine stand
today, you can find pictures not only of people getting
ready to have sex, but doing it in every conceivable
manner and place. Good reading material can be conveniently purchased; some physicians, therapists, and
educators now know about sex; and it is even considered legitimate, in some circles at least, to have sexual questions, concerns, and problems.

But most of us developed our sexual scripts or models (the organized totality of our sexual knowledge)
before we had access to accurate information. We
grabbed whatever information we could find, from
our friends and older boys (many of whom differed
from us only in having a larger store of misconceptions), from the media, from sexual humor, and from
any other sources at our disposal. Bit by bit we
constructed a sexual script for ourselves, something to
guide our sexual thoughts and behavior. Such scripts
are acquired at a relatively early age and quickly become entrenched and resistant to major change.

That a more permissive attitude now prevails may
seem to herald the end of sexual misinformation and
ignorance, and the beginning of a state of unprecedented sexual bliss. But such is in fact not the case.
Opportunities for obtaining more accurate information
have clearly expanded, thus making more possible the
development of more appropriate and personally satisfying sexual scripts. But all is still very far from well.
Many health professionals are still abysmally ignorant

about sex and much of the information disseminated by self-styled experts—like David Reuben and the anonymous authors of *The Sensuous Woman* and *The Sensuous Man*—is misleading, inaccurate and, in some cases, even dangerous. We are inundated with articles, books, courses, and programs about sex, but, because of the anxiety surrounding sexuality, most people are in no position to separate the wheat from the chaff.

And of sexual chaff there is no end. There seems to be no limit to the amount of nonsense people will believe about sex. Old misconceptions are discredited and disappear only to reappear under new labels or to be replaced by new ones at least as absurd. What sounds at first like liberation usually turns out on closer inspection to be a new and sometimes even harsher tyranny.

Because of the cultural uneasiness about sex—which affects us all, virgin and swinger alike—and because of our desperate desire to do sex the "right way" and not miss anything for fear that we be judged less than men, we tend to distort even information that is accurate. Perspective and personal evaluation ("Does this really fit and feel good for me?") are lost as we frantically attempt to prove our masculinity and sexiness. The fact that some women sometimes have multiple orgasms gets translated into an imperative ("I've got to make my partner have several orgasms every time"). A statistic demonstrating that men in a certain age bracket have sex 2.5 times a week on the average becomes an iron-clad rule. Options like open relationships and bisexuality become necessities or causes for concern.

The problem is cultural rather than personal. Whether we formed our basic sexual scripts in the last five years or forty years ago, we are all victims of the cultural imperative to prove our manhood and the unwillingness of society at large to present us with realistic and meaningful sexual scripts to follow.

The models of sex and masculinity that were and are presented to us are deficient in a great many ways, harmful to both us and our partners, and the main cause of our sexual dissatisfaction and problems. These models have little to do with what is possible or satisfying for human beings.

We had little choice. We tried to get the best possible information. We could not foresee the negative implications of what we were learning. We were too young, too naïve, too busy growing and living to have much perspective and to realize what was happening to us. Much of the time we were not even aware that we were learning anything. As we shall see in the next chapter, much of our sex education comes from sources not usually thought of as educational.

Not all of our sex education was negative, however. Although all of us have been influenced to some extent by the myths and fantasies discussed in the next two chapters, some of us were influenced less than others. Some men were fortunate in having understanding parents, teachers, lovers, or others from whom they were able to obtain information and the space to develop in their own way. Others, with little or no outside assistance, had to struggle harder to develop their sexuality in personally satisfying ways. And some of these men were able to replace early, destructive knowledge with models more consistent with their own personalities and values.

While we acknowledge these exceptions and salute the increasing number of men willing to deal with the sex-role stereotypes and sexual mythology that chains them, it is certain that these chains still exert an incredible influence on most of us. The sexual model we will be discussing guides much of our sexual behavior (including thoughts and feelings) even though we are usually unaware of its influence. In a real sense, the model is our problem. It is what prevents us from expressing and enjoying our sexuality in the most satisfying ways.

What has been learned can be unlearned and replaced by more personally appropriate knowledge. Actually, you don't really have to unlearn anything. All you need to do is recognize what is getting in your way and loosen its grip just a little bit. Much of sex therapy, and much of what occurs in workshops and courses on sex, is simply the use of techniques designed to gently unleash you from some of your early sexual learning and give you the opportunity to experience other ways of being sexual.

And that, in essence, is what this book is about.

3

It's Two Feet Long, Hard As Steel, and Can Go All Night: The Fantasy Model of Sex

In this and the following chapter we discuss the model of sex that is prevalent in our society. The model is rarely encountered in its entirety, but bits and pieces of it are found everywhere. Its purest exemplar is pornography (movies, books, and, more recently, comic books), but it also abounds in sexual humor, popular literature, those works of "good" fiction that deal explicitly with sex, and even in technical and scientific literature.

We believe that sexual learning takes place all the time. Whenever something happens that affects our subsequent behavior, thoughts, or feelings, learning has occurred. While we don't listen to or tell what used to be called dirty jokes in order to learn anything, the sexual messages are there and, because of our basic insecurity about sex and our sensitivity to anything sexual, the messages get through to us whether we realize it or not. And what is true about humor is also true for all the other sources of the sexual model. The fact that we are unaware of having learned anything is unimportant. In fact, some of the most important learning in our lives happens without our knowledge. Many of the things we believe are not learned but are simply "the way it is" are in fact learned but, because of our insistence to the contrary, extremely resistant to change.

An interesting fact that ensures that just about all men (and women) will learn the same model of sex is that all the media sources portray essentially the same sexual messages. What is picked up from one is reinforced by the others. Even if we never read a book and never saw a movie, we would still learn the model. It pervades our culture. Our friends learned it, as did our parents, and it would be a mistake of major proportions to assume that the professionals who talk and write about sex have completely escaped its tentacles.

There can be no question regarding the influence of the fantasy model of sex. In their highly regarded study *Pornography and Sexual Deviance,* Michael Goldstein and Harold Kant report that erotic literature and films are "often the only media" through which the roles of men and women in sex and "concrete models of the actual 'mechanics' of heterosexual relationships" are gained. Erotic literature is the primary source of sex education for many young people, as well as for many not so young. When we add the effects of sexual humor, popular literature, movies, television, and other media, we begin to get an idea of the immensity of the problem.

There has also been, at least up until very recently, a relative paucity of competing models. The variety of possibilities and problems of real sexuality—as opposed to the superhuman sexuality of the model—are detailed only infrequently. With the new openness about sex in the culture there is some hope that this may change in the future, but what we have seen so far gives us little cause for optimism. Which is not surprising since the people who write for and direct the media were brought up on the same sexual script as the rest of us, a fact to which their productions attest.

Enough introduction for now. The following quotation, from Harold Robbins's *The Betsy*, is useful for setting the proper mood for our discussion of the model. Try to keep in mind that this book is not only not pornographic by any of the usual definitions but can be conveniently purchased at many drugstores and supermarkets. It may also be helpful to know that Robbins is the best-selling author of fiction in the world. His works have sold well over 150 million copies. Considering this, he may be the most influential sex educator of our time.

Gently her fingers opened his union suit and he sprang out at her like an angry lion from its cage. Carefully she peeled back his foreskin, exposing his red and angry glans, and took him in both hands, one behind the other as if she were grasping a baseball bat. She stared at it in wonder. "C'est formidable. Un vrai canon." ...

... *Naked, he looked even more an animal than before. Shoulders, chest and belly covered with hair out of which sprang the massive erection.* ...

She almost fainted looking down at him. Slowly he began to lower her on him. Her legs came up ... as he began to enter her. ... It was as if a giant of white-hot steel were penetrating her vitals. She began to moan as it opened her and climbed higher into her body, past her womb, past her stomach, under her heart, up into her throat. She was panting now, like a bitch in heat. ...

[He then flings her onto the bed.] Then he was poised over her. ... His hands reached and grasped each of her heavy breasts as if he wanted to tear them from her body. She moaned in pain and writhed, her pelvis suddenly arching and thrusting toward him. Then he entered her again.

"Mon Dieu!" she cried, the tears springing into her eyes. "Mon Dieu!" She began to climax almost before he was fully inside her. Then she couldn't stop them, one coming rapidly after the other as he slammed into her with the force of the giant body press she had seen working in his factory. ... Somehow she became confused, the man and the machine they were one and the same and the strength was something else she had never known before. And finally, when orgasm after orgasm had racked her body into a searing sheet of

flame and she could bear no more, she cried out to him in French.

"Take your pleasure with me! . . . Quick, before I die!"

A roar came from deep inside his throat and his hands tightened on her breasts. She half screamed and her hands grabbed into the hair of his chest. Then all his weight seemed to fall in on her, crushing the breath from her body, and she felt the hot onrushing gusher of his semen turning her insides into viscous, flowing lava. She discovered herself climaxing again.

While this quote was not chosen randomly, there are literally thousands of similar ones that could have been used.

We now examine in greater detail some of the major components of this sexual fantasyland. In the rest of this chapter we deal with the model's prescriptions for male equipment and the sexual partner. In the next chapter, we talk about the process and goals of sex. Although we mainly use quotations from books to demonstrate our points, it is well to remember that the other sources of sexual information convey the same information and that some of those sources may have been more influential than books in your own education.

The Equipment

By equipment we mean penises, since the model teaches that they are all men need to have good sex. Presumably that bit of skin between your legs is the only sexual part of you.

It is not much of an exaggeration to say that penises in fantasyland come in only three sizes—large, gigantic, and so big you can barely get them through the doorway. This joke has been around at least since we were in high school: A woman tells the man she has been dating that she would never marry anyone unless he had twelve inches. To which he replies that he refuses to cut off four inches, even for her.

Penis size is frequently mentioned in jokes and literature, and of course bigger is always better. Average or small penises are noted only as objects of derision. A woman in Joyce Elbert's *Crazy Ladies* complains that the men she meets have such small penises that they might as well use their fingers, but then becomes ecstatic when she finds a man with "an erection a mile long."

Women, we are given to believe, crave nothing so much as a penis that might be mistaken for a telephone pole. They receive such monstrosities with thanksgiving and complete satisfaction. Who can forget that tender love scene in *The Godfather* where Sonny, the best-hung stud in town, gets together with Lucy, who has hitherto been unable to find a penis large enough to fill her up?

> *Her hand closed around an enormous, blood-gorged pole of muscle. It pulsated in her hand like an animal and almost weeping with grateful ecstasy she pointed it into her own wet, turgid flesh. The thrust of its entering, the unbelievable pleasure made her gasp . . . and then like a quiver, her body received the savage arrows of his lightning-like thrusts . . . arching her pelvis higher and higher until for the first time in her life she reached a shattering climax. . . .*

The fact that the penis is not a muscle and contains no muscular tissue at all is conveniently ignored, a clear example of how far from reality is the model.

Not only are fantasyland penises much larger than life, they also behave peculiarly. They are forever "pulsating," "throbbing," and leaping about. The mere sight or touch of a woman is sufficient to set the penis jumping, and whenever a man's fly is unzipped, his penis leaps out. From Harold Robbins's *The Inheritors:* ". . . she pulled open the buttons on his trousers. He sprang swollen into her hand. . . ." Nowhere does a penis merely mosey out for a look at what's happening.

The penis should also be unbelievably hard. It is often described as being hard as rock or steel, anything less apparently being inadequate. The fantasy penis is always totally full and firm, always ready to go.

Or to stay. The last characteristic of the idealized penis is its infinite capacity to satisfy, either by lasting for hours on end or by immediately regaining its hardness after ejaculation. Henry Miller gives this example of total control over the ejaculatory process:

> *I was in such a cold-blooded state of control that as she went through her spasms I poked it around inside her like a demon, up, sideways, down, in, out again, plunging, rearing, jabbing, snorting, and absolutely certain that I wouldn't come until I was damned good and ready.*

From *The Pearl* comes this example of a penis that never needed to rest: "I could not exhaust him; he was continually shooting his love juice into my . . . womb. . . ."

Wonderful instruments, these penises. Though they be like rock, they just keep rolling along.

The penis is the central figure—the hero, so to speak —of the fantasy model. Not the human penis, to be sure, but an organ of make-believe, conceived of, in the words of Dr. Steven Marcus, as "a magical instrument of infinite powers." The names given to these penises reflect their inhuman nature—tools, weapons, rods, ramrods, battering rams, shafts, coursers, and formidable machines. Somehow the humanity of the penis has been lost. The model makes it quite clear that the quality of a sexual experience and the measure of the man is a direct function of the size and power of that magical toy between his legs.

Real men with real penises compare themselves to the model and find themselves woefully lacking. Most men believe that their penises are not what they ought to be. They are not long enough or wide enough or hard enough, they do not spring forth with the requisite surging and throbbing, and they do not last long enough or recover fast enough. A recent magazine survey of over a thousand men found that "all male respondents, with the exception of the most extraordinarily endowed, expressed doubts about their own sexuality based on their penile size."

Given what we learned, this isn't surprising. The problem is that we think we should measure up to what are basically impossible standards. The penises in the model are products of fantasy and the real always loses when compared to the creations of human imagination.

But, you may be thinking, that isn't the whole story. What about the huge organs you've seen with your own eyes in pornographic movies and magazines? And in the movies some of those guys seem to last forever or regain their erections immediately after orgasm. Aren't these things for real? Sure, in a way. There is no question but that some men are more generously endowed than the rest of us and that they are sought after by those whose business it is to titillate the public. There are also all kinds of things that can be and are done to make the huge look even larger than it actually is. There is very little that cannot be accomplished through the magic of photography. And splicing works wonders in films. What looks like a continuous sequence in a movie is often the result of taping together segments filmed at different times. You'd be surprised how much film is wasted because the actors don't get erections, or come before they're supposed to. But the film you see looks perfect. What you see isn't necessarily what is when it comes to sex.

We don't want to gloss over the fact that there are some large penises around. It is also true that some men can last long periods of time or have relatively brief refractory periods. But such phenomena are statistically rare. There is no more reason to try to match them than there is to try to grow to be seven feet tall just because there are a few men of that height, or to try to run a four-minute mile because a few men have accomplished that feat.

Accepting your own merely human penis can be difficult. You know it is somewhat unpredictable and, even when functioning at its best, looks and feels more like a human penis than a battering ram or a mountain of stone. Not much when compared to the fantasies we are brought up on. But you do have one small advantage—you are alive and can enjoy yourself whereas the supermen of the model with their gigantic erections are unreal and feel nothing. Later in the book we give some exercises to assist you in learning more about your penis and enjoying it. For now, it might be helpful if you would look at your penis and ask whether you can live with it. After all, unless you are contemplating a transplant from a horse, it's the only penis you'll ever have and, whatever its characteristics, it can give you much pleasure.

The Partner

The women in fantasyland are all gorgeous and perfectly formed. A glance at the cartoons in any issue of *Playboy* or *Penthouse* makes the point succinctly: the women men desire are beautiful and flawlessly built; women who do not fit this mold are ridiculed.

Average-looking women, women who look older than twenty-two, those whose breasts sag or whose skin is not the model-conforming smooth, creamy, and silky —such women rarely appear in the world of sexual make-believe. It is a world where no one ages and no one wrinkles and no one loses her jutting breasts. In keeping with this notion, many of the women in popular literature keep peering into mirrors and noting that, though they have reached the advanced age of, say, thirty, there's nary a crease or wrinkle marring their charms.

Feminists and other women have long complained that men are too interested in physical appearance, paying more attention to "tits and ass" than to the personality and intelligence of women and being uninterested in women who do not fit the current standard of physical perfection. There is more than a bit of truth in this, for men have learned that sex is something one has only with young and beautiful women. Given all the brainwashing we have been subjected to, it is understandable that we should pay so much attention to physical attributes and that middle-aged and older men should so often prefer to go out with much younger women. On the other hand, it is a tribute to the resiliency and common sense of men that so many have been able to see through the propaganda and find happiness with women who don't fit the requirements of the fantasy script.

Women in the fantasy model are also portrayed as wanting sex all the time and wanting to be handled roughly, no matter how much they may request gentleness or protest the male's sexual advances. Such characteristics are regular features in pornography and also occur frequently in other sources of the fantasy model. The maid in Norman Mailer's *American Dream* resists Steven Rojack's sexual advances. But he overpowers her and is later rewarded for "taking her" by such statements as "You are absolutely a genius, Mr. Rojack," and "I love you a little bit."

D. H. Lawrence's Lady Chatterley, though "it cost her an effort to let him have his way and his will of her," allows her lover to have anal intercourse with her. It is a wonderful experience:

> [S]he had needed this phallic hunting out, she had secretly wanted it, and she had believed that she would never get it. . . . What liars poets and everybody were! They made one think one wanted sentiment. When what one supremely wanted was this piercing, consuming, rather awful sensuality. To find a man who dared do it, without shame or sin or final misgiving. If he had been ashamed afterwards . . . how awful!

The message couldn't be clearer if it were written across the sky in neon—never listen to what a woman says when it comes to sex. She means yes even if she says no. She wants to be taken despite her protestations, she wants roughness even when she asks for tenderness.

As the following joke indicates, contempt is the only reward for the man who takes a woman's resistance seriously.

A traveling salesman found lodging at a farmer's house and was told that he would have to sleep with the farmer's beautiful daughter. The salesman started having fantasies of a sex-filled night and eagerly awaited bedtime. But when it arrived the girl piled a few pillows between them on the bed and told him not to cross over them. He was disappointed but complied with her request. In the morning the girl was gone, and the salesman dressed and started to leave. As he left the house, he saw the girl doing some chores on the other side of a fence and called to her: "Wait a minute, I'll jump over this fence and give you a kiss good-bye." To which she contemptuously replied: "Hell, if you can't make it over three pillows, you ain't never going to get over the fence."

Men in the fantasy model are always rewarded for not listening to a woman rather than for taking her seriously. Is it any wonder that men in the real world have trouble knowing what to do when a woman says "No" or "Stop" or "Be more gentle"?

The idea that women shouldn't be listened to is also learned from, and reinforced by, the social game in which the woman, trying to protect her reputation and not appear "loose," resists the man's advances even when she is willing to have sex. She resists to comply with the rules of the game and, having satisfied the requirements, lets the man proceed. The understanding man develops as a result of this game is, don't listen to what she says.

The problem for the man is how to differentiate between sincere rejections and requests on the one hand, and those that are ambivalent or merely facades on the other hand. Since the task is difficult and since the risks in backing off when the rejection is not real are so grave, many men simply give up trying to make the distinction and forge ahead regardless of what the woman says.

Women are caught in a bind because many of them were taught that it is important to put up a show of resistance even when they don't mean it. In rewarding men for not listening to them, they add to the already considerable amount of deafness in the male population. And then they get angry because men don't take them seriously.

This is not to suggest that women are the culprits in this situation. They are doing what they were taught was necessary, while men are doing the same. The point is that our sexual scripts are harmful to both men and women, making it difficult for either to be honest and enjoy sex.

Another important characteristic of women in fantasyland is that they constantly validate their lovers' egos and sexual prowess in particular ways. They behave in a manner calculated to leave no doubt that their men are the greatest sex machines in the world. From James Baldwin's *Another Country:*

> Her hands . . . had their own way and grasped his friendly body, caressing and scratching and burning. . . . He felt a tremor in her belly, just beneath him, as though something had broken there, and it rolled tremendously upward, seeming to divide her breasts, as though he had split her all her length. And she moaned. . . . He began to gallop her, whinnying a little with delight. . . . Her moans gave way to sobs and cries. Vivaldo. Vivaldo. Vivaldo. She was over the edge. . . . "It never happened to me before—not like this, never."

And here is one of Henry Miller's many partners going through her innumerable gyrations:

> Moving with furious abandon, biting my lips, my throat, my ears, repeating like a crazed automaton, "Go on, give it to me . . . Oh God, give it, give it to me!" She went from one orgasm to another, pushing, thrusting, raising herself, rolling her ass . . . groaning, grunting, squealing like a pig, and then suddenly, thoroughly exhausted, begging me to shoot. "Shoot it . . . I'll go mad." . . . I shot a wad into the mouth of her womb that jolted her like an electric charge.

The women in the world of make-believe are always moaning and shrieking in ecstasy, demonstrating time and again what wonderful lovers their men are. In pornography, they frequently lose consciousness as they climax, the ultimate tribute to the potency of their lovers. Pornography sometimes also features women who

ejaculate (a physiological impossibility). Torrents of
"love juice" gush from the man and the woman and it
is a wonder they both don't drown.

It goes without saying that all women in the fantasy
model are multiply orgasmic through intercourse. Non-
orgasmic women exist, but only until a man who is big
enough and rough enough comes along to open them up
to the joys of sex. Women who are orgasmic only
through means other than intercourse are unheard of, a
very inadequate preparation for the realities of the
world.

That is the main problem with the model of the partner—it is not a good preparation for the real world.
The model ignores the fact that very few women meet
the specified criteria of beauty and that even those who
do will deviate further and further from them as they
age. The standard of physical perfection influences the
types of sexual partners men choose and/or makes
them feel deficient if they end up with someone who
does not meet all the specifications.

The model also leads men to expect that women will
behave in certain ways. But what if she never shrieks
and moans in sex? What if her orgasms do not resemble
an epileptic seizure? Suppose she doesn't have an orgasm every time they have sex or doesn't have orgasms
in intercourse? How is the man to know that he's a
good lover? His idea of a good lover is defined by the
fantasy script. What is he to think of himself when reality doesn't match the fantasy?

The stage is set for trouble. The man may feel inadequate and put pressure on his partner to live up to the
model. Questions are asked or implied: "How come
you don't want sex more often?" "Why don't you
make more noise (or shout obscenities)?" "Did the
earth move for you?" "Are you *sure* you wouldn't like
to have another orgasm?"

A man came to therapy literally dragging his wife
along. The problem according to him was that she was
multiply orgasmic with masturbation and with stimulation from his hand, but she usually had only one orgasm in intercourse. That she was perfectly content

with this state of affairs mattered not at all to him. He didn't know who was at fault but he wanted one or both of them fixed up so that she could have as many orgasms with intercourse as with manual stimulation. Only then would he feel adequate as a lover.

We want to make it clear that we are not saying that anything is wrong with fantasies per se, no matter how unrealistic they are. If you enjoy thinking about how life would be if you had a penis four feet wide and ten feet long, that's fine, as is fantasizing about being the greatest lover in the world, able to satisfy twenty women with a single spurt. Any fantasy is fine so long as you are aware that it is a fantasy and so long as it does not make you feel inadequate when reality does not conform to it.

The problem with the sexual model we are discussing is that it is not just a fantasy, one that can be turned on or off at will and that has little influence on behavior. It is rather the description of how our sexual world "should be" and it affects our thinking, feeling, and behavior. Many of us are unaware that the model is indeed a fantasy, one that has little to do with what is possible or desirable for human beings. Since we take the script for the way things ought to be, we measure ourselves by it, striving to match its standards and feeling badly when we don't. Instead of asking whether the model is physiologically feasible, personally satisfying, or enhancing of ourselves and our relationships, we ask what is wrong with us for not being able to meet its standards. And that is precisely why this model is so destructive.

4

The Fantasy
Model Continued:
The Process and
Goals of Sex

While most of us learned the same sexual model, the specific myths affect us differently. You may believe in some with a very firm conviction, while others may have little influence on you. We ask you to read carefully, to consider if and how each myth pertains to you and how it affects your sexual functioning and enjoyment.

The first two myths or rules are part of both the fantasy model of sex and the general model of masculinity taught in our culture. Their impact can be felt in all aspects of men's lives but we focus primarily on their influence in the sexual area.

Myth 1

Men Should Not Have, or at Least Not Express, Certain Feelings

While looking at the boats from a dock on San Francisco Bay, a four-year-old boy fell into the very cold water. After being fished out of the water by his father and others in the party, he was trembling, looking very scared and like he might cry. His father patted him on the back and loudly announced that "Billy doesn't cry; he's a big boy."

In ways like this, and from the media, we learn early that only a narrow range of emotion is permitted to us: aggressiveness, competitiveness, anger, joviality, and the feelings associated with being in control. As we grow older, sexual feelings are added to the list. Weakness, confusion, fear, vulnerability, tenderness, compassion, and sensuality are allowed only to girls and women. A boy who exhibits any such traits is likely to be made fun of and called a sissy or girl (and what could be more devastating?).

We learn this lesson well and there is no lack of later reminders lest we be tempted to deviate from the true path. To give but one example, newspapers and commentators throughout the country questioned Edmund Muskie's emotional stability because he had shed some tears during a speech when he was campaigning for the presidency. Other males who have publicly expressed fear, deep sadness, or any other feelings on the prohibited list have sometimes lost the respect of their peers and themselves.

We end up either consistently denying to ourselves that we have any of the taboo feelings or, if we do acknowledge them, we are careful to hide them from others and often worry about the consequences of being found out. We are convinced that others will find us unacceptable if we reveal certain feelings or qualities, and so we go through life blocking out huge portions of our beings.

It is no wonder that close relationships are, at least, very difficult for most men. Looking at the feelings prohibited to us, we can begin to understand why we have so much trouble relating to others. What kinds of relationships can be built on the basis of aggressiveness, competitiveness, anger, sex, and joviality? How can there be closeness without compassion, tenderness, caring, trust, vulnerability—all the emotions not allowed for men?

The point is simple and frightening: the socialization of males provides very little that is of value in the formation of intimate relationships.

Everyone suffers as a result of this. Women constantly complain about the inexpressiveness of their men and how this causes problems in relationships. What women often fail to understand is that it is not a case of stubbornness on the part of men. We simply were not and are not given the permission to be expressive that most women were. We were not allowed to acknowledge even to ourselves all those emotions labeled unmanly, which has resulted in an inability to recognize and differentiate among them. Many times we are aware of feeling something but, because of our lack of experience in dealing with feelings, we don't know exactly what we are feeling or how to find out. And even if we do find out, we aren't sure it would be acceptable to express the emotion.

It is often said that men don't communicate, which is only partly true. Men can communicate very well about certain things, like their jobs, sports, and the state of the world. But this isn't what is meant by those who fault men; they say men don't talk about their feelings and hopes and problems. That is generally true, but given what we have said, how could it be otherwise? Talking about feelings and concerns is itself considered feminine by the models we were raised on. And when it comes to sex, what's there to communicate?

In the fantasy model no one ever has much to say. Doing it is the only thing that matters, and aside from the "I'm going to do it to you" and "Do it to me harder and faster" routine, what could there possibly be to say? The superstuds in the model never feel fear or concern or tenderness or warmth, they never have problems, they never need to stop or rest. So where can a boy or man turn for an example of emotional or sexual communication? No place at all.

Our partners sometimes say that there is something machinelike about our sexual behavior and that something seems to be missing. What is usually missing is our human, feeling side: our likes and dislikes, our tenderness and concern, our fears (breathes there a man who has never been fearful in a sexual situation?), and sometimes our excitement and enthusiasm as well.

Because we learned that it is not right or manly for us to be ignorant or scared or tender, we try to hide these feelings under a mask of aggressive sexuality, cool confidence, or stony silence. This often backfires in sex. Our arousal systems and our erections, as we discuss later in greater detail, are extremely sensitive to certain feelings, especially anxiety. What is not expressed in other ways may well be expressed by a lack of interest or by a refusal to become or stay erect, or by a tendency to ejaculate very quickly. The tragedy is that often a simple acknowledgment of the feeling is all that is needed to resolve the difficulty.

Another problem created by this myth is that we tend to label any positive feelings we have toward another person as sexual. All of us—men, women, children—need support, validation, physical affection, tenderness, and the knowledge that we are loved and wanted. Sometimes these needs can best be met through sexual activity; many times they are best fulfilled in other ways. But since men were not taught to differentiate among these needs and since the needs themselves are suspect for us—is it really OK to want to be held or "just" to snuggle or to want to hear that she cares for me?—whenever one of them presses for expression, we assume that sex is what we want. In sex we can get some of these other needs met without raising any questions about our masculinity.

We often try for sex when that is not really what

we want or need. Sometimes a hug or hearing "I love
you" is much more satisfying than sex. It is more satisfying because it is more relevant to our needs at
the moment. If, on the other hand, we were to go
through a complete sex act just to get that hug, we
might well end up feeling disappointed and resentful.
After all, the best way to get a hug is to get a hug. But
if getting a hug is not legitimate, we may have to try
for sex or get nothing at all. We thus often do not get
our needs met, or go to ridiculous effort to get very
simple things. And in the process, we stay confused
about what we really want.

We miss so much by hanging on to this myth. We
miss opportunities to let our partners really know us,
and as long as we feel that parts of ourselves must never be revealed, we must constantly be on guard lest
some of our secret feelings or qualities sneak out. Being on guard all of one's life hardly seems to be the
best way to live. We miss the chance to be open about
our needs and have them met. So we go without the
support, the understanding, the physical affection, and,
in a word, the love we all want. And we overburden
sex, forcing it to meet needs that really aren't sexual.
Since, as we discuss later, our sexual systems are
fragile, they may function poorly when too much responsibility is placed on them.

Myth 2

In Sex,
As Elsewhere,
It's Performance
That Counts

As boys and men we are socialized in what Jay Mann
calls the three A's of manhood: Achieve, Achieve,
Achieve. We learn that it is by our performances and

productions that we will be judged. We are taught to accept or create tasks, to focus on the goals and work doggedly until they are reached. Nothing comes easily or by itself; only by trying and working hard can anything be accomplished. Feelings and any other factors that might get in the way are denied or ignored.

We are good at being achievement machines. Give us a job with a goal, some job specifications, and perhaps a time limit, and we are in business. And it works well in many areas; this orientation has been useful to us in getting through school, winning games, making money, and so forth.

The problem is that the performance ethic becomes the only way of doing things. Rather than a useful approach appropriate to some situations, it becomes our only approach, and, for many of us, our only way of being. We are uncomfortable with time and situations that are unstructured, with just letting things happen. We feel uneasy when we do not have a goal to strive toward. We have to make tasks of everything, since we feel at ease only when we have a job to do.

It is understandable that we should bring this performance orientation to sex. How else could we, given our training, handle such an anxiety-laden experience? And we get plenty of support from the sexual model because, being a predominantly male enterprise, it is about nothing so much as performance.

The goals—usually intercourse and orgasm—are the only important factors in make-believe sex. One does a minimum amount of what is needed to achieve these goals. You might have to wine and dine the woman, say sweet nothings you don't mean, and perhaps engage in some foreplay—but you keep it to a minimum and never lose sight of the reason you are going through all this uninteresting activity. There is actually little foreplay in most erotic materials, and just playing around with each other's bodies without any particular goals in mind is almost unheard-of.

The point is clearly made in this joke popular during World War II. A soldier on leave finds his wife exposing her breasts provocatively. "I haven't got time to chew the fat," he says, "just time to come and go."

Throughout his work, Henry Miller offers countless examples of goal-oriented sexuality. He goes immediately for the crotch. The fewer words and other preliminaries, the better. In the following example, he is visiting a woman he hardly knows to console her on the death of her husband. She has asked him to sit beside her on the couch.

Sitting there on the low sofa, the place flooded with soft lights, her big heaving loins rubbing against me, the Malaga pounding in my temples and all this crazy talk about Paul and how good he was, I finally bent over and without saying a word I raised her dress and slipped it into her. And as I got it into her and began to work it around she took to moaning like, a sort of delirious, sorrowful guilt punctuated with gasps and little shrieks of joy and anguish. . . .

The preoccupation with reaching goals that is induced by our performance orientation means that we tend to ignore or not fully participate in the process of sex (it is "only foreplay") and therefore miss out on experiences that might well be stimulating and pleasurable. We miss more than we realize. The willingness and ability to participate and "get into" the process is precisely what makes possible a full and enjoyable sexual response. Paradoxically, focusing on the goal to the exclusion of what comes before it makes attainment of the goal difficult or impossible.

The result of our goal orientation is an inability to focus on the present, since we have been trained always to attend to what is in the future. The tragedy is that even when we reach our goal—be it intercourse, orgasm, or something nonsexual like a certain status or income—we can't enjoy it because our goal orientation forces us to focus on yet another goal. We can never pay attention to where we are at the moment, which means that it is very difficult for us to enjoy anything.

We make work of sex. It becomes businesslike and mechanical, another job to be done, another goal to be achieved. As Roxie Hart says of her man in *Chicago,* "When Amos made love it was like he was fixin'

a carburetor." Rather than seeing sex as a way for
two people to relate and have fun, and asking how
much pleasure and closeness there was, we view it as
a performance and ask how hard the erection was,
how long we lasted, and how many orgasms she had.
When problems develop we look for mechanical aids
and advice to help us do it better, much as we read
manuals on how to care for our cars and other machines. The more we do this, the further we get from
our feelings, ourselves, and our partners. The more
this happens, the better the chances that sex will become boring and grim or that a dysfunction will develop.

Living in an advanced technological age, it is easy
to assume that what is needed to make sex more interesting and exciting is a technical solution—a pill
or shot, a new position or partner, a better foreplay
routine, and so on—when, in fact, in sex and all aspects of human relating what is really needed is the
willingness to get to know ourselves and our partners
better and to flow with or "get into" whatever contact
there is.

Preoccupation with reaching goals also means high
levels of anxiety, for anxiety is simply the fear that the
goals will not be reached. The greater the need to
achieve them, the greater the anxiety. Since anxiety
tends to block sexual interest and response, we are
caught in a bad bind: the more concerned we are
with performing well and the harder we try, the less
well things go. There is no doubt that it is this need to
perform, to do it right and reach the goals, that makes
sex so difficult for so many of us.

A last consequence of the performance ethic is that
we tend to place a high value on work and a much
lower value on pleasure. Many of us still believe deep
down that it is not quite right to be doing something
just for fun. As a result we set aside little time for
physical affection and sex. Other things—work, paying
bills, taking care of the children, doing maintenance
work around the house—all take precedence. Sex is
usually squeezed in between these "more important"
matters. Many men engage in sex only when they are

tired, in a hurry, or have other things on their minds. Is it surprising that they are not quite satisfied with their sexual experiences?

The alternative to performance orientation is easy to state but it goes against our training and is therefore not so easy to put into practice. Sex need not be a performance. There is no right way to do it and there are no particular goals to achieve. Sex can be whatever you and your partner want it to be at the moment, whatever best expresses and satisfies the two of you. All that is needed in this regard is the expenditure of a little time and energy to find out more about your sexual self. The information and exercises in this book are of course dedicated to this end.

Myth 3

The Man Must Take Charge of and Orchestrate Sex

I remember the first time a woman told me to relax and do nothing, that she wanted to make love to me. Even as I was agreeing to her proposal, I was busy doing things to her. I wanted to comply with her request but had tremendous difficulty being passive and letting her lead. Only then did it occur to me how busy I was in sex. I not only conducted the band but played all the instruments as well.

We learned that sex was our responsibility and that we had to do it all. We should initiate (and even if she initiates, we still have to do the rest), we have to turn her on, we have to turn ourselves on, we have to lead all the way (deciding which procedures and positions should be adopted), we have to give her at least one orgasm, and we have to produce our own orgasm. No need for any help from our partner, thank you.

This myth stems from two old ideas about the nature of masculinity: that being a man means being the leader and the active one (and the concomitant fear that not being in charge is a sign of inadequacy); and that a real man needs little or nothing from a woman, either in terms of information or stimulation.

All of this responsibility and activity are often experienced by us as burdens but are nonetheless difficult to relinquish because they exemplify so many of the masculine "virtues."

This myth leads to problems in relationships since the partner is denied the opportunity to be the initiating, active one. More and more women want to initiate and take charge, at least some of the time, and battles can develop when their partners refuse to let them do so.

Another problem deriving from this myth is that when we are so busy doing for our partners we often do not get anything for ourselves and do not get aroused or erect.

> Jim, a man in his forties who was in a sex therapy group because of erection problems, went on at great length about all the things he had done for his partner—touched her there, kissed her here, rubbed her somewhere else—and was perplexed by his lack of erection. When asked what she had done for him, he was stunned. It simply had not occurred to him that she wasn't the only one who needed to be touched and rubbed.

That it didn't occur to him is understandable since our basic sexual model teaches us that men don't need anything special to get aroused and erect. The thought of having sex or the mere sight of a woman should be all that is required. Only women need special attention to "get in the mood," or so the model says.

Many men believe that they should produce their own turn-on, that they should come to a sexual situation already excited and erect. This, they think, is the "normal" way, while getting an erection as a result of direct stimulation from the woman somehow indicates a deficiency.

Because of this conviction many of us, like Jim, do not get the stimulation we need. Being more passive and allowing our partners to stimulate us is particularly important if we have trouble getting or maintaining erections. For being more passive allows a greater focusing of attention on the incoming stimulation, and it is just such focusing that can often overcome the difficulty, as well as increase the amount of pleasure that is experienced.

We have also taken total responsibility for satisfying our partners. She *should* have an orgasm, at least one, and we feel guilty if she doesn't. And, since we were taught that being a man means knowing it all, we are reluctant to ask her what we should do to help her reach orgasm. Like Bill Cosby said: "I never thought of her showing me, because I'm a man and I don't want her to show me—I don't want *nobody* to show me, but I wish somebody would kinda slip me a note. . . ."

We look everywhere for that note. We read books, attend speeches, and talk to doctors and therapists to find out how to satisfy a woman. We look everywhere but the one place where we might get the answer—the woman herself. We are afraid to ask what she likes because such an admission of ignorance might raise questions about our manhood. After all, we should know what to do; the men in erotic literature and film don't have to ask their partners what turns them on, they just know.

What we need to learn is that there is no way to know in advance what will please a partner. All women are different and even the same woman will have different desires at different times. No matter how experienced we are and no matter how many books we have read, we are going to have to learn from her, just as she will need to learn from us what we like. We need to understand that a good lover is not one who already knows what to do (since such knowledge is simply not available beforehand) but one who is open to learning about his partner's needs and desires. If the information we desire is not spontaneously offered, we need to learn to ask for it.

It would also benefit men tremendously to understand that we have taken on too much responsibility in sex. Partner sex by definition is a two-person venture and it is a bit presumptuous for one of the parties to assume that he has to take charge of, and be account-able for, everything that happens. Women want to share in what happens—in fact, one of the major complaints women have about men in sex is their unwillingness to share more of the responsibility and themselves. It's really not true that you have to do it all by yourself.

Myth 4

A Man Always Wants and Is Always Ready to Have Sex

Erotic materials portray men as always wanting and always ready to have sex, the only problem being how to get enough of it. We have accepted this rule for ourselves and most of us believe that we should always be capable of responding sexually regardless of the time and place, our feelings about ourselves and our partners, or any other factors. We have thus accepted the status of machines, performing whenever the right button is pushed.

Most of us have acknowledged a woman's right to say no to sex (even if it made us angry and we tried to change her mind, it was still her right) and to set con-ditions as to when and how she would have sex with us. But we have been unable to take these rights for our-selves, to recognize that sometimes we are simply not interested in sex, and that sex is better for us under certain conditions than under others. We work very hard to live up to this myth of perpetual readiness and severely berate ourselves and wonder why we are in-adequate when we do not function according to plan.

It is not a question of adequacy. We simply are not sex machines and we cannot function as the fantasy model demands we do. Our sexual systems are highly complex, influenced by many factors and vulnerable to many kinds of interference. Just as each of us has a particular constellation of circumstances that allows us to do our best creative or productive work, and sets of conditions under which we carry out such necessary operations as digestion, elimination, and relaxation, we each also have a set of conditions that maximizes the probability of a full and satisfying sexual response. When these conditions are not fulfilled or at least approximated, we function poorly or not at all.

This is a hard pill for most of us to swallow since it runs counter to the deeply held conviction that a man is always capable sexually and that only women need conditions to be right. After all, the men in sexual fantasyland can do it anytime, any place, and with anybody. And we were also told that a man is one who is not deterred by adverse conditions; he grits his teeth and pushes on, bowling over or in some other way overcoming obstacles and difficulties. While this procedure may work in some areas, in sex it works not at all, for here the harder one tries, the less enjoyment and arousal there is.

While the idea of sexual conditions takes some getting used to (as does the related idea that sometimes you just aren't going to be interested), it's definitely worth the effort. Acceptance of these ideas is directly related to how much you get out of sex.

Myth 5

All Physical Contact Must Lead to Sex

Physical contact in the fantasy model serves only as a request or demand for, or a prelude to, sex. Cuddling, hugging, kissing, holding, caressing, and other types of physical affection that do not lead to sex are completely absent in pornography and rarely encountered in any erotic material. Touching is always portrayed as the first step toward sex. It is not seen as something valuable or pleasurable in its own right; it is useful only to the extent that it paves the way to a presumably grander event.

These beliefs about touching affect men much more strongly than women. There is a greater tolerance for females of all ages to touch and want to be touched. A girl or woman can ask for a hug, or to be held, without much hindrance (although some men are likely to get angry if she doesn't want to go further). But can you imagine a man asking "only" to be held and seriously meaning it? A lot of people would think that very strange. We are taught that only two types of physical contact are appropriate for males. One is aggressive and includes not only the rough contact in sports and fighting but also the mock violence men often display with one another (as when friends greet each other with a playful slap or punch). And the other is sexual. Physical contact that is neither sexual nor aggressive is truly a no-man's-land. According to what we were taught, it really isn't OK for a man to want only a hug or a caress.

The idea that touching is sexual is so deeply ingrained in us that many men refuse to engage in any physical contact whatsoever unless it is going to lead to sex. They think they are being considerate, not wanting to tease or, in the words of one man we worked with, "not wanting to start something I can't finish." A common phenomenon in couples where the men are experiencing sexual problems is the complete absence of any touching: no hugging, no kissing, and, often, sleeping at opposite sides of the bed.

As we discuss later, the myth that touching must lead to sex is harmful to everyone, but particularly to men since we have been most powerfully affected by it. It robs us of the joys of "just" touching, it confuses us as to what we really want at any given time, and it puts pressure on us to be sexual whenever we touch or are touched.

Myth 6

Sex Equals Intercourse

Both men and women learned that the main thing in sex is intercourse, and for most of us the two terms are synonymous. This is hardly surprising since almost all resources that deal with sex—medical books, textbooks, popular books and articles, as well as erotic materials—treat sex and intercourse as if they were the same thing. Kissing, hugging, and manual and oral stimulation of the genitals are all fine, but mainly as preliminaries to the ultimate goal: intercourse. The very term we use to describe these other activities—foreplay—clearly indicates their lowly status relative to intercourse. They are presumably important only as means to that main event.

The extent to which this myth pervades our culture can be measured by its place in the thinking of serious and intelligent sex therapists and researchers. Even Masters and Johnson show little understanding in their three books that real sex can be anything but intercourse.

In the past, when the goal of sex was conception, intercourse was absolutely necessary. You can't make babies without it. But times have changed and these days the goal of most sexual encounters is recreation rather than procreation. There is no longer any good reason why a sexual experience has to end in or include intercourse, unless that is what the participants desire.

This means that there is no "normal" or "natural" way for sex to proceed. There are always many choices that can be made regarding what is to be done, when, and how. And this, as the following story demonstrates, can be unnerving.

During the first few years that I was sexually active, I sometimes wondered about how homosexuals decided what to do in sex. I had a reasonably accurate idea of *what* they did, but it was unclear how they went about organizing what was to happen in a given encounter. They had so many possibilities to choose from and no normal or regular way like we heterosexuals did. I knew that heterosexual sex usually more or less followed the same routine: kissing and hugging, playing with her breasts and then between her legs, putting my finger in her vagina (no one seemed to know about the clitoris in those days) and then, either because of a signal from her or because I felt like it, insertion and intercourse. This was just the way it was supposed to be. I occasionally engaged in oral or manual stimulation to orgasm but only when circumstances were not conducive for intercourse. So I knew how the game was to be played and was certain that all other heterosexuals did it just the way I did. But I imagined that each homosexual encounter was preceded by a long negotiating session in which the partners decided who would do what, and in which order. What I didn't realize until years later was that I actually had as many options as they did but, because of the myth of coital primacy (sex must include intercourse), I wasn't able to see them. This realization was less of a thrill than you might imagine because it brought up the possibility of communicating with my partners about what I wanted and what they wanted, something I had little experience with, and that made me somewhat uncomfortable. I was barely secure in doing sex the "normal way"; the last thing I needed was the possibility of making choices and having to talk about my desires.

You may be wondering why we're making such an issue about this myth. Does it really make any difference if you use sex and intercourse synonymously or, in behavioral terms, think that every sexual act should include intercourse? The answer is yes, it makes a great deal of difference.

Belief in this myth can prevent us from discovering what we like.

For many years, while I enjoyed all kinds of sexual stimulation, I always insisted on "finishing" (coming) inside a vagina. I just "knew" that this was the best way. I was quite surprised when I finally allowed myself to climax with other types of stimulation. I enjoyed a sense of being done to or being taken care of that I rarely got with intercourse, and I found that I have the most explosive orgasms through hand stimulation. Of course, explosive orgasms and being taken care of are not the only things I want from sex, and intercourse is better at providing some of the other things I want. But now that I know what leads to what, I feel I have more options and can better choose one that will fit my wants at the moment.

Even if we know what we want, this myth can prevent us from getting it. Many men wonder what their partners will think if they say they are more interested in manual or oral stimulation than intercourse.

Because this myth defines intercourse as the goal and most important part of sex, it reinforces our performance orientation and makes it difficult for us to enjoy other parts of a sexual experience. Many men, when asked how it felt to touch their partners or be touched by them, have said that they didn't know because they were so busy thinking about getting to intercourse. In this way we rob ourselves of pleasure and of fully experiencing the stimulation necessary for an enjoyable sexual response.

Men are not the only ones hurt by this myth. Women who do not reach orgasm through intercourse but who respond best to manual or oral stimulation—and there are many such women—are put under tremendous pressure by the idea that intercourse is the "normal" way to have sex. It makes it difficult for them to tell their partners what they need. And we often feel that something must be wrong either with the woman or with us because she doesn't respond the "right" way.

We hope that what we have said will not be taken as an argument against intercourse. Intercourse can be a wonderful way of having sex. But it is only one way of relating sexually, rather than the only way, and at any given time it may not be the best or most appropriate.

Myth 7

Sex Requires an Erection

This is a corollary of the preceding myth since intercourse is the one sexual act that is impossible without an erection (this is a bit of an overstatement since it is possible to get a flaccid penis into a vagina, but it's not all that easy to do and it certainly doesn't conform to the usual meaning of intercourse). The fantasy model goes even further, however. It teaches that any kind of sex requires an erection.

The erection is considered by almost all men as the star performer in the drama of sex, and we all know what happens to a show when the star performer doesn't make an appearance. The whole show is cancelled or, to be a bit more accurate, the planned performance gives way to an impromptu tragedy, replete with wailing and self-blaming, usually ending with everyone feeling miserable. The woman may blame herself ("I'm not attractive or sexy enough to turn him on") or be thoroughly confused as to why her partner is so furious with himself. The man, angry and confused, may apologize profusely to no constructive purpose, start a fight with her, or go into a fit of sulking which can last hours or even days.

This myth puts tremendous pressure on the man and places him in an extremely vulnerable position. He thinks he absolutely must have an erection, he knows he can't control his penis, and he's also aware that there's no way to fake an erection or hide the lack of one. A most interesting situation, to say the least. We doubt that there is a man anywhere who has not wondered, right in the middle of some enjoyable sex play, if his penis was going to come through for him this time, and quivered at the prospect of its not doing so.

Of course erections are nice and we have nothing against them. Penises were designed to get hard and they usually do when your conditions are fulfilled. But sometimes they don't and you need to be able to take such situations in stride. The problem with this myth is that it creates too much pressure and it is precisely this desperate need to get an erection that makes erections difficult to get or maintain.

You need to learn that all is not lost when you don't have an erection. The penis is not the only sexual part of your body. You can do wonderful things for your lover with other parts of your body and you can enjoy her touching other parts of your body. A penis that is not hard can still feel very good when stimulated, and you might want to give this a try. Regardless of which particular options you choose, the main point is that lack of erection need not mean a miserable time. The experience can still be close, warm, and fun. Neither erection nor intercourse is necessary. Even if you are unwilling to give up the idea that an erect penis is the star of a sexual performance, we want to remind you that every star has an understudy, and understudies have been known to do very well when given a chance.

And, as you will see, the less important erections become, the less it matters to you whether or not you have one, the more abundant they become. Erections flourish best in a relaxed setting, where there is no pressure for anything in particular to happen.

Myth 8

Good Sex Is a Linear Progression of Increasing Excitement Terminated Only by Orgasm (The Myth of the Hard-Driving Fuck)

This myth is actually composed of several different ideas. The first holds that sex should be a process of continuously increasing excitement and passion. Whether the act lasts for minutes or hours, the arousal must continue to build. This notion is typical in erotic materials.

Because of this myth, the idea that sex can be leisurely, with breaks for resting, talking, laughing, or whatever, is foreign to many men. Some of us feel that there is something inherently wrong with a leisurely approach to sex, thinking that it connotes a lack of passion, spontaneity, or masculine vigor.

Here, as with all the myths, there is pressure to perform in ways that may be totally inappropriate to the circumstances. This idea overlooks a basic fact of human psychology, namely that attention and arousal cannot be maintained at very high levels for long periods of time and that as a result there is a natural tendency for them to wax and wane. The same is true of erections: they, too, may wax and wane during a sexual experience, especially as we get further away from our adolescence. But we are not always aware of this, so when we notice our arousal level or our erections subsiding, we panic and try to reestablish the excitement or erection. Such frantic efforts usually end in failure, for neither arousal nor erection can be coerced. How much better if we could just stop and cuddle or rest for a while.

Belief in this myth often gets in the way of developing better ejaculatory control. Such control is relatively easy to develop if the man is willing to stop stimulation when it gets very intense, resuming when the urge to ejaculate has subsided. But this myth makes no provision for stopping during sex.

John, a member of a sex therapy group for men wanting to develop ejaculatory control, had achieved good control with masturbation exercises. When I suggested it was time for him to employ the stop-start method in sex with his partner, he was astonished. He couldn't believe that I wanted him to stop during sex with his partner. Not being able to convince me that the idea was absurd, he turned to the female co-leader and asked indignantly: "What would you think if a man you were making love to said he wanted to stop . . . right in the middle of things?!"

The outcome of John's story is illuminating. After much hard work by the group leaders, he agreed to use the stop-start method with his partner, but only because it seemed necessary to resolve his long-standing problem of premature ejaculation. He followed through and gradually developed good control with her. To his great surprise, he found that he very much enjoyed this more leisurely approach to sex. Sex became a more relaxing and satisfying experience for him, and what began as a distasteful but necessary solution to a problem became an integral part of his sexual behavior. Other men have reported similar stories. Once they found that sex didn't have to follow any specific progression, they were free to discover the ways that best suited their partners and themselves.

Another part of this myth is that sex is wild and uncontrolled. This process is illustrated by the following selection from Harold Robbins:

> *I don't know how it happened but she was in my arms. Then it was like an atomic fire searing through us. We couldn't wait to get at each other. Our clothes made a trail up the stairs to the bedroom. We fell naked on the bed, tearing at each other like raging animals. Then we exploded and fell backward on the bed, gasping for breath.*

According to this scenario, someone must be out of control but it need not be the man and, in fact, he often is exactly the opposite. This makes sense because men have forever been taught the virtue of keeping their wits about them and not letting their feelings get the best of them. But since the fantasy model demands something or someone wild with passion, the role is often assigned to the woman.

Lust without limits is what the sexual model is about. Desire flows in torrents, sweeping everything in its path, and the exuberance frequently verges on or becomes violent. This is the realm of the hard-driving fuck, where better means harder and rougher. From Joyce Elbert's *Crazy Ladies:* "He was much bigger than Peter and he rammed it into her with such force that she screamed out in delicious agony. . . ." A recurring feature of the model is a situation where the woman tells the man that whatever he's doing hurts and then warms up to it and begs him to continue hurting her.

From the novelized version of the film *The Devil in Miss Jones* comes this sterling example:

"Just hold it there for a minute. . . . Yes, put it there. . . . Oh god, oh, Jesus, I can't take it—No, do it, it hurts, but do it. Do it now, do it more. . . . Ahh, it hurts, hurt me . . . faster . . . hurt me . . . hurt me . . . hurt me . . . HURT ME!"

This is a wonderful world indeed, where pain and pleasure are the same and where being pounded and split apart are delicious.

With all the grinding and slamming and banging portrayed in the media, and with the absence of good examples of more tender lovemaking, it is not surprising that many men think of sex as a rough-and-tough business, and that they will be most appreciated if they pummel the hell out of their partners. Since women in fantasyland are always grateful to the most aggressive and even violent lovers, and since there is a clear implication that a man who cannot brutalize a woman is something less than a man, there is considerable pressure for a man to restrain his more tender expressions of affection and give free rein to his more aggressive tendencies.

Aside from the violent parts of things, we should also consider the imperative, driven, and mindless way in which passion is presented. Here is an example from a recent sex manual called *Sexual Loving* by Joseph and Lois Bird:

Ideally, the husband enters the wife when the sex drive of both is near its peak. . . . And at this intensity, sexual actions become very self-centered. They are imperative. His overwhelming desire is to penetrate her fully. Her desire is to be penetrated. At that moment each becomes an almost totally sensual being. Nearly all sensations are concentrated in—or related to—the aroused genitals . . . in the flood of sexual sensations we tend to shut out everything else.

*Even what would be uncomfortable or painful under
other circumstances goes unnoticed in those seconds
. . . the concern and awareness which were dominant
during the preceding lovemaking give way, in large
part, to the imperious demands of self-satisfaction.*

There is nothing wrong with this kind of sex and
most people have probably experienced something like
it (although we hope you realized that the business
about penetration is only another way of saying that
sex equals intercourse). But this is just one kind of sex,
though it is usually portrayed as the only kind. Sex need
not be so driven, so urgent, so mindless, so focused in
the genitals. In fact, it seems that real sex is only rarely
this way. Usually it is simply not so imperious or
"spaced out." Sex can proceed in a more leisurely, gentler fashion, with irrelevant thoughts floating through
your mind, with awareness of things other than your
genitals, and with no overwhelming desire to do anything at all. And such experiences can be very pleasurable and certainly need not be cause for worry because
you were not consumed by passion. What's so wonderful about being consumed, anyway?

A universal rule of make-believe sex, and the last
part of this myth we're discussing, is that it must end
in at least one, but preferably more, orgasms for everyone. And these are no ordinary orgasms. They are
raging, exploding, and earthshaking. From Norman
Mailer's *American Dream:*

*I could not hold back, there was an explosion, furi-
ous, treacherous and hot as the gates of an icy
slalom with the speed at my heels overtaking my
nose, I had one of those splittings of a second where
the senses fly out and there in that instant the itch
reached into me and drew me out and I jammed up
her ass and came as if I'd been flung across the room.*

We don't understand what he said either, except that i
was quite a jolt. Here's a tender thought from Mickey
Spillane's *The Last Cop Out:*

*All she wanted was for him to enjoy, to take, to
spend, to rise to the heights of screaming physical*

pleasure where everything becomes blanked out in those nerve-shattering waves of orgiastic abandonment that left the body spasm-wracked and helpless.

One wonders how anyone could survive all this nerve-shattering, crushing violence.

Orgasms need not be explosive or violent to be part of fantasyland. In this passage, D. H. Lawrence provides the romantic version of unrealistic expectations:

Oh, and far down inside her the deeps parted and rolled asunder, in long, far-travelling billows, and ever, at the quick of her, the depths parted and rolled asunder . . . as the plunger went deeper and deeper, touching lower, and she was deeper and deeper and deeper disclosed, and heavier the billows of her rolled away to some shore, uncovering her . . . and further and further rolled the waves of herself away from herself, leaving her, till suddenly, in a soft, shuddering convulsion, the quick of all her plasm was touched . . . the consummation was upon her, and she was gone. She was gone, she was not, and she was born: a woman.

There are no ordinary, run-of-the-mill orgasms in most erotic materials. Every orgasm is explosive, body-wrenching and/or mind-blowing, and even better than the one before. Needless to say, such is not the way it is in the real world. But many of us take the fantasy as our goal and spare no effort to achieve the ultimate orgasm for ourselves or our partners. Compared to the fantasy, real orgasms can feel rather humdrum.

But there is much more to the orgasm story than that. Even if we do not believe in the fantasy type of orgasm, most of us are wedded to the idea that every sexual event must culminate in some kind of orgasm for our partners and most definitely for ourselves. Well, maybe not quite as far as she is concerned. We know a woman may not have an orgasm every time. But a man must beyond any doubt have a climax in every sex act. Otherwise, as is well known, he will suffer the painful and crippling conditions known as "blue balls" and "lover's nuts." At least that's what we were taught.

Actually, there is no good reason why a man must

have an orgasm every time he has sex. Despite the high school horror stories about blue balls and lover's nuts, they are rare conditions. They can be painful but they usually don't last very long. But because of the influence of those stories and because our sexual model presents almost no cases of men who do not ejaculate every time they have sex, we are convinced that we must come every time, no matter how much we have to work to make it happen.

Sometimes it becomes clear that an orgasm is not going to occur, at least not without great effort. But how many of us have toiled on anyway, frantically grabbing at our partners and every conceivable fantasy in a desperate attempt to come? Why not just stop when we are still feeling good? Orgasms can be wonderful, as can hard-driving fucks, but they are not always necessary or the best way to go. The same can be said of passionate, nonstop sex. It can be nice. But there is also something to be said for a gentler, nonlinear, less lustful approach.

Myth 9

Sex Should Be Natural and Spontaneous

Most of us believe that good sex should somehow just happen. The following quotation from Peter Benchley's *The Deep* well illustrates this notion. The participants met for the first time only a few hours earlier.

After lunch, they played tennis. . . . After tennis, they swam, had dinner, went for a walk on the beach, and then—as naturally as if the act were the next event in the day's athletic schedule—made noisy, sweaty love in Gail's bungalow.

The fantasy model teaches that sex is natural. There may be a need for initiation with an experienced partner, and we can always learn some new tricks, but basically we need do only what comes naturally. There should be no necessity for learning any skills, talking about sex, or taking any corrective measures, for there is nothing to learn and nothing to correct.

In our complex modern society, where everything seems so difficult and artificial, we yearn for something simple and spontaneous that requires no thought or conscious effort. What is more natural than wanting sex to be natural? One man we worked with echoed the sentiments of many when he said: "Why do I have to learn about my feelings and conditions? It seems so artificial. I should just be able to do it!" Why can't sex be natural?

Perhaps sex would be more natural and spontaneous if we had not been taught how *not* to be natural and spontaneous. Perhaps sex would be different for us had we not been bombarded with sexual restrictions, inaccuracies, unrealistic expectations, and double messages all of our lives. We really don't know. But we do know that we were taught about sex from the day we were born. We learned not only from the types of sources cited in this and the preceding chapter, but also from the way our parents touched us; from their reactions to our explorations of our own bodies; from their response to our game of "doctor" with the girl next door; from the way our parents related to each other; and from the images of men and women in the media.

Unfortunately, our learnings made us confused, conflicted, and nervous about the whole subject. Much of what we learned doesn't work or doesn't satisfy us. Talking about natural sex or "just doing it" makes little sense when all this is taken into account.

If natural is taken to mean without learning, sex will never be natural for us. As pointed out in Chapter 2, sex in humans and many other animals is largely a product of learning. Learning cannot be eliminated, but inaccurate and unsatisfying knowledge can be replaced by learning better suited to our needs.

"Spontaneity" and "passion," though having definitions quite different from "natural," are often used in a similar sense, implying a lack of preparation or learning. People often talk of spontaneous or passionate events as if they came out of nowhere, with absolutely no premeditation, training, or preparation. Although such usage has wide currency, it is in error. All acts of adults—whether the artistry of a Van Gogh, Rubinstein, or Nureyev, the grace and "naturalness" of great athletes, the ways we relate to one another—all of these are the result of years and years of training and preparation. It is so easy to overlook the tremendous amount of training and learning, of objectification and routine, and of sheer boring effort, that make any "spontaneous" action possible. Spontaneity and passion are *not* the result of knowing nothing and preparing nothing. Rather, they result from knowing the skills so well that you have forgotten them as skills; they have simply become part of you. Then, when an appropriate situation occurs, they come into play without thought or effort.

The problem with the naturalness myth is that it can get in the way of taking the steps necessary to get the type of sex life you want. Some men find it easier to sit around and bemoan their fate than to do something about it. Your sexual discontent is a product not of what you are but rather of what you learned. That learning can be moved aside to make way for a more satisfying sexual expressiveness.

Our last myth is not a product of the fantasy model. It is a recent idea inspired by the sexual revolution.

Myth 10

In This Enlightened Age, the Preceding Myths No Longer Have Any Influence on Us

Surely, many people say, in these days of increased openness about sex and wider availability of accurate information, the old sexual model must be losing its hold on people. It must be in the process of being replaced by saner and more realistic models.

It would give us great pleasure to agree with such statements but, unfortunately, they don't seem to be true. In many ways the pressure on men (and on women as well) is becoming worse.

Much of the explicitness of recent film and fiction serves only to give more detailed presentations of the same old myths, thus creating even more pressure than before to do it right. The old myths die slowly. You need only go to one pornographic film to check this out.

And a lot of nonsense is coming from people who one might hope would know better. In the old days, the experts were saying that sex, or too much sex, or certain kinds of sex, wasn't healthy. Now, in a complete about-face, many are saying you can't live, or live well, without it. Albert Ellis devotes the entire first chapter of his book *Sex and the Liberated Man* to the disadvantage of sexual abstinence. Ellis, like so many sex educators and therapists, is in the business of selling sex. He tries to make a case that abstinence will impair your physical and emotional health, your future sexual adequacy (presumably you might forget how to do it), and, aside from all this, "it also has grave social disadvantages." In support of his views he cites a number of authorities, including that well-known sex expert, Henry Miller. And, lest you still haven't been convinced, Ellis says interesting things like the following:

> But voluntary *abstinence remains an* unnecessary *evil: Accept* that *misery, and you seem off your rocker. You'd better see a psychologist, fast, than keep afflicting yourself with that kind of nonsense.*

That Ellis and others of his kind are for sex rather than against it may seem liberated, but it's only a modern version of tyranny. Their stance in favor of sex is as rigid as that of the people who used to be against sex and, in fact, their arguments and hysterical tone are remarkably similar.

Sex, we are told in many articles and books, is good for you. It's good exercise, a wonderful way of losing weight, the best way to get to know others, and, well, it's just good for you. The result is pressure to get into sex, whether or not you feel ready for it or interested in it. Just so long as you do it. We fail to see how freedom has been increased.

Group sex and open relationships have become chic in recent years, thus following the road paved in erotica where almost everyone has multiple partners and where in each work there is at least one scene in which sex is done in threesomes, foursomes, hordes, or whole villages. This is fine for people who like their sex communally, but many are feeling that they ought to do it even if they don't want to.

While we're on the subject of current fads, we should mention the resurgence of sado-masochism (S&M), also called bondage and discipline (B&D). Violence and brutality are regular fixtures in erotic material and are currently being peddled as methods for the enhancement of your sexual enjoyment. A recent publication, called *S-M: The Last Taboo,* argues for a repeal of the prohibition. Apparently the authors, and others, feel that there shouldn't be any prohibitions on behavior. That way we could all feel free to punch out anyone we don't like—or do like, as the case may be. In any event, it now appears that you're somewhat square if you haven't at least tied someone to a bed. If you're really with it, of course, you gave them a few smacks while they were helpless. All in the name of pleasure and liberation.

Much of the new pressure on men has to do with the scientific discovery of multiple orgasms in women. The phenomenon of multiple orgasms was a regular feature of pornography for over a hundred years but it became a big issue only after Masters and Johnson reported in 1966 that some women in their laboratory had experienced multiple orgasms with self-stimulation. Their data have been distorted and exaggerated almost beyond recognition. The message most commonly heard now is that all women have this capacity and it should be exercised every time they have sex. Guess who is supposed to produce all these orgasms (that's right: you) and how (right again: through intercourse).

Gail Sheehy, in her book *Passages,* provides a good example of this viewpoint. Although she is aware of the tremendous burden we place on erections, she is so enmeshed in the idea that sex equals intercourse that the best she can do is approvingly cite an example of how a woman can help a man insert a soft or partially erect penis into her vagina. Hard or soft, it just has to go in there. Throughout her chapter on sex, she indicates not the slightest understanding that sex can consist of anything other than penis-in-vagina.

And once it's in there, the man's task is very clear according to Sheehy: to bring his partner "to ecstasy again and again" or, put slightly differently, "through an ascending chain of orgasms." All we can make of this is there is an ascending chain of pressure and responsibility being put on men and women to act in certain ways, all of them rooted in the fantasy model of sex.

Our last example is perhaps the most tragic, for it comes from a therapist who has worked with men and professes sympathy for them. In his *Hazards of Being Male,* Herb Goldberg is appalled by statistics indicating that men in their forties spend more time shaving than having intercourse. "Surely, the male is cheating himself of a vital joy and is entitled to reclaim his full share of the primal pleasures of sex." In other words, you *should* spend more time in bed and perhaps less time shaving. The idea that men may be having as much sex as they want seems not to have occurred to him.

But this is only the beginning. Goldberg then goes on to something he calls fusion sex.

The experience of fusion sex is one of an intense, totally un-selfconscious sexual coming together during which the male is not focusing on or aware of having sex per se but is simply a part of a wholly spontaneous, ecstatic union or fusion with the female, one that often brings him to tears of joy.

In fusion sex there is the phenomenon of a seemingly endless potency, lasting sometimes for an entire

*weekend or several days during which time he remains
in bed making love continually. Men who have reported fusion sex to me describe the phenomenon of
ejaculating and then almost immediately becoming
erect again. They may have as many as twelve to
fifteen orgasms during a weekend's experience of fusion sex.*

You're right if you think this sounds familiar. Aside
from the tears of joy, it differs little from the examples
of fantasy sex we quoted earlier. But now it is coming
under the guise of social science.

Fusion sex is merely old nonsense with a new label.
We don't question the fact that it can happen, but such
experiences are rare and cannot be trained for or
planned. What's the point of writing about them? Surely we already have enough unrealistic expectations. All
that Goldberg and others who write of such things accomplish is to convince many men that they really
aren't getting as much out of sex as they should, and
they therefore should try harder, or try more things, or
else feel bad about all the joy they're supposedly missing.

We trust we have said enough to help you realize
that the old model of sex is very much with us today. It
may now be called liberation or freedom but it's still
the same old junk. What's sadly missing is any sense of
perspective on the role of sex in the lives of human
beings and any understanding of what freedom means.
Sex is not the most important thing in the world and it
is not necessarily good for you. Only the individual can
decide how and where sex should fit into his life, if at
all.

Freedom to be obliged to have sex is no freedom at
all and, in fact, is a contradiction. The same is true for
having to have sex in certain ways or under conditions
set by outside authorities. True freedom means the freedom to do or *not* do as you please, to not have sex
as well as to have it, and to have it in circumstances
of your own choosing. Freedom may be a wonderful
goal for humans to aspire to, but we seem little closer to
it in the sexual area than we were fifty years ago.

The chief difficulty with the fantasy model of sex is that it establishes standards for the way things ought to be, standards that ignore individual differences and that are highly unrealistic, thus setting the stage for disappointment and frustration when reality doesn't match the model. Ralph Keyes, in his excellent study of the influence of high school, *Is There Life After High School?*, makes the point succinctly: "Adult reality generally can't top our high school fantasies. Or match them. Or even come close. In fact, compared with high school's aspirations, sexual reality can really be a drag." High school aspirations are, of course, made up primarily of the fantasy model.

So many times, for both men and women, the reaction to their first sexual experience with a partner is: "Is that all there is to it?" Compared to the fantasies and expectations, it often isn't much. It takes time to adjust to reality and give up the unrealizable expectations. Some of us manage the transition with relative ease, although it is never easy, but many of us have great difficulty letting go of the fantasy.

We strive mightily to play the role we learned. We believe that there is some way of achieving the standards of the model, of having superhuman sex. Somehow, there's got to be a way. And we believe that everyone else knows the secret and is enjoying sexual delights we can barely imagine. So we get angry with ourselves and our partners for not being able to make the magic happen.

Despite our anger and despite whatever remedies we try, the disappointment often remains and even deepens. For in our search for the impossible, we forget the obvious and the important. We forget that in human events there are no right ways, no external scripts that will make us happy. We forget about ourselves, about discovering what we are about, about our own sexuality and the best ways of expressing it. In straining to make reality match our expectations, we lose contact with ourselves and our partners, robbing ourselves of any joyful experience. In our intentness to make sex better, we forget that sex is only a small part of life. We focus on it too much, not putting enough time and energy into other aspects of relating, thus cheating ourselves of opportunities to relate in ways that might bring us much satisfaction.

Are we then saying that there is no way of enhancing your sexuality, of making sex a more comfortable and joyful experience than it has been? Not really, but we are suggesting that changing your sex life may not lie in the direction you think. What is needed is not more exotic practices, techniques, or equipment, but rather a willingness to let go of the sexual script you learned and to create new ones that are more relevant to you. Will this, then, lead to passion-filled sex and the ultimate orgasm? Probably not. But it can lead to sex that accurately reflects your values, your body, and your personality—your self. Sex, like everything else, is limited in what it is and what it can produce. The secret, however, is not to try to increase its yield by adding more partners and equipment, but to "get into" and participate fully in whatever sexual expressions and activities seem appropriate to you. Such experiences are more likely to occur when you are aware of your sexual needs and wants and able to get them.

You may be in a place where "working on sex" to develop some new ways of thinking and acting seems appropriate. This "work" will not always be exciting. It may be boring at times and you may find yourself wondering if sex is becoming too mechanical or routine, or if you are being too self-conscious about it. It may be this way for a while.

What you need to keep in mind is that your training or work time need not be long. How long depends on a number of factors, but most of all on how much time you are willing to give each week. For most of the men we've worked with, a few hours a week for seven to ten weeks has been sufficient.

The process of acquiring new sexual skills is similar to learning most other skills. You may remember that when you were learning some skills that you are now proficient in—such as driving a car, playing tennis, talking to women—you were extremely self-conscious.

You were continually wondering what to talk about or what to do with your hands or feet. But if you persevered you reached a point where you forgot about your hands and feet and what to say. You could just get into the activity in a way that others called spontaneous. The same thing happens in learning sexual skills. At first there may be some confusion, routine, and self-consciousness. But as you learn the details, you forget them. They become part of you and you become free to get more involved in the activity. Then you are open to real spontaneity and abandon.

5

Where Are You Now?

Before you can start changing and growing sexually, it is necessary to examine where you are starting from. This may sound so obvious as to not warrant discussion, but it's unfortunately true that many people who want to change have only the foggiest notion of where they are and where they want to go.

One of the most important lessons to be learned from the remarkable success of the behavior therapies, of which sex therapy is the most successful stepchild, is that the probability of producing change is directly related to, first, a detailed assessment of your current situation and, second, the delineation of specific goals to be achieved. It is, of course, much easier to say something vague about wanting to be happy or to have a better sex life, but the chances of reaching such goals are slim indeed. What specifically would have to happen for you to feel happier or have better sex? That is the key question, since specific goals can be worked toward and achieved; vague generalities, on the other hand, do not lend themselves to planning for change.

Another important aspect of producing change involves dealing with the obstacles to change. There are always obstacles. If there were none, you would already be where you want to be and there would be no need for change. As we mentioned several times in the previous chapters, the main obstacles for men are the sexual fables that comprise the fantasy model of sex. It is essential that you recognize the influence these myths exert on your thinking and behavior. Obstacles can be successfully negotiated, but only when you are aware of which ones are doing what to you.

The exercise below will help you take the first step toward change by giving you an opportunity to examine where you are now. Once that step has been taken, you will be in a better position to set some specific goals for yourself.

EXERCISE 5–1: YOUR PRESENT SITUATION
Time Required: 1 to 2 hours

Write a detailed statement of your present sex life. The more detailed the better. Give concrete examples of all major points. Include the following items:

1. What do you like about your sex life? What parts of it give you pleasure?
2. What about it is not satisfying to you? Be specific as to when and how problems occur and how they make you feel.
3. Which of the myths in the last two chapters are helping to maintain the problems? How?
4. How are you dealing with the problems or unsatisfactory elements (e.g., are you avoiding sex, not asking for what you want, having sex a lot in order to prove that you're really OK)?

This exercise can be done as a list, essay, or in any other form. It doesn't have to be neat, and spelling and grammar don't count. It is for you alone.

If writing is difficult for you, do the exercise by talking into a tape recorder or by covering the material in a conversation with a friend. If you are in a relationship and communication with your partner is good, you might want to discuss the material with her. Obviously, if you do not feel your partner would be a supportive listener, you shouldn't do the exercise with her. Should you choose to do the exercise in conversation, your friend is to function primarily as a listener, reserving comment until you are finished.

If you read the exercise but did not take the time to do it, perhaps telling yourself that you'll go back and do it later, you might want to rethink that decision, particularly if you wish to make changes in your sexual behavior. Changes rarely come about through reading alone.

We wonder if you paid much attention to the first item in the exercise, the satisfactory aspects of your sex life. Men often skip that part, thinking that they should concentrate on what is not going well. That isn't necessarily the case. Surely there are some satisfactory aspects of your sexual behavior, and it's nice to get them on paper so that you can put everything in perspective. Also, sometimes the pleasurable parts offer the best clue about where to go next, as the following example illustrates.

Robin was fairly well satisfied with his sex life but wondered if there were ways of making it even better. In doing the first part of Exercise 5–1, he remembered an experience that he very much enjoyed: his partner giving him oral sex. This was a bit confusing since Robin and his partner often engaged in oral sex. What made this one experience stand out? It turned out that their usual pattern was simultaneous sex; whatever one did to the other was reciprocated at the same time. During the experience he recalled, however, they had not assumed their usual "69" position but he had just lain there and let her do all the work. And it had been one of the most enjoyable sexual experiences he had ever had. But, though it had occurred about two months before he came to see us, it had never been repeated. As we talked further, it became clear that Robin was interested in further exploration of nonsimultaneous sex but that he was so accustomed to being active in sex that this was unlikely to happen unless a program of exercise was established and followed. With our assistance, this was done. Robin and his partner gradually explored various aspects of being active and passive in sex. The process was not always smooth since Robin, like many men, sometimes found that being passive was uncomfortable (a man is not supposed to just lie there and be dependent on the woman's ministrations), but within a few weeks he and his partner felt that they had considerably increased their sexual options and enjoyment.

This example also underscores the necessity of being specific. Until it was discovered what in particular (his passivity) had made his recalled experience so special, it was impossible to know in which direction to go to help him enhance his sexuality.

We tried to be clever in our wording of the exercise to prevent you from using terms like impotence, premature ejaculation, insufficient enjoyment, and lack of interest. These labels are convenient to use, but they aren't very helpful. As we mentioned earlier, it's the specifics that count. When do you get an erection and when don't you? When are you interested or what are you interested in? What do you mean when you call yourself impotent or premature? It can make a lot of difference.

Arthur said in his initial interview that he was a premature ejaculator. When asked if he had any control over when he ejaculated, he answered affirmatively, indicating that he could last for thirty-five to forty minutes in intercourse. But that obviously wasn't sufficient, he maintained, since his wife climaxed only rarely. He thought that if he could last a few minutes longer, his wife would have more orgasms.

Arthur was looking in the wrong place. Teaching him to last for fifty minutes to two hours would probably have been a huge waste of time. Anyone who has some control over when he ejaculates or who can last for thirty minutes can by no stretch of the imagination be called a premature ejaculator. What Arthur didn't realize is that many women never have orgasms during intercourse and that many others reach orgasm this way only a small percentage of the time unless supplementary manual stimulation is applied simultaneously. Lasting for hours on end doesn't help the situation any and will probably only bore everyone. If you are labeling yourself premature, carefully examine what you mean by that and how realistic your goals are for lasting longer.

The same is true for erection problems. Do you believe you should have erections all the time, that you should get them without any direct stimulation, or that they should be as hard as steel? How realistic are your goals?

A sixty-year-old man came over a thousand miles to see us. His wife of thirty-two years had died less than a year before and, while he had had a few erections by himself since then, he did not get one on the few occasions when he had gone out with a woman. He wanted to get married again but felt it would be impossible until he was capable of having erections with a partner. The man was clearly depressed and we asked who or what turned him on. He couldn't think of anyone or anything. Upon questioning, he admitted that he had not felt sexually aroused since his wife died. We tried some sexual fantasies with him and they failed to evoke any interest. The same was true for erotic literature and movies. Nothing elicited the slightest degree of sexual interest, and yet he was convinced he should be able to get an erection. Needless to say, his goal was somewhat unrealistic. Not until he finished mourning for his wife was he able to get aroused and erect again.

This man did have a problem, but it wasn't sexual.

Since, as we have already discussed, men tend to sexualize everything, you will not be surprised to hear that men tend to make sexual problems out of things that really don't have that much to do with sex. We have seen men who insisted they had a sex problem when what quickly became evident was that they disliked or were angry at their partners. Sure, we can say there was a sex problem of sorts (they couldn't get or stay erect), but the primary problem was in the relationship. Their penises were not being contrary but rather were acting precisely the way they were designed to act. Hostility is not an atmosphere in which erections and good sex flourish. The angry feelings, or the situations that produce them, may have to be dealt with first. Until they are resolved, at least partially, better sex may be impossible.

In looking at the myths or rules that are maintaining your difficulties, perhaps you came up with some that were not discussed by us. That is fine. There are many,

many myths that get in the way of good sex, and we discussed only a few. The important thing is to recognize the ones that are getting in your way.

Terry was generally satisfied with sex but there was one aspect that, while not a major problem, was an annoyance. The first few times he had sex with a new partner, even if he was comfortable with her and felt very good about her, he could not have an orgasm. He could live with this situation but preferred not to if a solution was available. Terry knew a lot about what excited him and never had any problems coming through his own efforts. We asked what prevented him from using this knowledge with a partner. It turned out that he had tried telling his partners how to touch him and, while they did what he wanted, it still did not result in orgasm the first few times. We asked about the possibility of his touching himself while he was having sex with a partner (e.g., touching the base of his penis while having intercourse or using his hand as well as her hand or mouth when they were doing something else). It sounded reasonable to him but there was some resistance because one of his rules—a quite common myth in our culture—was that in partner sex you do not touch yourself. The resistance was worked through in a few sessions and the problem was resolved.

What is keeping you where you are is what you need to discover, whether or not we mentioned it or whether or not other people also believe in that rule. It can probably be moved out of the way so that you can get more from sex, but the chances are much improved if you can clearly identify it.

The last aspect of Exercise 5-1 is the role of solutions, how you are dealing with the problem. Home remedies frequently serve to maintain rather than resolve the problem. Trying to will an erection, for example, usually makes an erection impossible. The same is true of gritting your teeth and trying to hold back an ejaculation. Not letting your partner touch your penis because you fear she will find it too small or soft does nothing to resolve those fears and, in fact, often maintains or even increases their power.

Take a close look at how you answered the last item in the exercise. Is it possible that your "solution" is maintaining the difficulty? If so, what steps can you take to stop applying that solution?

Now that you have determined where you are starting from, you can set some goals you'd like to achieve. You should be aware that you need not achieve all of them right now. Changes can be made in steps, and short-range goals may be considerably less than what you would like in the long run.

Bob had never been able to ejaculate during intercourse and, during his current relationship, found that he rarely could maintain an erection for more than a few minutes. Although he wanted to resolve the ejaculation problem, it seemed logical to deal only with the erection problem first. Once that was resolved and he was able to have intercourse, we could deal with the remaining difficulty.

To put the lesson from that example in other words, don't take on too much at once. That will only serve to disappoint and frustrate you. Go slowly, taking small steps. Be realistic: you can only do so much at a time. Also, be sure your goals are in fact *your* goals, not standards of someone else's choosing.

The following exercise will help you be more specific about your goals.

EXERCISE 5–2: YOUR GOALS FOR
. A BETTER SEX LIFE
Time Required: 30 to 45 minutes

Write a letter to an imaginary friend telling him or her how you would like your sex life to be. Be wary if it sounds anything like the fantasy material we discussed in Chapters 3 and 4. Discuss the aspects you would like to change, listing how you would like them to be different. If there is a need, separate immediate and long-range goals.

Do not be brief. Discuss your wishes in detail and be very specific about any changes you plan. Note any obstacles that might get in the way of reaching your goals. Mention any concerns you may have about reaching your goals. Is it possible that there would be negative aspects to making the changes? This is not uncommon and, should there be even a slight hint

that problems could occur as a result of making changes, read
the part of Chapter 22 called "The Uses of Sex Problems."

Now that you have set some goals for yourself, you
have laid the foundation for change. Keep your answers
to the last two exercises; you may wish to refer back to
them later.

Before going further, you should consider the following issues.

—If you found possible negative consequences *for*
making sexual changes, you should follow the suggestions in Chapter 22. Trying to make changes before you are more comfortable with the probable
outcome may be very difficult.

—Since whatever can get in the way probably will,
pay careful attention to any obstacles to change you
noted in Exercise 5–1. Are there any ways of pre-
cluding their appearance or at least of mitigating
their influence?

—If you suffer from a serious illness or injury, have
had surgery recently, are taking medication of any
sort, or have reason to question your health in any
way, get a complete physical examination and read
Chapter 21. When you see your doctor, discuss
your sexual problem with him and ask him to check
for possible physiological causes. If your doctor is
not comfortable discussing sexual matters or does
not seem knowledgeable in this area (and many
doctors fall into these categories), ask him to refer
you to one who is. It is up to you to get complete
and understandable information about the issues that
concern you. Ask questions, ask for clarification
when you do not understand; be sure you get what
you are paying for. It is important that you try not
to be intimidated by the doctor's professionalism or
his apparent lack of time. Even if you are intimidated, as most of us are in the presence of physicians, attempt to get the information.

—Look at your priorities and time schedule to determine how you can devote the two to five hours a

week we'll ask for sexual exercises. You should make
sure that you can spend the time leisurely and without interruption.

Many men, although claiming that sex is very
important to them, allow very little time for it in their
schedules. This usually does not make for enjoyable
sex. The time you set aside should be prime time.
Be good to yourself.

—If you are in a relationship, you might want to discuss your plans for change with your partner. While
not absolutely essential, it is preferred, since you will
progress much faster if your partner is informed and
willing to cooperate when necessary.

If you find that the two of you are unable to
agree on the importance or goals of change, or that
you have difficulty talking about the subject, read
Chapter 12, "Dealing with a Partner," now. It is
important that the two of you agree on the nature of
the problem and how it's going to be resolved. If
there is substantial disagreement—if, for example,
you believe there is a sexual problem but she feels
the difficulties lie in other areas—it will be very difficult to make progress in resolving anything. Talk it
out and decide where you should put your energy.

6

Your Conditions
for Good Sex and
How to Get Them

This chapter is one of the most important in the book. It presents a way of looking at sex that is different from the one most of us learned. Having a better sex life very much depends on understanding and being able to apply what is in this chapter.

As we mentioned in Chapter 4, men learned that they should be able to perform on demand. Given a willing partner, we should become aroused and erect, ready and able to have a good sexual experience. While girls and women had all sorts of special requirements (needing to trust us, to feel loved, and so on) we were less complex and didn't need anything "special." If she was willing, that was sufficient to get our sexual apparatus working. And if that wasn't sufficient, we tried frantically to kick the machinery into operation by trying harder, by working at it. Then we began to worry. What was wrong with us that it required so much effort to become aroused or erect? Why didn't it happen spontaneously the way it was supposed to?

The truth is that it was never supposed to work the way we were taught. We men are not as simple as we

have been led to believe. We are complex human
beings, with diverse styles, needs, likes, and dislikes.
This is as true in sex as in other areas, but because of
what we learned about how we were supposed to be
sexually most of us don't know this. When sex doesn't
work out the way we like, we are all too ready to assume that something is wrong with us for not responding the way we think we should, rather than to look at
the situation to discover what about it might be blocking our sexual responses.

Let's look at what is needed for a satisfying sexual response in more detail so you can get a better idea of
what facilitates or blocks such a response. The two
basic ingredients are arousal and a relatively open nervous system.

Arousal (synonymous with desire, excitement, and
turn-on) is not easy to define. It is not the same as
erection. Arousal and erection are separate systems.
They often go together—you feel excited and get an
erection—but not always, and it is crucial to separate
them in your thinking.

Arousal refers to feelings, a desire to touch someone
and have sex with her. It is often experienced as a pull
or surge toward a lover and it can also be more ab-
stract, with the desire or pull being present but without
a specific partner in mind. Men have described arousal
in these ways: "a wanting to be with her, to be close
to her, to merge with her"; "a warm tingling sensation
in my penis and elsewhere"; "an overall feeling that
I want her"; "feels like my blood is racing and I can
feel my heart beat"; "my whole body comes alive in a
special way."

Your own experiences of arousal may or may not
be similar to these examples. The important thing is
that you know when you are sexually excited. What
specific sensations or feelings tell you that you're in a
sexual mood?

Men often think they are turned-on when they aren't.
Because of our training, we frequently look to the situation rather than to our feelings to determine if we're
interested in sex. If the situation is one that our edu-

cation defined as sexy (e.g., having an attractive woman indicating that she wants sex with us) we assume that we are, or should be, aroused, without checking to see if that is indeed the case.

The importance of arousal can hardly be overstated, yet it is commonly overlooked. We are all so caught up in the myth that men (and, more recently, women as well) will automatically be turned-on in a situation the fantasy model defines as sexual that we often forget to ask whether we really are interested.

Despite this cultural blindness, however, you need to check your interest if you desire a better sex life. Before launching into a sexual experience, ask yourself if you *feel* aroused (remembering that feeling is not the same as thinking) or if there is some potential for becoming excited. If not, better do something other than sex. Otherwise, you risk the possibility of not enjoying the sex or not functioning well.

The second ingredient for good sex is an uncluttered nervous system that will allow your arousal to be reflected in your bodily state (e.g., getting an erection) and let you fully experience what is happening.

Let's say a man is looking at something, perhaps his partner's legs, that usually excites him. If his nervous system is obstructed—by concerns about something that happened at work, for example—seeing her legs may not feel sexual and, in fact, her legs may hardly be noticed at all. He's looking at her legs but the perception has no impact on him. This is an example of how a cluttered nervous system can block arousal.

But let's assume that man does experience his partner's legs as sexy and feels turned-on. For this feeling to have an impact on the state of his penis, a message has to be sent to it through his nervous system. The message says, in effect, "This feels great, so get hard." As the man continues looking at his partner, or as this is replaced by other types of stimulation—touching, talking, fantasy, and so forth—more and more similar messages are sent and received, producing and maintaining a state of arousal and erection.

Simple enough, but there is a slight hitch. The message to the penis must be clearly sent and received. If his nervous system is obstructed, the messages to the penis don't get through properly.

There are many things that can clutter the nervous system so that sexual messages don't get through. Alcohol and many other drugs are well-known culprits. Other common factors are guilt about sex, anger at partner, preoccupation with other matters, fatigue, and poor physical health.

The most common obstructor of the nervous system during sex, however, is nervous tension or anxiety. This includes any doubts or concerns about the situation and one's acceptability and performance ("Will the kids walk in?" "Will she think I'm as good as her other lovers?" "Can I last long enough for her?").

Such concerns, if they are strong, throw the whole nervous system into a tizzy, obstructing the transmission of sexual messages to the penis and other areas. Regarding the penis, the messages may not get through at all or only a few may get there; you may not get an erection, or it may not be as firm as usual, or you may quickly lose it. Anxiety, anger, and other feelings can also stimulate the processes involved in ejaculation, triggering quick ejaculations. Any efforts to get or keep an erection, or to hold back ejaculation, usually only add another layer of tension to whatever is already there, thus making it even more likely that something will go wrong.

An obstructed nervous system can also block enjoyment. There are men who can function even when they are unaroused and/or their nervous systems are cluttered up with anxiety, concerns, or anger. For reasons we don't understand, they are able to bypass many of the requirements that other men have. They can function no matter how nervous or bored or angry they are. These feelings affect their nervous system in a different way—they function but they don't feel much. They feel little closeness, love, joy, or excitement. Theirs may seem like a wonderful situation, since they can function almost anytime regardless of the situation, but you need only to talk to one or two of them to realize they get very little from their sexual encounters.

Erections, ejaculatory control, and feelings of arousal and enjoyment cannot be directed by force of will. We cannot coerce an erection or force ourselves to get turned-on or to enjoy an experience. This is a crucial point and one that is difficult for many men to accept, since it goes counter to our training. As mentioned in our discussion of the performance orientation, we men learned to get things done by giving direct commands to our minds and bodies. ("Don't get rattled; stay calm." "You can do it; push harder.") This system works well enough much of the time, but only with those parts that we can directly control.

For better or worse, our arousal, erection, ejaculation, and feeling systems cannot be controlled in this way. They do not take orders. In fact, attempts to direct them a certain way more often than not result in their doing just the contrary. If you have any doubts about this, it is important that you put the proposition to the test. Whenever you want, try to will arousal, erection, good feelings, or to hold back an ejaculation. Beg, threaten, sweet-talk, issue any kind of command you like, and observe the results. Then perhaps you'll be more open to considering the idea that this isn't the best way to deal with sex.

So what can you do to have better sex? Very simply, you need to discover the conditions under which you are most able to become aroused or erect or experience good feelings. A "condition" is anything at all that makes a difference to you sexually. It can involve your physical and emotional state, how you feel about your partner, what you think you can expect from her, the type of stimulation you want, the setting you are in, or anything else. A condition is anything that makes you more relaxed, more comfortable, more confident, more sexual, more open to your experience in a sexual situation. Another way of looking at conditions is that they are the factors that clear your nervous system of unnecessary clutter, leaving it open to receive and transmit sexual messages in ways that will result in satisfying sex for you.

We sometimes conveniently ignore the fact that even machines have conditions, requirements that allow them to function at their best. Our highly valued cars, for example, have requirements in terms of type of gas, oil, servicing, and ways and places they should and should not be driven. Yet we seem more tolerant of their needs than of our own. We don't call our car stupid or bad or impotent if it doesn't run with an empty gas tank. We simply accept the fact that it needs gas to run and we meet this requirement. But when it comes to ourselves, we have a different set of standards and don't hesitate to call ourselves inadequate or bad or impotent if we don't function the way we think we should, no matter how poorly the situation meets our requirements.

Mort, a man in his early thirties with erection problems, had no trouble understanding the idea of conditions . . . for his boat. He was very proud of his possession and could talk eloquently about all of its requirements, which he was happy to meet in order to get the best possible performance from it. On the other hand, when it came to his penis, he couldn't understand why it didn't operate the way he wanted. That a boat should have all sorts of special needs he could understand, but a penis, well, it should just work all the time and not need any special attention. It took him a while to understand that a penis is, if anything, more sensitive and more vulnerable than a boat, and that its needs have to be attended to for it to function satisfactorily.

The reason that Mort and so many of the rest of us have trouble accepting our sexual needs as valid is that they run counter to the fantasy model, to the way we were taught "it ought to be." There is no tolerance in the model, and therefore very little in ourselves, for individual variations or needs. Which means, when you get right to the essence of it, that our model has little room for individuals at all.

It seems obvious to say that we all have our individual preferences, styles, and needs; they are what make us the unique person that we are. The problem is that, except in those rare cases where our own styles and desires are similar to those glorified in the model, we tend to be ashamed of them. We have been carefully taught to feel guilty for having any special or unusual needs (which means anything that does not fit the model).

We try to hide the parts of ourselves that do not conform to our sexual script in order to spare ourselves and others from seeing how "inadequate" or "strange" we are. We try to pretend that we don't need or want what in fact we do, that we aren't who we really are.

It is worth repeating what we said in Chapters 3 and 4. Compared to the sexual model we learned, we are all inadequate and deficient. None of us can measure up to its absurd standards. The problem is not in us, but in the model we compare ourselves to, a model that, to be charitable, is utter nonsense and unfit for human consumption.

It is perfectly acceptable to be yourself, to have your own desires, anxieties, concerns, and style. They need not be viewed as deficiencies or, as one man called them, "weirdnesses." They are merely expressions of your uniqueness. Your special requirements or conditions, in sexual and other areas, are a large part of what you call your "self," and the less of it you feel bad about and want to hide, the easier your life will be.

We realize that at this point some readers may be confused. They will recall times in their lives when arousal, conditions, and feelings didn't have to be considered. They were usually aroused in sexual situations, they functioned well, and they enjoyed themselves. What happened? We can't really answer that question, but the phenomenon is a common one. Many men function automatically—that is, without regard for any particular conditions or, as we mentioned earlier, without even needing to be aroused—for a while. And then the system breaks down. We aren't sure why the automatic functioning ceases, although it is clear that it often involves a trauma of some sort—divorce, infidelity on the part of a partner, loss of job, or one sexual experience that goes poorly. Whatever the cause, it appears from our experience that automatic functioning, once disrupted, cannot be restored, at least not in the same way it existed before the disruption. The man is forced to start paying attention to factors he once could ignore: e.g., whether he is aroused, relaxed, and getting the proper stimulation. Of course, as time goes on and these factors become a regular part of his thinking, his functioning will become less self-conscious and, therefore, more automatic. But it will now include some elements previously ignored.

Your sexual systems were designed to work for you and allow you to have good sex. All you need to do is determine the conditions under which they can best satisfy you. Here is an example of how one man discovered this.

Jan had never had a sexual dysfunction but both he and his wife of two years felt that they weren't having as much sex as they wanted and that it wasn't as enjoyable as it was in the past. His wife complained that he rarely initiated sex and often turned down her invitations. It turned out that Jan had many times felt interested in sex but had not acted on it and was now trying to quash even the interest. What, we asked, would have to change so that he would feel free to have sex when he felt in the mood? This was his answer: "I'd just have to know that we wouldn't get locked into the same routine every time. When I think about what sex will be like, I lose all interest. It's always the same routine. I have to spend lots of time getting her ready for intercourse, even when she initiates, and it all goes according to the same ritual. I enjoy it this way sometimes, but it's the thought that it always has to be this way that gets me. I know I probably shouldn't say this, but sometimes I'd like a quick screw, with no foreplay or messing around. Sometimes I'd like just a blow-job, without having to do anything in return right away. I guess I mainly want the feeling of some freedom. I want to know that there are some possibilities other than the same old stuff."

Jan was stating his conditions for being more interested in sex. It was interesting to watch his wife while he talked. Although they had good communication in most areas of their relationship, sex was something they hadn't been able to talk about. His wife at first looked shocked—she had never heard him say these things—but then started smiling and finally was laughing wildly: she felt precisely the way he did. It rarely works out this quickly, but the important thing was that once his conditions were met, once he knew that sex could go in many different ways, his interest returned and sex became more enjoyable.

Before presenting two exercises that will help you discover your conditions for good sex, we want to mention a difficulty that you may encounter. You may find yourself coming up with things you wish were not true. Some of your conditions may at first strike you as old-fashioned, feminine, strange, or something else that you feel is bad or inappropriate. Whatever your feelings, it is best to write the conditions out and give them serious consideration. We say this because it is our experience that most conditions are easier to accept and fulfill than to change. Unless your conditions involve pain or harm to you or your partner, the chances are very good that, no matter how new or unusual they seem to you now, you can learn to accept them and find effective ways of meeting them.

The two exercises that follow have been very useful to many men for discovering their conditions. Read them both and then do the one that you like best. The first one is stated in general terms. If you have been having a problem in a specific area, e.g., arousal, erection, or enjoyment, you might want to direct the exercise toward it.

EXERCISE 6–1: CONDITIONS ESSAY
Time Required: 45 minutes

Compare the three or four best sexual experiences you have had with an equal number of ones that did not turn out well, and list all the factors that differentiate between the good and bad ones (for example, "In all the good experiences, I knew the women well; this wasn't true in the bad ones"). The elements that characterize the good experiences and are lacking in the bad ones are your conditions for good sex. Be sure to be as specific as possible. If you have not had any good experiences, or if it is difficult to remember them in sufficient detail, simply use your imagination and list those things you think would be necessary and helpful for you to have good sex.

Whether you use comparisons or your imagination, consider

all these areas: your physical health; amount of anxiety or tension; use of alcohol and other drugs; your feelings about yourself; the extent to which you were preoccupied with other matters; fears about performance, pregnancy, and venereal disease; your feelings about your partner (how much you are turned-on to her; your conviction that she cares for you; your confidence that she will not put you down if you are not a perfect lover; and any anger or resentment toward her).

When you have finished with your list, put it away for a day or two, then reread it and see if there is anything you want to change or add. Now go through each item and reword it so that it is specific enough to be put into practice. Let's assume that one of your conditions is "knowing it won't be a disaster if I don't get an erection." This is too vague. You need to ask yourself: "What would have to happen for me to know that it won't be a disaster if I don't get an erection?"

One man we worked with answered that question like this: "First, I'd have to know that she was interested in more of me than just my sexual performance and, second, that she could take a lack of erection in stride without getting angry." This was still too general. We asked him what he would have to do in order to feel confident that she was interested in him as a person and that she wouldn't be angered by a soft penis. He came up with more specific ideas: "I'd have to spend some time with her before we got into sex. If we got along well and I felt she liked being with me and doing things with me, then I'd know she was interested in more than just my cock. I'd also need to talk to her about sex, to tell her that I don't always get an erection, and also that her satisfaction is very important to me. I'd want to know if she would let me take care of her orally if my penis wasn't working. If she reacted well to this, I'd feel comfortable." His hitherto vague conditions were now workable. He could take his time with his partner before getting into sex and, with a little help from us, was able to have the conversation he wanted. He followed through beautifully, he met his conditions, and his sex life improved rather dramatically.

The importance of being specific cannot be overemphasized. If your conditions are too general to be put into practice, you obviously will be unable to attain them.

The next exercise may strike you as a bit odd when you first read it. We hope you won't let this put you off. It has worked extremely well for many men—most of whom thought it was strange indeed when they first heard it—and it can also be lots of fun.

EXERCISE 6–2: LETTER FROM YOUR PENIS
Time Required: 60 to 75 minutes

This letter (or list) is to be written from the point of view of your penis. Yes, you read it right, from the point of view of your penis. So before beginning take a minute or two to imagine what it's like to be your penis. Try to put yourself in its place. Imagine yourself dangling there between your owner's legs. What would that be like? Then address yourself to the question given below and let yourself write whatever comes to you. It is important that you write with as little censoring and editing as possible. Just write whatever comes, no matter how messy, ungrammatical, illogical, or silly it seems. As much as possible let your penis do the writing, so to speak.

The question to be answered is: HOW DOES MY OWNER MISTREAT ME? Be as specific as possible, giving examples whenever appropriate. Spend no more than 45 minutes on this question. When you are done, put your letter away for a day or two.

When you come back to the letter, reread it and add anything you want. Then again take the point of view of your penis and spend 15 to 30 minutes answering this question: HOW COULD MY OWNER TREAT ME BETTER?

From these two letters you should be able to come up with a fairly complete list of your conditions for good sex. Spend as much time as you need to make them specific enough to be workable.

There are two conditions that are absolute musts, no matter what your situation or concern. Please add them to your list if you did not come up with them yourself. NEVER TRY TO USE YOUR PENIS IN SEX WHEN YOU ARE NOT AROUSED, and NEVER TRY TO USE YOUR PENIS IN SEX WHEN YOU ARE ANXIOUS. These are other ways of saying that you should involve your penis only when you are turned-on and reasonably relaxed. Flouting these conditions is an excellent way of getting into a war with your penis, a war you cannot possibly win.

Check your list of conditions again. How many of the items are absolutely necessary and how many are not? You probably need to attend to only the most important ones. Most men we've worked with have found that meeting one, two, or three of the most important ones are all they need to improve their sex lives.

The implication of discovering your conditions is simple. You are going to have to learn to deal with sexual situations so that your most important conditions are met or at least approximated. How well you function and how much you enjoy are directly related to the extent to which these conditions are fulfilled.

At this point you may be feeling discouraged. Knowing your conditions sometimes has this effect at first. Do some of the items on your list surprise you, make you wonder if you're weird, or leave you feeling that you'll never be able to meet them? Such reactions are common. We were trained to think that we had no special requirements, so it's no surprise that we get concerned when we find that we do. Here are two typical responses:

I guess I always sort of knew about these things but I never saw them so clearly or took them seriously. Now I'm worried. Seems like it would take lots of work to get them all set up.

Some of this sounds so feminine. Trust, closeness, knowing she likes me—those are things I expect to hear from my sister. Do you really think there are women who would go to bed with me with this damn list of stuff?

It can be upsetting to learn that we are quite human and have very human kinds of requirements. It is natural to wish that things were different, that meeting conditions was not necessary. Before you get depressed or throw part of your list away, consider the items carefully. Are you really less of a man because you have such needs? If you answer in the affirmative, you should clearly delineate just what is your image of a man. Is it at all human? Does it make any sense for you to compare yourself to such a standard?

Consider your conditions again. Is it at all conceivable for you to honor them without giving up your membership in the male sex? Do you really believe there are no women who could accept you and your conditions?

While you are thinking about these heavy questions, you may find some comfort in the following story, the source of which we no longer remember:

A world-famous bullfighter, the epitome of masculinity in his culture, entertained some guests at his villa one evening. After dinner he disappeared and one of the male guests went in search of him. He found the bullfighter in the kitchen, wearing an apron and washing dishes. The guest was appalled and blurted out, "How can you be doing such a feminine thing?" To which the bullfighter replied, looking down his nose at the guest: "Whatever I do is masculine."

The bullfighter made an important point. Whatever he does, and whatever you do, is an expression of yourself. Since you are both male, how could it be feminine? Wearing an apron and washing dishes, taking care of children, wanting gentleness and emotional closeness in sex, or almost anything else—if it is an expression of a male, how could it be other than masculine?

That the bullfighter's guest or you or anyone else thinks otherwise is only because you have accepted certain social fictions—sex-role stereotypes—as valid. Such fictions may have had some useful functions in the past, but it is painfully clear that the present demands more flexible arrangements. John Wayne, Harold Robbins, Henry Miller, and the rest of their kind are no longer relevant, if indeed they ever were.

And it still isn't easy. It is difficult to admit needing things that contradict the myths and stereotypes we learned so well. It becomes easier, however, when we realize that the myths themselves are what limit our functioning and enjoyment, in sex and elsewhere. It is precisely through our conditions—our needs and desires—that we can express our maleness, our humanness, our selves. And it may help to know that not one of the men we have worked with felt that he lost any of his masculinity in the process of fulfilling his conditions.

Many, in fact, spontaneously reported that once they could accept and express their conditions, they felt more like men than ever before.

Greg never had any problems functioning sexually—he was a swinger by any standard—but he rarely experienced any joy in his activities. He was well versed in the techniques and tricks of sex, he always had erections, he could last forever, and his partners often complimented him on his virtuosity. He got little, however, beyond the knowledge that he was "a great fuck." Even his orgasms felt "only like a few muscle contractions." Greg thought that conditions were "dumb" but, since nothing else worked, he reluctantly set out discovering his. He found that he needed to like and care for his partner, feelings he had spent most of his life running away from. He feared getting involved with women and therefore only had sex with those he found attractive but didn't like. It was a long, hard struggle for Greg to overcome some of his fears of caring and involvement, but he made it to the point where he could enjoy sex and relating to his partners on many levels.

Several months after he terminated therapy, Greg asked for an appointment to deal with another issue. In the course of the session, he said the following about his sexuality. "It's strange looking back at where I was. I thought I was the biggest cocksman in town. But now I know the horrible price I paid for all those performances with women I didn't care for. It's like I buried a big part of me, all my feelings, so I could play the role. Now I've mellowed out and settled down. I love Jenny and we've been thinking about living together. She satisfies all my sexual desires. Sex is great with her. I'm not performing—actually, I'm having less sex than ever before in my life—but I enjoy it so much. It's really fine and I feel more of a man than ever. Not the kind of rowdy, show-off I was before, but more quiet, more secure. I like it better this way."

Meeting Your Conditions: Basic Assertiveness

Conditions fall into two general categories: those that can be dealt with entirely on your own, and those that require you to deal with a partner. Examples of the first type would include requests from your penis for some nonsexual contact with you (such as talking to it or light touching) or for gentler treatment in masturbation. These and similar goals can be accomplished without anyone else's knowledge or participation. Sometimes these are easily dealt with and sometimes not. It mainly depends on your willingness to take the time and energy to be good to yourself. We give an exercise later in the chapter to help you with this.

The second class of conditions, those requiring a partner's participation, may be more difficult. Let's say that one of your conditions is not to have sex when you are tired. This is easily accomplished if your partner never takes the initiative. But suppose you are tired and she indicates that she wants sex. You now have to deal with her. Many men deal with such a situation either by not dealing with it—that is, by acquiescing to the partner's requests and ignoring their conditions—or by pretending not to notice the partner's advances. Done often enough, the first method can lead to a dysfunction or a dislike of sex, while the second can leave the partner feeling confused and rejected. In neither case is the man honoring both his conditions and his partner.

Men have a reputation for being able to get what they want and to stand up for their own interests. That's what being a man is about, isn't it? Sadly, we have found that when it comes to sex, men are rarely able to do what is best for them, rarely able to communicate their needs and feelings to their partners. However assertive they may be at work or in other areas of their lives, most men have difficulty getting their sexual needs met. They are so focused on acting the way they think a "real man" should or on pleasing their partners that they often do not get what they want.

We have come a long way from the heyday of the "Slam, bam, thank you, ma'm" performances. Now women are supposed to have orgasms and we feel it is our responsibility to provide them. It is true that there are still some men around who are totally inconsiderate of and insensitive to their partners' needs, but their ranks seem to be dwindling rapidly. The pendulum has swung far in the opposite direction and most men feel under tremendous pressure to satisfy their partners. If they don't, they feel guilty and label themselves failures.

Because of the pressure to satisfy their partners' needs and live up to the standards of the fantasy model, men often sacrifice their own enjoyment. Thus we find men making love when they don't want to, when they are too tense to fully respond, in ways they don't like, and sometimes even with partners they find unattractive—usually with the excuse that "she expected it, so what else could I do?" Such self-sacrifices rarely make for good sex.

If you think we are joking or that meeting your conditions will be easy, consider the following questions seriously:

—Could you let your partner know that you are not in the mood for sex even though she is interested?
—Could you tell her that you don't want intercourse but would like some other form of sex?
—Could you indicate in a clear way that you want to stop in the midst of a sexual experience?
—Could you let her know that certain feelings (anger, anxiety, boredom, etc.) are interfering with your sexual feelings and functioning?
—Could you give her directions how to stimulate you in ways you find more pleasurable?
—Could you ask her to tell or show you how she likes to be stimulated?

If you answered yes to some or all of these questions, we have another one for you. Could you tell her these things in such a way that did not leave her feeling humiliated, disliked, or undesirable? If you can honestly answer yes, you are one of the fortunate few. These are generally situations that men find difficult to handle.

The trick is to learn to assert yourself in sex, to learn to get the conditions you need and not go along with situations that make you uncomfortable—and to do so in ways that do not crush your partner. Assertiveness is not rudeness, bullying, or aggression. Being assertive does not mean that you won't consider your partner's needs or satisfy her. It does mean, however, that you are going to pay serious attention to your own needs. It does mean that you will express your desires directly and try to get what you want. Your partner may not always be responsive and compromises will have to be negotiated. This may be new for you but you will find that they can be worked out in ways that honor both of you.

So often in sex today the situation is that each partner is focused primarily on the other's satisfaction. The woman is trying to figure out what the man wants and expects, while he is busily trying to determine how to satisfy her. Each is looking out for the other and neither is taking care of his or her own needs. So much time and effort is spent on the other that both partners are unlikely even to be aware of what they themselves want. A lot of mind reading and guesswork are necessarily involved since neither partner is willing to be direct about what is wanted. That, we have been taught, is selfish and to be avoided. While such altruism may sound lofty and virtuous, the result is usually somewhat less than satisfying for both participants. If both could start paying more attention to getting their own needs met—a little selfishness, if you like—sex would be so much better for both.

Meeting your conditions and asserting yourself sexually are parts of a larger concept: being good to yourself. We men are always so busy doing our tasks—work, studies, chores around the house, taking care of bills, and so on—that we rarely take sufficient time to get what we need and enjoy, and this is directly related to the problems we have in sex.

The following exercise is intended to give you the

opportunity to do some of the things that please you. Though important in its own right, it is also good preparation for the exercise that follows it, which deals with asserting yourself with others.

EXERCISE 6–3: DOING SOME THINGS YOU ENJOY
Time Required: Variable

This week do one or two things that you really want to do and that are fun for you. The main criteria are that you enjoy them and they not be work-related. They may or may not involve other people.

Here are some examples of what some men have done with this exercise. Robert, who was working himself to death, took a few hours to lie in bed and watch television. Stan went fishing, an activity he loved as a young man but had "been too busy to do" in the last twelve years. Lou, always busy doing something "useful" and "constructive," allowed himself three hours a week for fun things that were absolutely useless, like reading mysteries and science fiction. And George, who loved animals, spent a relaxed afternoon at the zoo.

Your activities may or may not be similar to these examples. As long as you enjoy them, you're on the right track.

If you have trouble thinking of things you like to do, think back over your past and see if there were any activities you once liked but have given up. You might want to try some of them again. Or ask yourself what you would do if you had a million dollars and didn't have to work.

Do at least one or two enjoyable things per week as long as you follow the programs in this book. We hope you will continue taking time for yourself long after you have forgotten the book.

Now that you've had some practice being good to yourself, it is time to begin asserting yourself with others, which is just another way of being good to yourself. The next exercise was developed by our friend and colleague Lonnie Barbach and is the best we have found to help you learn to assert yourself with others and get your sexual conditions met. It is long and a bit complex, so we suggest you read it and the discussion that follows it carefully before putting it into practice.

EXERCISE 6–4: YES'S AND NO'S
Time Required: Variable, but usually no
more than a few minutes a week

Yes's: A Yes involves getting or attempting to get something you want from someone, which you ordinarily would not allow yourself to ask for. It can literally be anything at all so long as you really want it and it's something you usually don't ask for. The assignment lies in the request, not the response. Even if your request is rejected, you have done a Yes by asking. Some examples of Yes's are: asking someone to give or loan you something, like a book, record, or money; asking someone to spend time with you or listen to a problem; asking for a certain type of stimulation or sexual activity.

The following example is a good illustration of how one man went from doing enjoyable things for himself to asking others for things he wanted and, finally, to getting his needs met in sex.

Roy had worked hard all his life building up his construction firm, taking very little time off for personal pleasure, and asking little from anyone except for business reasons. While he at first saw no connection between this pattern and his lifelong problem with erections, he agreed to do some things that pleased him. He took off three hours from work on Saturday mornings to do some reading, an activity he had enjoyed in his youth but had not done for years. He was pleasantly surprised at how much pleasure he still derived from reading. Another nice thing for himself involved coming home from work earlier than usual a few days a week so he could do sexual exercises while he still had some energy. He soon found he could come home at a reasonable hour, every evening, with plenty of time for reading, doing sexual exercises, and spending some time with his family. He also found, and this is typical, that his work suffered not at all; if anything, he was getting more done at work than before and in much less time. In therapy we talked about the kinds of things he had once enjoyed, like sailing and fishing, and he used some of his Yes's to ask his wife and friends to join him in some of these long-forgotten activities. As he became more confident about asserting himself, Roy started talking to his wife about what he wanted in sex. In time, all of his conditions were met and his sex life showed considerable improvement.

No's: A No is a refusal to do something that you don't want to do but usually go along with, perhaps to prevent an argument, to preserve your nice-guy image, or for some other reason. If you habitually loan money to a friend not because you want to but because you fear what he will think of you if you refuse, turning him down the next time he asks would be a No.

We all do many things we don't want to do. Some of them are necessary since the consequences of not doing them are quite serious (not paying your income taxes, for example). But there are many other things we don't like that we really don't have to put up with. The No's will give you an opportunity to turn some of them down. Being able to say no is very important in sex: going along with things you don't like in sex is one of the best ways not to get turned-on and to lose interest in the whole subject.

While most No's are in response to direct requests from others, some are not. You probably do some things because of expectations built up long ago. Refusing to continue these behaviors, even though no direct requests are made, is a No.

Maggie and Fred had for years driven thirty miles every Sunday night to have dinner with his parents. This had been going on so long that invitations were no longer extended. It was simply understood by all that Maggie and Fred would show up Sunday at five o'clock. In therapy both said they would prefer to spend their Sunday evenings in other ways, but they were worried how his parents would feel if they stopped coming to dinner every week. It was pointed out to Maggie and Fred that this worry controlled their lives. Most of their time was taken up meeting the needs and expectations of their parents, children, and friends. Even though they didn't like many of the things they were doing, they couldn't change because of their fear of hurting someone's feelings. They were far better at respecting everyone else's feelings than they were at taking care of their own. After some talk, Fred told his parents that although he and Maggie would be happy to consider individual invitations, they would no longer be coming every Sunday. His parents were disappointed and hurt, but Fred stuck to his position. This No turned out to be very important to this couple. After dealing with his parents, they were able to make similar changes in other important relationships and start living their lives more in accordance with their own desires. They learned that you can't satisfy everyone else's needs and that they can live with the occasional disappointment friends and others express toward them. Two years after that first No to his parents, their marriage and sex life are better than ever.

SUGGESTIONS FOR DOING YES'S AND NO'S

1. Do two Yes's and two No's the first week. After that, do three of each a week. As you do them, you will discover what is easy and what is difficult for you. Since there is no benefit in endlessly repeating easy items, gradually include more difficult ones. If, for example, after a week or two you find that Yes's are easy for you but No's are hard, you can do only No's, six a week.

2. Start small. Discouragement is the only reward for trying to change the world in a week. Start with items that are easy, even trivial, and gradually work up to topics and items that are more difficult. Unless you believe that you are already quite assertive, do not do any sexual Yes's and No's the first few weeks. Wait until you are comfortable doing them in other areas.

3. Use your common sense. There are situations where the consequences for being assertive may be very serious. We suggest you don't say no when the highway patrol pulls you over for speeding or when a thief demands your money unless, of course, you are willing to accept the consequences.

4. Continue doing Yes's and No's until you feel confident of being able to get your sexual conditions fulfilled. This may take anywhere from two to twelve weeks. Since this exercise takes only a few minutes a week, it is simple to do while you continue with other exercises in the book.

POSSIBLE PROBLEMS

1. You don't find anything to say yes or no to. If there is nothing for you to ask for or reject, then your life is precisely the way you want it and you are probably perfectly content. Or maybe you're not looking hard enough. You might find it helpful to take some time every night to review the events of the day and see if there's anything you wanted that you didn't ask for or anything you did that you wish you hadn't.

2. You try to do too much too soon. This is the most common problem in doing this exercise. It cannot be sufficiently emphasized that you should start with relatively easy situations and only slowly work up to more difficult ones. For example, if asking someone to loan you something is difficult, don't start out by asking for $1,000 or the use of his car. Start with something you are more comfortable with, perhaps the loan of a book or a dollar. Since this is an extremely important exercise, do it in such a way that will allow you to progress and feel good about it.

3. **You feel bad about being rejected.** You will undoubtedly get turned down some of the time when doing Yes's. If you are getting rejected almost every time, this either means that you are asking for too much or from the wrong people, or that you are asking in such a way that defeats your aim. You should carefully read the discussion that follows the exercise.

If you are getting rejected some of the time, there's probably nothing to be done about it. It is a basic fact of life that neither you nor anyone else is going to get everything he wants. And it may not feel good. The negative feelings about being rejected will probably diminish as you realize that you are also getting some of the things you wanted, but they will never disappear entirely. The only thing to be concerned about is if your fears of rejection prevent you from asking for what you want. The only way to get what you want is to ask, and this inevitably entails some unfulfilled desires, some hurt and disappointment. The alternative, however, is far worse for most people: less disappointment perhaps, but also far fewer of the things desired. The choice is yours to make.

4. **You feel guilty about being assertive.** Contrary to popular opinion, women do not have a monopoly on feelings of guilt. Many men feel bad when they start putting their own interests first. In some extreme cases, dealing with this guilt requires professional assistance. For most men, however, these feelings will diminish in frequency and intensity as they get more practice in using their assertive skills. If you are feeling guilty, it may help if you write down what rules you have broken (guilt usually involves a rule that has been violated: something you "should" have done but didn't or something you "shouldn't" have done but did). For example, "I should always put a woman's needs before my own," or "It's not nice to try to get what I want; it's selfish, and no one will like me." Seeing these rules in writing can help you understand the absurdity of the standards you are trying to meet.

Being assertive means expressing yourself directly in appropriate ways. It means avoiding the extreme position of being so compliant and mousy that you don't get your needs met and also avoiding the other extreme of being so overbearing and aggressive that you trample over the rights of others. This middle position of assertiveness, however, is by no means a thin line. There are almost an infinite number of ways to express directly and appropriately what you want and what you don't want, and you can find those that feel most comfortable and work best for you. The Yes's and No's exercise will provide you with many chances to try different approaches and evaluate their effectiveness.

Below are some guidelines that have been helpful to the men with whom we've worked. Try them out and see which are most useful to you. The examples, here and throughout the book, are real. They were reported by men we've talked to and worked with.

1. *Be direct and to the point.* Beating around the bush may be easier, but it's likely to confuse the other person regarding what you are saying, thus making a positive response less likely. Try an approach like these:

(A) John, could you give me a ride home tonight? My car is being fixed and I took a cab here.

(B) I'm sorry but I'm working on something that's very important to me and I just don't have the time to give you a massage tonight.

Not like this:

(C) Gee, Molly, you want me to help you move to-morrow. . . . Well . . . that's Saturday and I was thinking of going to the beach to relax. . . . Hmmm, I guess I could go to the beach some other time. . . . Tomorrow, huh? . . . I'm not sure. . . .

The speaker in example C is not giving a clear message. He probably hopes that Molly will notice his ambivalence and withdraw her request. By not directly expressing himself, he's putting himself at Molly's mercy. If she doesn't tell him to forget it, he may well find himself helping with the moving, even though he doesn't want to.

2. *Don't blame, just say what you want or don't want.* You are much more likely to get an affirmative and understanding response when you put your request in the most positive terms possible. For example:

(A) Honey, it's been a long time since you and I spent some time together without the kids or anyone else. I'd like to have a few days just with you, the way we used to before we were married. What about going to Mendocino next weekend and leaving the kids at home?

Calling people names or blaming them is not useful in most cases. Here's a negative version of example A:

(B) Goddamn it, I'm sick and tired of having the kids around the house all the time, along with all your stupid relatives. Why the hell don't you tell them to stay at their own homes sometimes? Another Sunday like this, with twelve people in the house, and you better believe it, I won't be coming home anymore!

The men in examples A and B really wanted the same thing, but they expressed themselves rather differently. While example B looks extreme on paper, we have heard similar speeches too many times to think that they are unusual. You won't be surprised to hear that while one of these men had a lovely weekend with his wife in Mendocino, the other got a battle that raged for almost a month.

And like requests, rejections are more effective (and less painful to all concerned) when they are put in the most positive way possible. For example:

(C) You look wonderful and I'm getting tempted. But I'd rather not make love now. I'm tired and I have to be at work early tomorrow. Tell you what, if you're free tomorrow afternoon, I can come home early and we can stay in bed as long as we want. That way, I'll be rested and can give you the attention you deserve.

Not like this:

(D) I don't know what it is about you, but you're always wanting sex when I'm tired or have to get up early in the morning. The last few weeks I've had lots of free time and could have gotten interested in sex, but did you show any interest? No. Now when I'm tired and up to my neck in worries, now you get interested. I think there's something wrong with you.

Both men are saying no, but the man in example C is doing it in a way that is probably acceptable to his partner and is also working out a compromise. The man in D is clearly headed for trouble with his partner.

3. *Give a reason for your request or rejection.* People tend to respond more positively if they understand the reasons for your yes's and no's. Note, however, that giving a reason is not the same as telling a lie. All of the constructive examples given so far include reasons.

4. *Be firm and persistent.* Many people give up too easily after making a request or giving a rejection, especially when they encounter resistance or do not immediately achieve their goal. Persistence often pays off. Like this:

(A) Touch me there but a little harder. . . . That's better but I'd like it still harder. . . . I think you might be afraid of hurting me. I'd like it harder and you don't have to worry about hurting me. . . . Here, let me show you how hard I want it. . . . Wow, that's much better, really feels good.

Not like this:

(B) Touch me there but a little harder. . . . Hmmm . . . is that harder? . . . I don't know . . . I guess that's OK. . . . Could you, well, no, it's OK the way it is . . . yeh, it's fine [and, of course, it isn't].

The man in B is settling for less than he wants. He'll feel dissatisfied, and perhaps angry or resentful as well. The man in A is being clear, firm, and persistent, and he's getting what he wants. Being firm, however, does not mean being stupid:

(C) Touch me there but a little harder. . . . Harder, I said! . . . That's not harder. Don't you think I know what I want? . . . Can't you do anything right?

There's simply no reason to carry on this way.

Being firm is particularly important when doing No's. Some people will try to sweet-talk you into changing your mind or make you feel guilty for rejecting their request. Here's an example:

(D) I'm sorry, Mary, I'd like to help you out but I have to teach a class at eight in the morning and I don't see how I could take you to the airport at two A.M.

(Mary says you're her last hope. No one else can take her and there's no other flight she can take. She'll have to call off her trip if you don't take her. Besides, she's done you some favors.)

I know you've done me some favors, and I'm grateful. And I realize you're in a bind. I would like to help you but I'm not willing to go at that hour on Tuesday morning. If you like, I could take you at midnight and you could wait at the airport for the plane, or I could take you on another morning, but not Tuesday.

But won't Mary be angry, disappointed, or frustrated? Probably. And there's nothing you can do about it except to take her to the airport when she wants to go. But that's going to make you unhappy. This is a clear case of having to decide whose needs come first. You have tried to do what you could for Mary without sacrificing your sleep. You have even offered her some alternatives, which leads us to our next guideline.

5. *When doing No's, offer alternatives if you want to.* If you are unwilling to grant a request as it is given but are willing to do something else, say so. The man in example 4D has done this: he offered to take Mary to the airport at two different times that were more convenient to him and that might be of help to her. If nothing else, the offering of alternatives can help ease any guilt you are feeling about rejecting the other person's original request. You are not totally refusing to help but are offering a compromise. If a compromise is not acceptable, if your friend wants what she wants precisely the way she asked for it, you can feel easier about saying no.

Offer alternatives only if you mean them. Otherwise, someone may call your bluff and you'll have to deliver.

If you simply don't want to have anything to do with taking Mary to the airport, regardless of the time or day, better say so.

6. *Express your appreciation when your requests are granted.* When you do a Yes and the response is positive, be sure to indicate your appreciation. Long speeches and gushing sentimentality are not needed, just a simple "I appreciate this" or "Thank you for taking the time." Such expressions let the other person know you recognize his or her efforts and are grateful for them, which usually will have the effect of making him or her more open to future requests from you.

These suggestions and examples should be sufficient to help you begin to get your conditions met. We return to this subject in Chapter 12, with further discussion of how to assert yourself in sexual situations and how to communicate with sexual partners.

If after giving the Yes's and No's a fair trial for at least four or five weeks, you are still having great difficulty doing them, you might want to consult one of several good books on assertiveness. *Your Perfect Right, Don't Say Yes When You Mean No,* and I *Can If I Want To* have been helpful to some of our clients.

Before leaving the issue of expressing yourself, we need to give further attention to positive expressiveness. Being able to do Yes's and No's is absolutely necessary for getting your conditions fulfilled and enhancing your sex life. At the same time, it is very important to express approval, praise, appreciation, and caring. Much of what passes for assertiveness training overlooks the necessity for balancing expressions of wants and rejections with expressions of liking and approval.

This is an especially difficult area for men. Our social scripts give us permission to be assertive. We still have difficulty with it, especially in the sexual area, but at least we have the permission. But where is the permission to say, "I care for you," "I feel good when I'm with you," or "I really appreciate your help"? The answer is that there hasn't been much permission or even tolerance. The strong, silent heroes we were given as models didn't say such things.

Expressing approval, support, and liking seems, well, feminine to many men. We know that women express such thoughts and feelings, and we like it when they are directed at us, but we aren't sure it's OK for a man to say such things. And besides, we haven't had much practice doing it.

An exercise we've used for years in group therapy involves the men pairing up and role-playing, asking their "partner" to stimulate the men's arms. We set the situation, which usually involves the "partners" not doing it quite the way asked for, so the man must keep correcting "her" with further instructions. Many of the men have trouble getting their "partners" to do it the way they want, and this is what we expected. What surprised us at first was the reaction we invariably got when we gave this situation: "She's doing it perfectly now, just the way you want. It feels wonderful. What do you do now?" Their reaction: dead silence. So we try again. "She's doing exactly what you want. It feels great. Can you somehow express how good it feels or how much you appreciate what she's doing?" At this point, some of them, with difficulty, give some positive feedback. Others continue to have troubles even after we give them specific examples of what they might say or do.

It may be difficult at first but giving positive feedback is well worth the effort. It makes you more balanced and makes it easier for others to hear and respond to your requests and rejections. If can also ease any guilt you have about asserting yourself, since you know that you also express things the other person likes to hear. Other people can understand you better; they get more information about you when you give compliments and praise. And last, expressing yourself in positive ways broadens your ability to express a wide range of emotions, a type of expressiveness most men lack and one that is greatly admired by women.

A few more examples of what we are talking about:

I appreciated your help with this project. It sure eased my burden.

That outfit looks wonderful on you.

It's nice to know I can turn to you when I have a problem.

It feels wonderful when you touch me like that.

You look so beautiful when you come. It makes me feel good.

I'm glad you're in my life.

Sound corny or mushy? Maybe, but only when such responses are not sincere. We are not suggesting you lie in order to gain some advantage with others; rather, we are saying that you must like and approve of some of the things that people around you are doing, particularly those you are closest to, and that you should make sure you are letting them know about it. Do you verbalize the good feelings you have for others as much as you could? Do people know that you like and appreciate them? Do they know you are thankful when they do something for you?

If you think you are not doing as much in this area as you'd like, you can assign yourself the task of giving one or two positive expressions every day. As time goes on, the practice will become automatic, but at first it may be difficult. You may have to spend a bit of time thinking about what you like and are grateful for in particular persons before you go to tell them. And you may find yourself coming up with reasons why you don't have to tell them ("She already knows I care— I'm living with her—so what's the point of telling her?" "I show my appreciation and love in action, so why should I use words?"). Expressing feelings through nonverbal means is fine, but words can add a lot, too.

The message is: express yourself. Your likes and dislikes, and your approval, support, thanks, and love.

7

The Physical
Aspects of Sex

Any sexual activity is an elaborate combination of physical and psychological factors. Feelings, thoughts (yes, it's really OK to think during sex), and physical changes are all part of sex. Yet it is surprising how often one or the other aspect is ignored. We have heard talks on sex that so focused on the feelings of the participants that one could easily forget that sex has anything to do with the rubbing of bodies. On the other hand, and perhaps more commonly, sex is treated as though getting one set of plumbing fixtures to mesh with another and produce a grand splash is the only thing that matters.

Both the physical and psychological are important. They do not always work together and, indeed, may be at complete odds with one another, but they both need to be considered if you are to understand yourself and have good sex.

This chapter is designed to give you a better understanding of, and appreciation for, your sexual anatomy and physiology. Such knowledge has proved helpful to most of the men with whom we have worked. At the same time, we try to place the physical in a psychological perspective, for one without the other is quite meaningless.

Women are not the only ones concerned about their physical appearance. Many men are dissatisfied with their bodies. They believe that they are too fat, too thin, not muscular enough, too short, or too tall. We have even talked to a few who refused to wear short-sleeve shirts because they felt their biceps were insufficiently developed.

If you are greatly dissatisfied with your body, you might ask yourself how you think it ought to be—i.e., what are the standards to which you are comparing yourself? Are they realistic for you? Are you really willing to put in the time and effort to change the way you look?

You might want to take a careful look at yourself in a mirror, slowly going over each part and seeing how you feel about it. Is there any chance that you can accept yourself the way you are right now? Any chance that you could accept the fact that your waist will never be slimmer, your arms never bigger, your head never hairier? And be sure to ask where you got the idea that you should look different than you do. Whatever the sources, must they run your life? You will not suddenly like all those parts you didn't like before. The question is whether you can accept them the way they are, even if you don't like them. If you can accept yourself the way you are, you can at least stop nagging yourself to do something about it, and get on with your life.

While we are on the subject of bodies, we'd like to ask you to consider yours from another vantage point. We men have been trained to think that our only sexual part is between our legs. When we think of sex, we almost automatically think of our penises and what we want to put them into. There's good reason for us to think this way since it is precisely what the fantasy model of sex teaches, but the truth is that such thinking is unnecessarily narrow. We can give and receive sensual and sexual pleasure with many other parts of our bodies. We haven't had much permission to explore areas other than our crotches, but there are many possibilities. Can you image what it might be like to have your face, neck, chest and nipples, stomach, legs, and the areas between your toes touched, stroked, and perhaps kissed and licked by your partner? Any chance you'd be willing to try out some of these activities with her?

It is also true that our mouths, hands, legs, hair, and so on can be exquisite instruments for giving pleasure. You might try running your hair across the sensitive parts of your partner's body. Or sucking her finger or having her suck yours. No, it's not the same as having your penis sucked, but many men who have tried it reported that it was interesting, to say the least. All or most of your body can give and receive pleasure. Your penis doesn't have to carry the whole load. Consider your body and see if this isn't true for you.

Which brings us to the next point we want to discuss, the true nature of the human penis, perhaps the most misunderstood organ in the male body. Penises have had a bad press lately. The popular and scientific literature tells us that impotence is reaching epidemic proportions; and even those penises not so afflicted still don't perform the way they should—they come too fast or not at all, or in some other way they don't measure up to expectations.

The truth is that nothing is wrong with penises. It is our thinking about them, the expectations and goals we have set for them, that is terribly mistaken. Both men and women have absorbed the erroneous notions about penises we discussed in Chapter 3, and berate real penises for not living up to these superhuman standards.

Let us then consider the penis, probably the laziest part of a man. Your heart, lungs, and brain are working all the time, even when you sleep, and you would be in serious trouble if they stopped for even a few minutes. Less impressive parts of you—your liver, kidneys, stomach, knees, and elbows, for example—are busy working for you much of the time. In contrast, most of the time your penis does exactly nothing. While it serves as a tube through which urine passes, it has no active part in the process. And a penis is not necessary for your survival. Even if you didn't have one, or had one that never became erect, you could live a long, healthy, and perhaps happy life. So, despite fashionable ideas of penises being necessary and always active, hopping about with lots of throbbing and crashing, the real penis is much given to rest and relaxation.

The major exception is the adolescent penis, a creature known to act with great peculiarity. It may be in a state of almost constant erection, regardless of the appropriateness of the situation. Teenage penises seem to take a perverse joy in getting hard at the wrong times, causing their owners much embarrassment. But after adolescence, penises revert to form, being more likely to cause embarrassment by their lack of activity than by their exuberance.

Penises are also somewhat mercurial. They sometimes get erect in the absence of any identifiable sexual stimulus or any interest on the part of their owners. They almost always get hard when their owners dream (about four or five times a night) whether or not the dreams have any sexual content. (While we're talking about dreams, we want to mention that morning erections, often called "piss-hards," are not, as the name implies, due to having a full bladder. The best evidence available indicates that morning erections are simply the erections that accompany the last dream of the night. Why penises get hard when you dream is something that has not been answered with any certainty.) Penises can also become erect during periods of general excitement as, for example, before or during a rock concert or sports event.

The other side of the coin is only too well known. There you are, trembling with lust, feeling passion in every corpuscle . . . and there's old penis, snoring away and feeling not a thing. What we're talking about, of course, is the distinction between arousal and erection. As we said in the last chapter, they are separate systems. Don't confuse them.

The lack of response in your penis usually causes great confusion and frustration. You think you're turned-on and can't figure out what's wrong. Your partner, also having been taught that desire should produce an erection in you, may think that she is not attractive or that you don't like her. Actually, especially if you don't know each other well, the situation may be just the reverse. You may find her particularly attractive and want very much to please her. But this may arouse concerns about whether you are equal to the task, and these concerns are precisely what can cause your penis to go into a deep sleep.

On the other hand, having an erection is no reason to assume you want sex. You may or you may not. You need to check your feelings to find out.

There is nothing wrong with using an erection even if you do not have accompanying feelings of desire, but your penis may not stay erect for long if the feelings do not develop as you get into sex. If that's going to be a problem for you, it's probably best not to have sex until you feel aroused.

Implicit in what we've said is the idea that your penis is a relatively frail instrument. It bears little resemblance to the fantasy model's bars of steel that can be knocked around and handled with impunity. Like any other part of you, it needs attention and consideration.

Here's what one penis (in the penis letter exercise) had to say to its owner, a man who hadn't had a good sexual experience in five years:

I never feel included. You don't care about me and don't pay any attention to me. Only when you want to fuck do you show any interest, and then it's only to scream and yell that I better come through for you. Usually you pay more attention to your goddamn knees and ankles than to me. Why should I do anything for you? I'd like a little attention and some consideration for my needs. I'd be much more willing to do what you want if I felt that you cared about me. Please pay some attention to me.

Another example:

A man in one of the first sex therapy groups we did was in the habit of calling his penis "you little son of a bitch" and threatening it with all sorts of dire consequences when it did not meet his expectations. Needless to say, the more he did this, the less his penis worked. Here is what came out when he did the penis letter exercise:

"I'm sick and tired of being called names and threatened. Don't you think I have feelings? I try to do my best and you don't do a damn thing for me or yourself. You get into the weirdest sexual situations that anyone can imagine and expect me to perform. And when I refuse, you get all huffy and start yelling at me. Christ, you don't even like most of the women you want me to screw! And do you ever ask me how I feel about them? Never! Well, the hell with you, Charlie. I'm putting you on notice right now. Either start treating me with some respect and get into situations that interest both of us, or I'm never going to do anything for you again. And, despite all your threats, you know there's not a thing you can do about it. If you want to start off on a new track with me, the first thing you can do is apologize for all the insults you've thrown my way."

If your penis doesn't work the way you want it to, remember that it's trying to tell you something. It's not your enemy. It was made for sex, it likes sex. If it's not working the way you like, it's telling you that there is something wrong with the way you are going about sex. If you want better sex, you need to start deciphering your penis's message.

Now on to sexual anatomy, a department in which men differ as much as they do in other areas like weight, height, color, amount of hair, and proportion of muscular to fatty tissue. Penises come in a variety of shapes and sizes (as do testicles), and about the only thing most penises have in common is that they are the wrong size or shape as far as their owners are concerned. In the many hours we have spent talking to men in and out of therapy, we have heard every conceivable complaint about penises. They are too small (the most common complaint), too large, too thin, too thick, stand up at too small (or great) an angle when erect, bend too much to the right, or left, or in the middle, or don't get hard enough when they erect.

A large portion of our concern about our penises undoubtedly stems from the silliness conveyed in the

sources we explored in Chapter 3. Confronted by phal-
luses of superhuman dimensions, we feel inadequate
when we survey our own merely human organs.

It is also true that most of us lack information about
what a "normal" or average penis is like. Almost all of
us have seen other penises in locker rooms or similar
situations and we somehow come away with the conviction that everyone else's is larger or better formed (forgetting to take into account that we view others' from a
very different perspective than when we look down at
our own). And, when you think about it, it's clear
that most of us have never seen another erect penis, or
at least not a typical one. The erections we are likely
to have viewed, in pornographic films or pictures, are
hardly representative. Given the absence of reasonable
models or standards, there is good reason for us to
wonder about the adequacy of our own penises.

Figures 1 and 2 (pages 116 and 117) illustrate some
of the variability of human penises in the flaccid and
erect states. Yours may or may not closely resemble the
drawings, but the chances are at least 999 in 1,000
that it is perfectly normal and quite capable of giving
you and your partner much joy.

Your penis is the right size and shape for your body.
It is as it is, and if you can accept it and worry less
about how it compares to others (whose owners share
the same concerns you have), it will serve you well.
We will give you an exercise to help you become more
familiar with your penis and see how you feel about it,
but first we want to discuss some of the more important features of your sexual anatomy.

Figure 3 (page 118) represents the typical male genital anatomy.

The external sex organs consist of the penis and the
scrotum, the latter containing the testes. The penis
contains three cylinders of spongy tissue surrounded by
a tough fibrous covering. During sexual excitement, the
spongy tissues become engorged with blood, causing the
penis to expand. Since the fibrous sheath covering the
spongy tissues will expand only so far, as the tissues
fill with blood they press against the sheath, making
the penis hard. The process is quite similar to what oc-

curs when you fill a bicycle or car tire with air. The tube in the tire (comparable to the spongy tissues in the penis), if not constrained by the tire (comparable to the fibrous sheath in the penis), would keep expanding until it burst. Since it is constrained by the tire, it can only expand so far and becomes hard.

If you study the diagram carefully you will notice that the penis extends far into the body, almost to the rectum. You can feel this portion of your penis if, when you have an erection, you press a finger up into the area behind your scrotum.

The penis has no muscle in it and therefore cannot be enlarged by exercise. However, although not shown in the diagram, the part of the penis inside the body is surrounded by muscles which can be strengthened by exercise. At the end of the chapter we present an exercise that will help you do this; it will not increase the size of your penis, but it does have some benefits which we discuss later.

For many men the head is the most sensitive part of the penis, especially around the ridge that connects it to the shaft of the penis.

The major internal sex organs consist of the testes, vas deferens, seminal vesicles, Cowper's glands, prostate gland, and urethra.

The testes produce sperm and the hormone testosterone. The vas deferens are two firm tubes that extend from the testes to the prostate. The sperm travel through the tubes and are stored at their upper ends until they mix with the secretions of the seminal vesicles and prostate just prior to ejaculation. It used to be thought that sperm were stored in the seminal vesicles, but this idea has been abandoned. The exact purpose of the vesicles is unclear, but it is known that they contribute a portion of the ejaculate. The secretions of the prostate comprise most of the seminal fluid or ejaculate, giving it its whitish color and its odor. The sperm actually account for only a tiny fraction of the seminal fluid or ejaculate, which explains why a man who has had a vasectomy still ejaculates about the same amount of fluid as before the operation.

It is believed that the Cowper's glands secrete a

Figure 1:
FLACCID PENISES

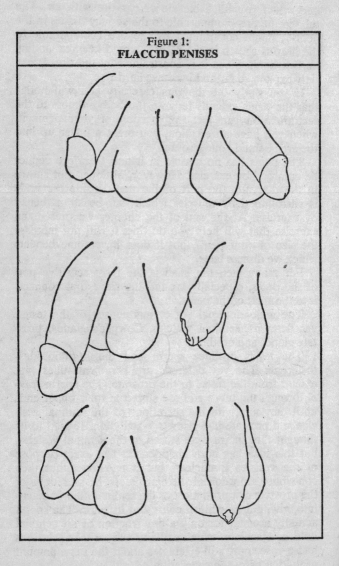

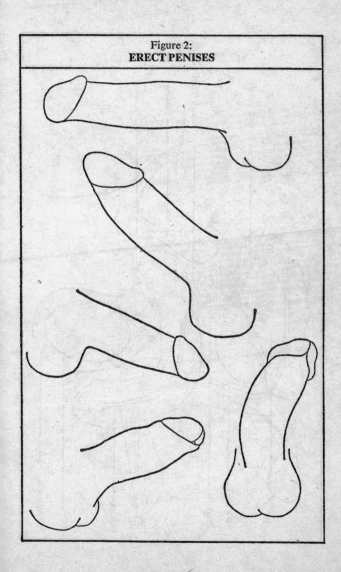

Figure 2:
ERECT PENISES

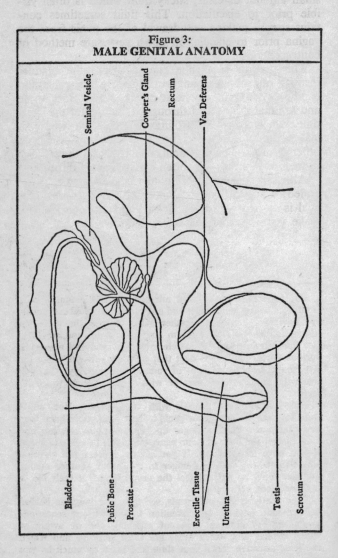

Figure 3:
MALE GENITAL ANATOMY

Seminal Vesicle

Cowper's Gland

Rectum

Vas Deferens

Bladder

Pubic Bone

Prostate

Erectile Tissue

Urethra

Testis

Scrotum

small amount of clear, sticky fluid which is often visible prior to ejaculation. This fluid sometimes contains sperm, making withdrawal of the penis from the vagina prior to ejaculation not a very safe method of contraception.

The urethra is a tube running from the bladder through one of the spongy cylinders in the penis and ending in a slit in the head of the penis. Both urine and seminal fluid travel through it, but not at the same time. The prostate surrounds the urethra where it leaves the bladder, and prostate problems—such as inflammation or enlargement, which are quite common in men over fifty—very often cause urinary difficulties.

Although this description has been somewhat simplified, it is sufficiently detailed for our purposes. Our goal is to help you understand yourself better, not to make you an expert on male anatomy. The following exercise will help you further that knowledge.

EXERCISE 7-1: EXPLORING YOUR GENITALS
Time Required: 30 to 45 minutes

Undress and, using a hand mirror, carefully examine your genitals. Look at your penis and scrotum from different angles. See how everything fits together. Also look at the perineum (the area between the scrotum and the anus) and anything else that interests you. Then determine how you feel about the various parts. Can you accept that perhaps you don't like the size, shape, or color of some of your sexual anatomy? Can you live with them without forever wishing that things were different?

Now explore your genitals with your fingers. You might want to press in above your penis to feel your pubic bone, and you might also press a finger up between your scrotum and anus to feel the bulb of your penis (although this is easier felt if you have an erection). If you gently squeeze the scrotum above the testes, with one finger in front and another behind the sac, you'll be able to feel the vas deferens; it feels like a cord or piece of wire.

Then gently stroke your penis, scrotum, and the area behind the scrotum, paying close attention to the various sensations produced. Try different types of touching and be aware of which strokes and which areas are most sensitive and which are least sensitive. Take your time and learn as much as you can.

If you become aroused and/or get an erection, that's fine.

Continue with the exercise and be aware of how sensitivities change when you go from the unaroused to the aroused state. Discover as much as possible about how and where you like to be touched.

If you had a lot of trouble accepting the way your genitals look, it would probably be worth your time to ask yourself what makes you think they ought to be different than they are. A fantasy, something you read or heard or saw? Also ask yourself who, aside from yourself, would be happy if they were different. How do you know they would? Consider the sources of your discontent. Are they so important to you that you are willing to continue making yourself miserable over something you can't change? Then go back to the mirror and do the exercise again. Is it possible to accept yourself the way you are? We hope you can gain some self-acceptance because, like it or not, there are no genital transplants and we are all stuck with what we got. Which, if you think about it carefully and identify the expectations that make you wish it were different, really isn't all that bad.

We now go to the changes that usually occur as a man goes through a sexual experience. This is a difficult area to discuss since the popularizations of the research data on this subject have in many ways been confusing and misleading.

In their pioneering work, *Human Sexual Response,* Masters and Johnson described the physiological changes a man goes through during sex in terms of a sexual response cycle arbitrarily divided into four phases: excitement, plateau, orgasm, and resolution. You may have read or heard about this cycle and seen the diagram used to illustrate it, a copy of which is included here.

Masters and Johnson's work in this area has been uncritically accepted by most people in the sex field. Almost all the books and articles that deal with sex merely summarize their description and classification scheme without noting variations or raising questions. The problem is that while Masters and Johnson's research constitutes a milestone in sex research, it suf-

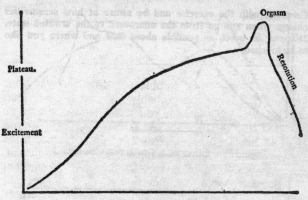

Figure 4: Male sexual response
Adapted from *Human Sexual Responses,*
by William H. Masters and Virginia E. Johnson, 1966.

fers from a number of limitations, some of which they noted in their book but which have been neglected by those who summarize their findings. The classification of their findings into a response cycle with four phases is probably the weakest part of their work. Many men's changes do not fit neatly into the phases, and some people have asked us what was wrong with them for not fitting the model.

Our ideas about sexual response conform to what Kinsey had to say on the subject: "There is nothing more characteristic of sexual response than the fact that it is not the same in any two individuals." There is no right or normal way to have a sexual experience. Your body's responses are the result of a complex interaction among many variables including, for example, your physical and emotional state at the time, what your partner does and how you feel about it, and your feelings about her. In contrast to Masters and Johnson's notion that there is only one type of male sexual response cycle, we believe that there are many possible cycles, a few of which are diagrammed in Figures 5 and 6.

The main changes that occur during a sexual experience are the result of vasocongestion, the accumu-

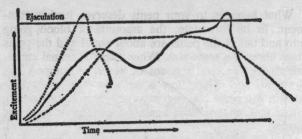

Figure 5: Other male sexual response cycles

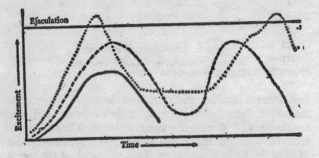

Figure 6: More male sexual response cycles

lation of blood in various parts of the body. Muscular tension increases and other changes also occur. Ejaculation reverses the blood flow and releases the tension, but these phenomena happen even without ejaculation or orgasm, though more slowly.

A sexual response begins when you receive some form of sexual stimulation. The stimulation can be in the form of a touch, smell, sight, thought, fantasy, or almost anything else that has sexual significance for you. Provided that you are open to a sexual experience, that your conditions are met, certain changes begin to occur.

An increased volume of blood is pumped into various parts of your body, increasing their size and often their sensitivity to stimulation. Your penis is not the only area so affected. Your lips, ear lobes, and breasts are other areas that may become engorged with blood.

What happens to your penis deserves further comment. In its soft state, the amounts of blood going into and out of the penis are about equal and the penis stays about the same size. When there is sexual stimulation, an increased amount of blood is pumped into the penis and the outflow is reduced. The spongy tissues in the penis become engorged with blood, getting larger and, as they push against their fibrous covering, harder.

Full erection may or may not occur early in a sexual experience. In many young men, erection is almost instantaneous; they get hard as soon as they get any stimulation. With increasing age, however, it may take the penis longer to get hard, and it may also take more direct stimulation of the penis to reach full erection. There is nothing wrong with either the shorter or longer route to an erection.

The scrotal sac and testes go through some interesting changes during a sexual experience. The skin of the sac thickens and contracts, while the testes increase in size because of the engorgement of blood. The testes are also pulled up within the sac until they press against the wall of the pelvis. This elevation of the testes anticipates ejaculation and is necessary for it to occur.

Increased muscular tension can be observed in various parts of your body. You may notice, for example, that you are tensing your stomach or leg muscles. There may be involuntary contractions or spasms in your pelvis and buttocks, and also in your facial muscles. As the excitement builds, pelvis thrusting begins and becomes involuntary as you approach ejaculation (although some men unconsciously inhibit these movements).

Other bodily changes include increased blood pressure, heartbeat, and breathing rate. Some men have nipple erection; and a sex flush, a reddening of the skin that looks like a rash, may appear on the upper part of the body.

All bodily changes are reversible. You might reach a peak of excitement and erection and then, because you were distracted, stopped to talk, weren't getting the most exciting type of stimulation, or if the experi-

ence went on for a long time, you might lose some of
your erection and experience other changes that reflect
the lowered level of excitement. This is not something
to get concerned about. You can probably return to a
higher state of excitement when you reinstate the conditions and activities that got you there in the first
place.

What you are feeling while all this is going on is another matter. Sometimes you feel extremely excited,
very much into all the sensations, and are having a
grand time. At other times, it may feel good, but you
are also aware that your mind wanders now and again,
seeming to be only partially involved in the experience.
On other occasions, you may be but little involved in
what's happening, perhaps experiencing it as boring
or as disconnected from you, as if it were happening to
someone else. Sexual experiences do not always feel
the same, ranging from wonderful to good-but-not-
exceptional to hardly-worth-the-effort. Expecting a
mind-blowing experience every time is a sure way of
keeping yourself in a state of perpetual frustration.
But there is no reason to go through bad experiences.
If it doesn't feel good at all, it might be best to stop
and see what you really want. Perhaps sex is not for
you at the moment, or perhaps a different kind of sexual activity would please you more.

What would happen if you got very excited and
did not go on to orgasm? Many men believe that the
lack of orgasm would lead to the condition commonly
called blue balls or lover's nuts: pain, discomfort, or
soreness in the testes. This belief is easy to understand when you realize that the fantasy model of sex
almost invariably includes orgasm for the male. The
implication seems to be that its absence would be
disastrous.

In fact, it is not disastrous. There may be some
soreness or pain, but this is rare. You might want to
think back over your sexual experiences and see if this
is true for you. Be sure to include all instances where,
whether with masturbation or with a partner, you got

very aroused and did not ejaculate. How many times was there pain? Probably very few, although those are the ones we tend to remember. Try to keep in mind that it's not necessary to ejaculate every time you have sex. It's nice when it happens but there's no reason to try to force it. You and your partner will probably feel better stopping while you are still feeling good. Working at producing an ejaculation has a way of making sex boring or frustrating.

Ejaculation is a spinal reflex which, as we mentioned earlier, reverses the flow of blood in the body, draining it away from the penis and other engorged areas, and releases the muscular tension that has been built up. Two distinct steps are involved in ejaculation. In the first, the prostate, seminal vesicles, and vas deferens contract, pouring their contents into the urethra; the sperm mix with the secretions of the seminal vesicles and the prostate to form the ejaculate. The contractions are the beginning of ejaculation and are often interpreted by the man as "It's starting" or "I'm going to come." Masters and Johnson have called this ejaculatory inevitability. Since the ejaculatory process is already in motion, ejaculation is indeed inevitable. Nothing can stop it once the point of inevitability has been reached.

During the second step of the ejaculatory process, the fluid is propelled through the urethra by strong contractions of the muscles in the pelvis. The semen may spurt several inches or even feet beyond the tip of the penis, or it may just ooze out. The number of contractions, the amount of ejaculate, and the force with which it is ejaculated are dependent on a number of factors, including age and amount of time since the last ejaculation.

Ejaculation involves more of the body than just the penis and internal genitalia. Respiration, blood pressure, and heartbeat rate increase as the man approaches ejaculation, usually peaking at the moment of ejaculation. Involuntary muscle contractions and spasms may occur in various parts of the body, including the legs, stomach, arms, and back. Ejaculation is a total body response, not just something that happens in the crotch.

Most authorities have accepted the contention of Masters and Johnson that while women have several different patterns of orgasmic response, only one type of ejaculatory response is possible for men. We disagree with this thinking, having ourselves experienced different ejaculatory patterns and having heard from a number of other men that they sometimes have ejaculations substantially different from the Masters and Johnson standard. Sometimes the excitement is so intense before ejaculation that it in itself feels like a long orgasm, and the actual ejaculation not only doesn't add anything to it but is experienced as a letdown. Another variant seems similar in some ways to multiple orgasms in women—a number of peaks that feel like mild orgasms are experienced, with ejaculation occurring only during the last one. Still another pattern involves continued pelvic contractions far beyond the usual number and long after the last of the ejaculate has appeared. Such contractions are accompanied by feelings of intense pleasure, sometimes as pleasurable as those accompanying the ejaculation.

We strongly believe that future research in this area will confirm that there are many different ejaculatory patterns in men. Whichever pattern or patterns you experience are perfectly normal. There is no one right way.

While ejaculation and orgasm are often used synonymously even by some sex experts, we find it useful to distinguish between them. Ejaculation is the physical process involved in propelling the semen through the penis. Orgasm refers to what you feel. Generally the two go together; you ejaculate and enjoy very pleasurable feelings. But one can occur without the other. You can have orgasms without ejaculating. Some men have trained themselves to do this and, according to their reports, have been able to have multiple orgasms like women. And some men, who have trained themselves carefully to tune into their sensations during sex, say that they sometimes notice very high peaks of feeling long before ejaculation. Were they not so indoctrinated in the idea that orgasm occurs only with pelvic contractions and ejaculation, they would be inclined to call these peaks orgasms.

The reverse situation is more common, where the man ejaculates—there's the white stuff to prove it—but feels very little. If this happens infrequently, there's nothing to worry about. But a number of men have consulted us about the possibility of enhancing their orgasms, and this question deserves comment. Even when you get past the unrealistic expectations (orgasms rarely feel like what D. H. Lawrence or other purveyors of fantasy sex lead you to think they'll be like), it is clear that many men do not experience as much feeling with their ejaculations as is possible. Near the end of this chapter we offer some suggestions that have been helpful in increasing orgasmic feeling.

After ejaculation, your body starts to return to where it was before the sexual experience began. As blood flows out of it, your penis returns to its nonerect state. The rate at which this occurs depends on many factors and varies from time to time. Sometimes your erection may go down immediately, while at other times it may stay relatively firm for many minutes after ejaculation.

The scrotal sac and testes descend to their normal position. Blood pressure and pulse and breathing rate gradually return to their prearousal levels. The sex flush disappears and a thin film of perspiration may appear over much of your body.

During this period of resolution many men experience feelings of lassitude and deep relaxation, and for some this immediately leads to sleep, often to the chagrin of their partners. For some of the men we've worked with, it's been clear that falling asleep directly after orgasm has been an escape from activities—cuddling, relaxed talk, relating without a goal—with which they were uncomfortable. Once they became more comfortable doing these things, they tended to stay awake longer most of the time. And sometimes, of course, sleep is just the best thing to do after sex.

In situations where high levels of stimulation continue after orgasm, some men, particularly younger ones, may not go through a clearly defined resolution period. They may begin to get aroused and erect again fairly quickly. For most men, however, once ejaculation has occurred, a definite period of rest—called a refractory period—is necessary before they can again respond to sexual stimulation. The length of the refractory period varies according to a number of factors, including age and amount of time since last ejaculation.

When there has been excitement and no orgasm, the resolution period usually takes longer. The muscular tension and accumulation of blood are released more slowly than when there has been an ejaculation. Because of this, you may feel a bit congested in the pelvis and perhaps a little tense or jittery. If it's more than this, you might want to consider how much of it is psychological, due to feelings of disappointment or anger because you think you should have come.

We now return to the enhancement of orgasms, but first let us repeat that the bombs-bursting and mind-blowing orgasms of the fantasy model are not what we have in mind. We are simply dealing with methods that are helpful for increasing bodily sensations or the experience of such sensations during ejaculation.

One of the best ways to increase the enjoyment of any experience is to fully participate in it, to really be there when it is occurring. Since many people seem to be someplace else during sex—thinking about other matters, wondering if they are doing it right or if their partner is satisfied—their pleasure can be enhanced by paying more attention to their sensations. Many of the exercises in the book are designed to help you focus on your sensations. Doing them as suggested will increase your awareness of what you are experiencing, making your orgasms, as well as the rest of your sexual experiences, more enjoyable.

Other methods involve relaxing the degree of control that many men exercise on themselves during sex. Men often seem to try to keep their bodies and feelings under control by limiting their movements, breathing, and sound, so much so that a number of women have told us that they usually can't tell if their partners have had an orgasm. Restricting your body in such ways tends to reduce feeling, and therefore pleasure. Check to see if you are controlling your breathing—by slowing it down or even holding your breath during orgasm—or restricting your movements, or suppressing noises. If you are, you might want to allow yourself to do the opposite the next time you have sex. Don't try to let go of all your controls at once; just do one thing you've been preventing yourself from doing before. Perhaps there are some moans or grunts or cries that want to come out; let one or two come out the first time you try this. Or perhaps you can allow your body greater leeway in moving the way it wants. And be sure you breathe (good advice under any circumstances). If you notice that your breathing is slow before or during orgasm, experiment with taking quick breaths, panting, during these times. Gradually relax more of your controls and see if you aren't experiencing fuller orgasms.

The last method of increasing the orgasmic experience is the strengthening of the pelvic muscles that produce the ejaculation by their contractions. The exercise we use for this also serves other important functions and has an interesting history. It was developed by a gynecologist, Dr. Arnold Kegel, for women who had trouble holding their urine after childbirth. Many of his patients reported greater sexual enjoyment as a result of doing the exercise, and this led Dr. Kegel to consider the importance of the pelvic musculature to female sexual responsiveness. In the years since then, thousands of women have increased their sexual responsiveness by doing the Kegel exercise.

We tried the Kegel exercise ourselves out of curiosity and, since it produced interesting results, started suggesting it to clients. Regular practice strengthens the muscles that surround the penis and improves the circulation of blood in the pelvis, a factor of obvious importance since increased flow of blood to the penis is what makes an erection.

The exercise has been useful for several types of situations and problems. Many men who practiced it report stronger and more pleasurable orgasms. Others have used it to develop better ejaculatory control, a point we discuss further in Chapter 15. And it's also been helpful to men with erection problems and those who didn't experience much feeling in their pelvises.

EXERCISE 7-2: KEGELS
Time Required: A few minutes a day

First you need to get in touch with your pelvic muscles, and there are two ways of doing this. One way is simply to contract your buttocks as you sit or stand. Pretend that you are in danger of having a bowel movement but need to keep it in until you can get to a bathroom. The muscles you squeeze to hold it in are the ones you will use in the exercise. The other way of getting in touch with these muscles is to stop and start the flow several times next time you urinate. The muscles you squeeze to stop the flow are the ones you're interested in.

The exercise itself is quite simple. Start by squeezing and releasing the muscles fifteen times. There is no need to hold the contraction for now; just squeeze and let go. Do one set of fifteen twice a day. At first, you may also be squeezing your stomach and thigh muscles. It will take a few days until you acquire the coordination to squeeze only the pelvic muscles. When this happens, you can do the exercise unobtrusively anywhere—while driving a car, watching television, reading, at a meeting, and so forth.

Do the Kegels every day, gradually increasing the number until you can do at least sixty or seventy twice a day. Build up slowly; we have known a few men who tried to do too many the first few days and developed sore muscles.

When you can do sixty or seventy comfortably, you can also do a slight variation. Instead of immediately releasing the contraction, hold it for a count of three, then relax and repeat. Work up to sixty or seventy of these twice a day.

You can do both the long and short Kegels, making two sets of each per day, or alternate between them, doing the long one day and the short the next.

Some men have developed rather extraordinary control over their penises by experimenting with the muscular movements. They can move their penises back and forth and from side to side. We're not sure what good this does, but some people like to experiment.

Continue doing the long and short Kegels for at least six weeks. Results usually aren't noticeable for a month or more. As you continue doing them, they will become automatic and require no conscious attention or effort.

8

Touching

To be held is support;
to be touched is contact;
to be touched sensitively
is to be cared for.

Our culture is highly sexual but not very sensual (sensual defined here as body contact that is pleasurable but not erotic). While the manipulation and union of genitals is greatly valued and much discussed, there has been, at least until very recently, an almost wholesale disregard for the uses and pleasures of other kinds of physical contact. For many adults, only two kinds of touching seem acceptable: the superficial and ritualized (shaking hands, a pat on the back, a hug when greeting and leaving) and the sexual (anything that is a prelude to or part of sexual activity). We have sexualized touching to the point where all but the most superficial types of touch are thought to be sexual invitations.

Several astute observers of the American scene have claimed that we suffer from sensory starvation, a lack of nonsexual touching, and worse, that most of us are unaware of how damaging this state of affairs is. Touching is important to us throughout our lives and, strange as it may sound now, the amount and quality of our nonsexual touching experiences are intimately related to how satisfied we are with our sexual activities.

The importance of touching in human life can hardly be overemphasized. The tactile sense is the first to develop: an embryo is sensitive to touch long before it can see and hear, long before it even has eyes and ears. Touching is essential for healthy development. Babies who have not received sufficient tactile stimulation—hugging, cuddling, kissing—do not develop normally and many do not grow at all; the mortality rate for babies deprived of touching is extremely high. In the months after birth, touching can literally mean the difference between life and death. Parents, especially mothers, seem to understand this instinctively and engage in a lot of physical contact with their babies. Unfortunately, this lasts for only a few years, after which there is a sharp decline.

The child's training about touching begins fairly early, as he starts to hear what soon becomes a familiar litany. "Don't touch this, it'll hurt you." "Don't touch that, you'll break it." "Don't touch yourself, it's naughty." "Don't touch him (or her), it's not nice." Over and over he hears, "Don't touch!" Where touching was once a source of pleasure to him, his first knowledge of being cared for and his main way of exploring the world, it now becomes a problem: touching provokes his parents' wrath. So he starts to feel inhibited about touching and guilty about the pleasures derived from it.

The rule not to touch is also taught by an important omission. The child may rarely see anyone else touching. Aside from perfunctory hugs or pecks on the cheek, many children don't see their parents being physically affectionate. While there are many exceptions—with some people reporting lots of physical affection between their parents—we have been astonished by the number of people we have talked to who could barely recall even a few instances of physical affection in their homes. The child also sees that he isn't being touched much either. Perhaps a small peck from his mother before he goes to bed, and being held if he hurts himself, but only in the very early years, and that's about it. He soon learns that when adults talk about getting in touch or keeping in touch, they certainly don't mean it literally.

Another message is also conveyed to the child: touching is sexual. If he does see his parents touching, it is followed by embarrassment (and what is he to make of that?) or by their going off to the bedroom, telling him they don't want to be disturbed. It doesn't take him long to figure out what that means. And the media, from which he learns so much, reinforce the message. People hug, then kiss, then they have sex. Slowly, but very surely, the child acquires the societal understanding about touching: it is sexual.

Although America is a particularly nontouching society and the restrictions we have discussed apply to almost everyone, it is evident that boys fare much worse in this drama than girls. Boys generally get much less touching than girls. Their mothers are likely to stop touching sons at a much earlier age than they stop touching daughters. The reluctance to continue being physically affectionate with sons seems to stem from two reasons. First, some mothers fear that their sons will interpret the touching as sexual and that this may be a cause of later psychological difficulties. Second, mothers as well as fathers know the masculine model and fear that too much "mothering" may make sissies of their sons. A real man shouldn't need to be hugged or held, so the boy has to be weaned early from such "feminine" or "childish" practices.

Fathers, having lived in a culture that is terrified of affectionate physical contact between males, do not touch their sons much after infancy. Since it is the father whom the boy will try to emulate, a very powerful lesson is transmitted by this lack of touching. The boy also does not see other males touching. He sees that men shake hands and pat one another on the back, and nothing else. Again, he learns something about touching. A girl, on the other hand, sees other females touching. She sees her mother hugging and kissing relatives and friends, and this is reinforced by seeing and reading about other women being physically affectionate. The lesson she learns is somewhat different from that learned by boys.

Girls also have far greater permission to experience their own sensuality—not, of course, by touching "down there," but in many other ways. It's considered normal and acceptable for a girl to derive physical pleasure from wearing frilly clothes, from washing herself or brushing her hair, and from trying out different scents on herself. These concessions may seem small, but they are far more than is permitted for boys.

Boys learn that physical contact is acceptable only in sports and sex. There are no taboos against touching if you are playing football, or wrestling, or boxing, or in some other way being rough. One cause, as well as result, of this notion can be seen in the way fathers handle their sons. They often seem uncomfortable just holding or cuddling their boys, being more at ease when throwing them around or engaging in mock wrestling or boxing bouts. Since roughness is what we learned, it's no surprise that we often show affection by being rough, by wrestling with our lovers and playfully punching our friends. And it's no surprise that we're often rough in sex, less gentle than our partners would like.

The main way for a man to have physical contact is by having sex, and the equating of touching and sex causes no end of problems for us. As discussed earlier, it hinders the expression of physical affection between parents and children, for the parents are concerned about the possible sexual implications. It also gets in the way of physical contact between both same-sex and opposite-sex friends. Men who have been friends for twenty years are often afraid to touch one another because, as one man put it, "Other people might think I was gay. Hell, even I might begin to wonder." And to touch a woman friend might be construed as sexual by her, by you, and by God knows whom else. The link between sex and physical affection even works to keep lovers from touching each other. Since touching is seen not so much as a thing in itself but as the first step toward intercourse, many people won't touch unless they feel ready and willing to "go all the way."

The taboo on touching except as a part of sex confuses us about what we want and how to get it. Ashley Montagu, a pioneer in the exploration of the importance of touching, says in his book *Touching* that "it is highly probable that . . . the frenetic preoccupation with sex that characterizes Western culture is in many cases not the expression of a sexual interest at all, but rather a search for the satisfaction of the need for contact." And this seems to be truer for men than women.

In growing up, girls more so than boys were allowed to express and explore their desire for physical contact. Having the permission, girls learned to differentiate their needs for support, comfort, validation, a sense of connection with another, and similar needs from the need for sex. In fact, given the way girls were brought up, sex was the one need they had trouble noticing and expressing. Boys developed in the opposite direction. Wanting sex was legitimate, even encouraged, while such things as wanting to be held or loved or to know they were not alone were unacceptable.

These needs did not disappear in boys and men. They simply went underground and got reorganized and relabeled. Wanting a hug or to feel close to another sounded too effeminate, but wanting sex was the epitome of masculinity; and in sex you could get some of these other things as well. After years of practice, the man just never felt a need for closeness or comfort or support. All he wanted was—sex. Whenever he felt something that might be called warm or close or loving, he read it as indicating a desire for—sex.

This may seem like a brilliant feat of engineering, but the result too often for too many men has been a frustrating confusion about what they want, and therefore an inability to meet many of their needs. One place where this is especially evident is in the relations between men. Many men are realizing that they want something from other men: closeness, understanding, camaraderie, support, and so forth. But as soon as they start getting any of these things, they very often pull back in fear and sometimes come into therapy to discuss their "latent homosexual feelings." This is especially true of men who have engaged in some physical contact with other men and found it pleasurable. Because touching is so closely tied to sex in our thinking, they decide that what they really want from other men is sex and, since that is unacceptable to them, they should just stay away from men. What they fail to see is that touching need not be sexual, any more than feelings of love or closeness or caring need to be sexual. One can hug or cuddle a man or a woman or a child, or animal for that matter, and not have sex. Touching serves many functions, sex being only one and probably not the most important.

But, we have been asked, cannot touching lead to sexual feelings and erections? Of course, it often does, but that in itself doesn't mean a lot nor does it imply a necessary course of action. In the first place, an erection can be caused by lots of things and does not necessarily indicate a desire for sex. Your erections need not run your life. Men often have such limited ideas about what erections mean and what must be done about them. The following story proved very helpful to many of the men we worked with in workshops dealing with male friendships, where there was great concern about what it meant if a man got aroused or erect when touching or being with another man.

As a teenager, John frequently rode on buses. The vibrations of the bus, sometimes combined with adolescent sex fantasies, often produced an erection. Despite the erection, and despite the fact that it was often accompanied by feelings of arousal, he somehow managed to contain himself and never became a busfucker.

The second point we want to make is that even if your feelings about someone are sometimes clearly sexual, you don't have to act on them. It is possible for all of us to be turned-on by many different people and even things. We have talked to men who became aroused and erect while stroking a child or pet, and to a few who have become aroused while listening to music or watching a sunset. And neither they nor you have to do anything about such events except, if you wish, appreciate the good feelings.

It has become clear to us that men need different things from different types of people. They need men as well as women, though perhaps for different reasons, and many feel incomplete unless they can also relate to people much older as well as those much younger than themselves. It seems a great tragedy that we separate ourselves from those we want to be with because of our fears about what being close and touching imply. They need indicate nothing more than what they obviously are, and we don't mean sex.

Even lovers don't seem to touch as much as they want. This is not usually true in the beginning of a relationship where the couple seems unable to keep their hands off each other: they are always holding hands, kissing, hugging, and so on. But when the relationship becomes sexual, the nonsexual touching often declines rather sharply. The following observation by Masters and Johnson in their book *The Pleasure Bond* is consistent with our own:

> *Once a sexual relationship has been established, most young couples use touch as little more than a wordless way to communicate a willingness, a wish or a demand to make love. It is functional; beyond that, it seems of limited value and is regarded, especially by men, as a waste of time and effort, an unnecessary postponement of intercourse.*

Interestingly, many men and women will admit, the men usually with some embarrassment, that they really would like more nonsexual affection. But the men wonder if it's OK for a man to feel that way and they fear "leading their partners on." One man put it this way:

> I've gotten through the thing about men not needing touching. I know I like to be held without wanting to have sex. But I'm afraid that the woman will get turned-on and want to have sex. Then, if I'm not in

that space, she'll get mad at me or at least be disappointed. I just don't feel it's right to lead her on.

Now look at what the woman he was seeing at the time said.

I guess I'm just an old-fashioned woman but I just love to be held and touched. It's much more important to me than sex. But I'm almost afraid to touch Ralph. He thinks that I want sex and immediately starts into the foreplay routine. Or else, if he's not in a sexual mood, he runs away. . . . Really, he starts making excuses about having to get up early or just happens to remember that he forgot something and gets busy taking out the garbage or doing some other chore. You'd think I was asking for a two-hour screw rather than some snuggling.

The problem was that neither of them was asking for anything, at least not in a way that was clear to the other. They were busily not getting what they wanted even though, as far as touching went, they both wanted the same thing.

And what does touching have to do with the quality of your sexual behavior? Probably quite a bit. For most people, sex is best, and the chances for avoiding sexual problems highest, when they have sex only when their conditions are met and when sex is really what they want. When you use sex as a way of fulfilling nonsexual needs—e.g., the need for support, love, physical contact—you run the risk of disappointment, sex that isn't quite satisfying, and perhaps even the beginning of a sexual problem. Your penis may be uninterested in your desire for some cuddling and may refuse to respond. And, when you think about it, going through a whole sexual experience just to get a hug is a lot of unnecessary exertion.

When physical contact and affection are restricted to your lover, and then only as a part of sexual activity, sex takes on an exaggerated importance. You expect and want it to meet all the needs that aren't being met elsewhere. Sex can become weighed down with these expectations. As we have said a number of times, our sexual systems are fragile and do not work well when too great a burden is placed on them. Get your *sexual* needs and desires fulfilled in sex; satisfy your needs for *other* kinds of contact and affection in more appropriate ways.

Ask yourself if you'd like more touching than you are currently getting. If the answer is yes, all you have to do is start touching more. Choose someone you care about—whether a partner, relative, or close friend—and next time you are with that person touch a bit more than you have before. Don't try to do too much too soon. If you haven't touched at all before, a pat on the hand or back or shoulder may be sufficient the first time. When you see that person again, go a bit further. You may wish to talk to your friend about wanting to touch more; if so, do it. If you've already engaged in some touching with the person and simply want to do more, just do it. There may be a specific type of touching you want. It may take some courage, but see if you can try to get it.

A couple told us this story at a men's conference. They had always done lots of touching but the man had wanted something that took him months to ask for. Since he was almost a foot taller than the woman, he always felt like the giver or comforter whenever they hugged, even in bed. He wanted to experience the feeling of being the smaller person, the one being comforted. He finally got up the nerve to deal with this one day when his partner was standing on a chair. He went over and put his arms around her and she hugged back. This was a very pleasant experience for him so he told her about his secret desire. It made a lot of sense to her that he sometimes wanted to be "mothered" this way and they have since incorporated this into their touching activities. It turned out that she very much enjoys being the taller one and "mothering" him.

Another thing you can do is to ask yourself what you really want when you think you want sex. Is it closeness to someone you care about? Compassion? Understanding? Support? A feeling of connectedness? Knowing that she cares? Physical contact? Intercourse? Orgasm?

When you have some idea of what you want, ask what is the best way of getting it now. Would a hug do? Being held? A conversation? Giving or getting a massage?

The results of such questioning can be amusing as well as informative, as indicated by this example.

A few years ago, I taught two three-hour classes one day a week, with an office hour sandwiched in between. I was drained by the end of the day and could barely crawl to my car. But I noticed that about an hour before the end of the second class I started feeling very aroused and thinking how nice it would be to have sex when I got home. One day, when I was feeling particularly tired and having the sexual fantasies, I thought: "This is crazy. I don't have the energy to stand up or do anything. What makes me think I want sex? I wonder what's going on?" As I started to drive my car home, I got my answer, in the form of another fantasy. When I got home, the fantasy went, a woman greeted me warmly, helped me undress and guided me to a bath she had drawn. Then she lovingly washed and dried me, after which she spoon-fed me supper. When that was over, she tucked me in bed, turned out the lights, and left. The fantasy ended with me falling asleep, feeling very good and well cared for. As soon as I had this fantasy, I realized it expressed my needs far better than the sexual fantasies. I was tired and felt I had put out all day, trying to care for the needs of my students. I now wanted someone to take care of me. Sex was about the last thing I wanted but, even so, my first clue that I wanted anything was a feeling of sexual arousal.

Of course, sometimes you're going to be clear that sex is exactly what you want and, when that's the case, sex is what you should have. But we encourage you to consider these other possibilities since men so often ignore them and think of sex when they would, in fact, be happier with something else.

To help you discover more about what you can get from touching, we offer a few simple exercises. You might want to try them regardless of what specific changes you want to make in your sexual behavior.

A good way of getting back into touching is to start

touching yourself. This is the way you learned about yourself as an infant, and there is much to be said for it as a means of giving yourself pleasure. Unfortunately, most adult men touch themselves only when they masturbate, when the touching is confined to a very small portion of their anatomy.

EXERCISE 8–1: SELF BODY-RUB WITH LOTION
Time Required: 30 to 45 minutes

Get undressed, put some kind of lubricant on your hands (hand or body lotion is fine), sit or lie down, and begin to stroke yourself. Touch and stroke all the parts of your body that are readily accessible. Vary the types of strokes and pressures. Try very light touches, circular movements, both long and short strokes, slaps, and so forth. Play around with different types of touches and try to keep your attention on the skin immediately under where your hand is touching. Just be in touch with what it feels like. Go slowly and experience the sensations. Be aware of how and where you most like to be touched.

You may include your genitals in the touching, but do not spend a disproportionate amount of time on them.

Although this exercise is not intended to produce arousal or erection, it sometimes does. Whatever happens in this regard is fine. Should you become aroused, just enjoy it. Do not masturbate while doing the exercise, however.

Do this exercise one or two times. What did you learn about yourself? Did you learn some things you'd like to share with a partner? Are there any types of touching you'd like to continue giving yourself on a more or less regular basis?

There are many ways of including pleasurable self-touching in your daily life. You may, in fact, already be doing some of the things we suggest, but perhaps you are not taking the time to experience the enjoyable sensations produced. Washing and combing your hair, soaking in a hot bath, taking a shower, and drying yourself are activities that lend themselves to experiencing the sensations of touch, but only if done leisurely and with some awareness of your feelings at the time. Most men simply rush through these activities, with little or no awareness of what they feel. Try to take your time.

All of these activities can also be done with a partner. If you've never washed your partner's hair and had her wash yours, or if you've never bathed or showered together, you may want to try it. You may be surprised at how much fun can be derived from such simple experiences.

Another way of getting more experience with touching is to get a professional massage. This can be especially valuable if you have trouble being passive; the masseur or masseuse will help you just to receive. A good massage can also be a marvelous means of reducing tension.

Should you decide to get a massage, be careful where you go. Most so-called massage parlors are nothing but houses of prostitution, a fine example of how sex and touching have become confused. Legitimate masseurs and masseuses do not offer sex, and their advertisements do not feature naked women or promises of blowing your mind (or something else).

It is very important in doing touching exercises with your partner that both of you understand that they are not to end in sex. Otherwise, there is a risk that one of you will feel misunderstood or misled. Also, when touching is merely a prelude to sex, there is a tendency not fully to "get into it" or experience it, since you're looking forward to the "more important" activity that is to follow. When you're more comfortable with both touching and sex, and with getting your various needs met, you can do whatever you want, sometimes touching for its own sake and sometimes using it as a prelude to sex. But in the beginning, it's best to be clear that touching is not to lead to anything else.

One of our students, Penny Schuchman, gave the name "nondemand snuggling" to the instructions we gave couples for being physically affectionate without going on to sex. Snuggling refers to any type of physical contact that is pleasurable or comforting, while nondemand means that there is to be no expectation, request, or demand that it lead to sexual activity. Nondemand snuggling is simply touching for its own sake, the type of contact we have been discussing in this chapter. Here is an exercise that will assist you in cultivating it.

EXERCISE 8–2: NONDEMAND SNUGGLING
Time Required: Variable, but usually 5 to 20 minutes

Tell your partner you do not want sex but would like to be close to her. Whether you are clothed or not is up to you. Pick a comfortable place—sitting or lying on a sofa, bed, or the floor—and be close in any way that you want. You might want to hold each other with little or no movement or activity, or you may prefer that one or both of you lightly stroke the other (leaving out breasts and genitals).

Use your imagination and try different things. Perhaps putting your head in her lap, or vice versa, doing some back-scratching, toe-pulling, scalp-rubbing, or maybe just lying next to one another. Try whatever you want, but take it slow: give yourself a chance to experience and savor the sensations. Make sure you are passive at least part of the time, just experiencing what is happening.

Continue for as long as you want and stop when you feel like it. Should one or both of you fall asleep during the experience, that is fine.

People sometimes get sexually aroused during the exercise and that can be nice. Do not have sex. Just continue doing what you are doing.

If this experience is new for you, a few minutes is sufficient the first few times you do it. Gradually increase the amount of time until you are comfortable with ten to twenty minutes of snuggling.

If you don't have a partner, you might want to consider doing the exercise with a friend. In any case, you should think about how you will do it when you are in a relationship. The chances are that sex will be better in a new relationship if you do lots of snuggling before you get to sex.

We wonder if you found yourself being very active during the exercise. Many men find it difficult to be passive, sometimes just to lie still and experience their partners' touching them. If that is true for you, try lying on your hands next time you do the exercise. Being passive may feel very strange to you, so proceed gradually, increasing the amount of passive time as you feel comfortable doing so. You can, of course, do something for your partner before or after. It is very

important for both your sensual and sexual enjoyment that you develop the capacity to do nothing except experience your partner's touching you.

The next exercise is more formalized and detailed
than the preceding one but the general goal remains
the same. It is important that it be done as described
and that it not lead to sex. If you do not have a partner, you might want to do it with a friend. If you
follow this option, feel free to exclude the genitals if
that will make you more comfortable.

EXERCISE 8–3: NONSIMULTANEOUS BODY-RUBS
Time Required: 30 to 60 minutes

In both steps of the exercise, one of you gives a light, stroking body-rub to the other. How light depends on individual
preferences, but you should avoid the heavy, kneading type
of rubbing usually called massage.

You will need a warm room, a comfortable place for the
receiver to lie, and a lubricant (hand lotion, massage oil, or
baby powder).

First you must decide who will give and who will receive
in a particular session. The nonsimultaneous in the title of the
exercise means that the distinction between giver and receiver
must be rigidly adhered to. The receiver is not to touch or do
anything else to or for the giver, except as specified in the
instructions.

Since the receiver may not feel like doing anything active after the session, we suggest you not plan to have two sessions
back to back. It is usually best to wait at least an hour between
sessions.

The goal of both steps is to allow you to experience touching
and being touched without any other ends in mind. The giver
should focus on his touching and the receiver on the sensations produced by being touched.

You may or may not get turned-on, you may or may not enjoy the experience. Whatever happens is fine. Just keep in mind
that this exercise is not a prelude to anything. It is simply
what it is.

Step A: The giver touches, strokes, and rubs his partner for
his own pleasure, doing whatever he wants. The receiver
should accept what is done without comment unless there is
pain or discomfort, in which case she should ask the giver to
discontinue what he is doing.

The giver should use this opportunity to explore his partner's body with different types of touch, pressure, and rhythm.

Touch where and how you want to for your own pleasure. Discover what you like to do.

Spend at least thirty minutes per session. When time is up, take a few minutes talking about what the experience was like for each of you. You should both say what you liked most and least about the experience, and also indicate any difficulties you experienced—e.g., in being active or passive or in doing what you wanted. This talking is useful for learning how to communicate better about physical preferences; include it after every session and be as specific as possible.

Give and receive at least one rub before going on to the next step.

Step B: Here the receiver is in complete control, giving directions on where and how he wants to be touched, while the giver simply follows the instructions.

The receiver should use this opportunity to discover where and how he likes to be touched. You can ask for anything at all as long as there is not a disproportionate amount of attention given to the genitals. Try new things and places even if you're not sure how they will feel. If you've ever wondered how it would feel to have the areas between your toes touched, or how a light touch would do on your lower back, or anything else, now is the time to find out. Make sure you are getting precisely what you want, no matter how many times you have to give instructions or demonstrate to the giver.

The giver should do everything that is asked so long as it is not obnoxious or uncomfortable for her. She should also feel free to ask for more specific instructions if needed.

Spend at least thirty minutes per session and, as in Step A, take some time afterward to share your feelings about what the experience was like. This may be more complex than in Step A for there are sometimes problems around the giving and following of instructions. If such difficulties are present, use this time to deal with them. The receiver should be as clear as possible about what he wanted and the giver should talk about the difficulties encountered in following the instructions. The better you can resolve these issues now, the easier it will be for you when you do exercises dealing more directly with genital touching.

You should each give and get at least two rubs and be comfortable with both giving and following directions before leaving this exercise.

POSSIBLE PROBLEMS (in Step B)

1. Receiver does not give sufficient feedback to giver. As receiver, you should give as much feedback as you are comfortable with, indicating not only desired changes but also when the stroking is just as you want it. For example: "A little

higher and a bit lighter . . . that's the right place but lighter yet . . . that's perfect, just like that."

If you have trouble giving instructions because you feel guilty, see point 2.

2. Receiver feels guilty about getting and tries to take care of the giver. Many people have trouble receiving, feeling that they don't deserve it, that they are being selfish, or that the giver is really bored and doesn't want to give to them. In response to these feelings, they may try to make it easier for the giver by not giving instructions or by cutting the session short, or they may try to repay the giver by doing something for her (e.g., rubbing her or saying nice things when they should just be receiving). Try to resist doing these "nice" things, as they only hinder progress. It will probably be useful to talk to your partner about what is going on, your feelings about just receiving, your concerns about what she is thinking, and so on.

If you absolutely must pay some dues (i.e., take care of the giver), do so before or after the session, not during it. Some men find it easier to receive if they have already done something for their partner, so you may want to give her a rub in the morning if she is going to do one for you later in the day.

3. Giver has trouble following directions. This can happen for a number of reasons. If you are not clear about what your partner is asking for, request clarification. If you are clear but have some trouble complying, talk it out with her; let her know what's getting in your way and see if something can be worked out (and remember that you should not do anything that is distasteful or uncomfortable for you).

A problem encountered by many men is that they try to do what is asked and then get frustrated and angry when they are corrected. Try to remember that the exercise encourages exploration. We want the receiver to ask for many different things, to make corrections, and to feel free to change her mind. And the giver must therefore be willing to follow the changes and corrections.

Being the giver is often frustrating. You may feel like a child, trying your best to do what is asked but somehow being unable to satisfy your partner. This is due in part to the fact that we often touch another the way *we* want, without considering what *they* want. Learning to follow detailed instructions, which may not even be clear to the receiver, is a bit difficult and may be new to you. Like any new experience or skill, it takes time and patience.

You may have experienced more difficulty than anticipated in giving directions on how and where you wanted to be touched. Let's use an example of scratching an itch to see how this can happen. When you scratch your own itch, you make use of an automatic, nonverbal, self-correcting feedback loop. Your nervous system has precise and accurate information on where the itch is and what should be done to relieve it, and it guides your hand accordingly. There is continuous feedback regarding the itch and the efforts to relieve it, causing corrective action as needed, moving the position of your scratching fingers, their pace, pressure, and so on. All this is done without words, without conscious effort, and perhaps even without your knowledge.

The situation is radically changed when your partner is scratching you. Her nervous system gets no information about the itch or her efforts to relieve it other than what you show or tell her. To supply the information to her, you need to make verbal what was automatic and nonverbal when you did it yourself. And this can be frustrating. Practice and learning are required to unscramble the automatic feedback loop so that it is, first, clear to you, and second, so that it is understandable to your partner. It may help to keep in mind that there's no way your partner can know what you want unless you tell her. She simply does not have access to the continuous stream of information that your body is supplying to you. You, of course, may not have much experience in making explicit the nonverbal messages of your nervous system. Continued practice will definitely help and we hope you can learn to enjoy it.

Most of the men we have worked with found the touching exercises enjoyable and real eye-openers. They had forgotten how much fun it can be to touch and be touched.

Jack, a man in his forties who had come for therapy with his wife, agreed to try the touching exercises only after he was convinced that they would help in the treatment of his erection problems. The first time he and his wife snuggled, he became disappointed and then furious because he didn't get an erection. He strongly believed that the purpose of any kind of physical contact was to arouse him so that he could have intercourse. He was then told that the snuggling

was to continue and that he should do everything possible to prevent himself from getting an erection.
There was to be no genital contact whatever. Jack was
at a loss to understand what was going on but agreed
to find out what this touching stuff was about. It
wasn't easy for him, for he believed in all the male
myths more strongly than most men, but he gradually
got more comfortable with touching. Within a few
weeks, he even admitted that he was enjoying the new
physical closeness with his wife. She was overjoyed; for
the eighteen years of their married life she had been
unable to get any physical contact from him except
when he wanted sex, and this was the main cause of her
coldness and sarcasm. As she became less critical, he
became more aroused, and in less than two months
they were having very enjoyable sex. But the real surprise was what Jack said in a phone conversation six
months after the end of therapy.

"I owe you a lot. Sex is fine, and that's great. But
there's more. This closeness and cuddling stuff is really
something. I never would have believed that I, of all
people, would like it. Never even occurred to me to try
it. Our lives are better because of it. I've gotten ad-
dicted to having my feet rubbed and licked and it's
great. And this you'll never believe: it's helped us with
our kids. They were really shocked when I started
touching them, but they've gotten used to it and we all
touch more now. When my boy came home from college, I hugged him at the door. He must have thought
I was nuts but he's gotten used to the idea and now we
always hug when we see each other. Makes us feel
closer."

If your experiences with touching are different from
Jack's, if they're not enjoyable for you, try to determine what is standing in your way. Your image of
how you should be as a man? The idea that touching
is only for women and children? The myth that touching is only acceptable as the prelude to intercourse?
The notion that touching should be a mind-blowing experience? Once you've found the obstacle, determine
if there is something you can do to move it out of
the way a little bit, and do it.

We are not prescribing touching as a panacea for
all your ills or as a compulsory ritual that should be

followed whether you like it or not. Rather, we view touching as a very important human need, probably much more basic than the need for sex, a need you should be free to fulfill in ways and with people of your own choosing. It won't change the world and it won't solve all your problems, but it may help you feel better and bring you a bit closer to the important people in your world. Men need touching as much as anyone else, and there is no good reason to deprive yourself in this area.

Touch [say Masters and Johnson] is an end in itself. It is a primary form of communication, a silent voice that avoids the pitfall of words while expressing the feelings of the moment. It bridges the physical separateness from which no human being is spared, literally establishing a sense of solidarity between two individuals.

Get in touch with those you care for. Stay in touch. Literally.

9

The Importance
of Relaxation

Although modern living has benefited us in many ways, it has also had many negative effects. The pace of living has accelerated at an alarming rate. Life has become more hectic, and the pressures of daily living seem considerably greater than in the past. We are tense and distraught much of the time, struggling to keep up with the treadmill of our lives and resorting to a vast array of chemical uppers and downers, including tobacco and alcohol, to help us cope with our tensions. But the tensions and anxieties remain, affecting almost all areas of our lives.

Nervous tension is not compatible with good sex. It can prevent you from becoming aroused, from experiencing the pleasurable sensations that would be available were you not so tense, and it tends to have a soporific effect on your penis.

Many men have sex when they are tense because of time pressure, some unfinished business with their partner, something that happened at work or with the kids, or for some other reason. Sex under such conditions frequently is not very satisfying and sometimes it doesn't work at all.

We cannot sufficiently emphasize the importance of

being relaxed in sex. Attempting to engage in sex when you are irritated or anxious is one of the best ways we know to have a miserable experience. Good sex is extremely difficult to come by under these circumstances; your arousal, erection, and ejaculation systems simply do not function well when you are feeling tense.

Let's talk a bit about what we mean by tension and relaxation. People differ greatly in this regard. Some are generally easygoing and relaxed, while others are tense and keyed-up most of the time. But even the most relaxed person is more relaxed at some times than at others, and even the most high-strung person is sometimes less tense. As far as sex goes, the important things, regardless of whether you are generally tense or relaxed, are that you be able to recognize when you are more tense than usual for you and that you be able to do something to relax yourself.

Relaxation and tension, as we use the terms, are relative states. You are to consider your own behavior as the standard, being aware that what is tense or relaxed for you may have little to do with what others are like when they employ these terms.

There are two general types of indicators of tension that will help you determine how tense you are in a given situation. The first type consists of physical indicators. People differ as to where in their bodies they experience tension, but some common signs are tensing of the neck and shoulder muscles, a knotty feeling in the stomach, sweaty palms, and clenching of teeth. Whether or not these examples fit for you, tension always has some physical manifestations and you need to determine what yours are.

Your thoughts are the second kind of indicator of tension. The following thoughts all indicate some degree of concern or anxiety: "Will it stay hard?" "Am I going to be able to last?" "Will she like me?" "Am I going to be able to carry this off?"

Have you ever experienced some of the physical symptoms described above in a sexual situation? Or asked yourself questions similar to the ones we cited? If so, you were probably experiencing tension or anxiety. There is nothing to be concerned about if the experiences were fleeting—if, for example, the question of whether you would last merely floated through your mind. But if it stayed on and nagged at you, the chances are good that you would enjoy sex more if you learned more about relaxing.

It may help you to consider the feelings you experienced in some nonsexual situations to get a better idea of how tension manifests itself in you. How do you feel when you sit in the dentist's chair waiting for him to start drilling? Does your body tense up in some way? Do you hold your breath? Grasp the arms of the chair? Do you wonder if it's going to hurt despite the Novocain? Or consider what you feel when your boss calls you into his office to discuss a mistake you made. And what happens to you when you have to finish a project by a certain time and are aware that you have more work than time left? Consider these questions carefully; they will give you a good understanding of what tension means to you.

Now, to look at the other side of things, give some thought to situations in which you felt free of cares and worries. Perhaps when you wake up late on a Sunday morning knowing there isn't anything for you to do that day. Or when you're lying on the beach during a vacation. Or perhaps after a good sexual experience. How do your body and your mind feel on such occasions?

Although the particular examples we gave may not fit for you, we're sure you can think of similar situations that will help you define what maximum tension and relaxation mean to you.

The following exercise is a useful tool for becoming more aware of your tension/relaxation state.

EXERCISE 9–1: DETERMINING HOW RELAXED YOU ARE
Time Required: 5 to 10 minutes

The first few times you do the exercise, make sure you have privacy and will not be interrupted. Once you are accustomed to it, you can do it any time, any place, even if others are present. The exercise should be done at least ten times, but twenty or thirty times are not too often.

Without changing your posture, breathing, or muscle tension, focus your attention on the part of your body that is most tense. Resist the temptation to relax that part; just experience it the way it is for a few seconds. Now check to see if any other part of your body is as tense or nearly as tense as the part you first focused on. Pay attention to this part, just experiencing it, for a few seconds, again without changing it. Next, spend a few minutes on the rest of your body—feet, calves, thighs, buttocks, back, stomach, chest, hands, arms, shoulders, neck, face, scalp, and insides—asking of each part if it is tense or relaxed. If it feels relaxed, could it feel more relaxed? If tense, more tense? Don't try to make it more relaxed or tense, just determine if it's possible that it could change.

Finally, get in touch with your breathing without changing it. Become aware of how you are breathing. Deeply or shallowly? Slowly or quickly? Is your chest moving? Your stomach? Are you unable to detect movement in either?

POSSIBLE PROBLEMS

1. You find yourself wanting to do something about what you discover. This tendency comes from being judgmental about what you find, e.g., "I shouldn't be so tense," "My breathing should be slower." These judgments may have little to do with reality and, even when they are correct, trying to do something about them gets in the way of the goal of the exercise, being aware of tension and relaxation. You will have plenty of opportunities to make changes in your level of relaxation later. For now, just try to accept what you find. If the temptation to change something is there, just let it be there and continue with the exercise.

2. You find your mind wandering away from the parts of your body you want to focus on. Everyone's mind wanders during such exercises and it is not a problem. When you are aware that your attention has drifted off, just gently bring it back and continue where you left off. You will have to do this a number of times during the course of the exercise, and that is fine. Of course, should your wandering be due to factors over which you have some control, e.g., the radio playing or the dog barking, you should take care of these distractions before continuing.

Doing this exercise may be the first time you have paid attention to your body without asking it to *do* something. You will be asked to do more of this type of attending, which we call focusing, in other exercises in the book. It may sometimes be difficult—for men have learned too well how to do and too little about how to be—but it will get easier with practice. Just take it slow and bring your mind back when it wanders.

Now that you have learned to check on your level of tension, let's explore some ways of lessening tension. There are many approaches to relaxation and, as our society grows ever more stressful, increasing numbers of people are turning to them. Among the more popular are meditation, yoga exercises, self-hypnosis, and tai-chi. All of these can be effective if practiced properly and consistently; if you are already involved in one or more of them and found them helpful, we encourage you to continue.

Here are some other effective ways of helping you become more relaxed.

A lot of the anxiety that men experience in sex has to do with trying to please or impress their partners. You want to do it well for her and get concerned about what may happen if you don't. As paradoxical as it sounds, probably the best way of dealing with such tension is to tell your partner about it. Just express what you are feeling: e.g., "Honey, I know you were disappointed last time and I want it to be good for you tonight. But I'm trying so hard, and I'm so concerned that you'll get mad if I don't stay hard, that I'm worrying like crazy and can't even concentrate on what's happening." Sometimes the acknowledgment will in itself reduce your anxiety. Or perhaps your statement will lead to a conversation regarding her feelings and expectations, as well as yours, and this may contribute to better feelings on both sides. You might find that she wasn't expecting the kind of performance you imagined.

Most men find it at least a bit difficult to express their feelings in this way. We learned that we weren't supposed to feel fear or concern, let alone express them. And it's true that there is some risk involved; though not likely, it is possible that your partner won't like what you say or will have the expectations you fear or will feel very disappointed. You have to decide if the potential benefits outweigh the risks. One way or another, you need to reduce your tension if you are to have good sex. Telling your partner about your concern isn't the only way, but it's one of the best. It may be of interest to you to know that of the thousands of instances we know of where men talked to their partners about their tense feelings in sex, there were only a few where the situation was not improved as a result of the talking.

Another type of talking, the kind involved in clearing up unfinished business, is also very helpful in making sex more satisfying. Every relationship is bound to include disappointments, frustrations, and hostilities. The feelings are inevitable but they get handled in different ways. At one extreme, some couples almost immediately deal with any negative feelings that come up. They may talk or scream or do something else, but the bad feelings are dealt with and no backlog results. Each day begins with a more or less clean slate. Other couples do just the opposite. They almost never deal with their negative emotions and, as a result, carry around resentment and hostility from years ago. Each new experience of frustration or anger just gets piled on top of the already existing heap which more and more begins to resemble Mount Everest. The feelings may be expressed in sarcasm or seemingly reasonable complaints, or they may not, but the aura of tension and hostility is often so thick that strangers immediately sense that something is wrong.

Sex usually does not go well in such situations, assuming that there is any sex. The tension and anger may interfere with one or both partners' arousal systems, causing a lack of sexual interest, or with the systems governing erection or orgasm. Simple relaxation exercises are usually not very effective in such cases. Much more beneficial are talks about the sources of one's discontent and negotiations for reaching a resolution of some of the problems.

Rob, age forty-two, came to therapy for help with his sexual relationship with his wife. For the past two years, whenever they had sex he would either not get an erection, get one but lose it quickly, or come very fast. He felt very tense in sex and he also reported feeling tense whenever he was around his wife, although he said he cared for her deeply and wanted to make the marriage work. His wife, Margaret, was asked to come in for a few sessions, and the following story emerged.

Rob had been somewhat dissatisfied with their sexual relationship since the beginning of their marriage. Margaret had been inexperienced sexually and reacted negatively to his desires for oral and anal sex. Rob, instead of trying to work it out with her, had an affair with a woman he worked with, feeling that Margaret's primness had driven him to it. Margaret was deeply hurt by the affair and was angry at Rob not only for having sex with another woman but also for not being more patient with her. None of these feelings had been discussed or worked out prior to their coming to therapy, and they had been the basis for ever-increasing tension between Rob and Margaret. Rob felt guilty about the affair and feared Margaret's anger. So he acted very carefully around her, trying not to show too much that he cared for her; he didn't want to give her a chance to reject him. Margaret took his withdrawal as a rejection of her; she wanted, but wasn't getting, his assurance that he loved her rather than the woman with whom he had the affair. All of these feelings, not expressed directly, formed a wall of tension between them all of the time, but especially in sex. The wall began to crumble when they told each other what they had been feeling and what they wanted. Margaret was surprised to hear that Rob cared as much as he did, that the other woman meant very little to him, and that he certainly would not want another affair. Rob was surprised that Margaret still wanted his love and, lo and behold, was quite willing to experiment with new sexual practices if he could respect her inexperience and get into new things slowly. These talks continued for six therapy sessions; the tension between them was reduced to a manageable level and sex became good.

This was a case where less direct methods did not work. Before coming to see us, Rob had been to several therapists, one of whom taught him self-hypnosis and another of whom had given him autogenic training (a form of relaxation training). Such methods were insufficient to deal with the strong and pervasive tension in the relationship. It had to be dealt with directly, by airing grievances and desires and making satisfactory arrangements for future behavior.

If there's a lot of unfinished business between you and your partner, consider how it affects your sexual activities and what you want to do about it. You might benefit from doing what Rob and Margaret did, with or without professional help.

Two more tension-producing situations deserve comment. We have found that many men find it difficult to separate work and leisure. They bring the worries, pressures, and frustrations of their jobs home with them and, in this state of tenseness, interpret anything their families do as more demands and pressure. Needless to say, they are hard to be with, sexually or otherwise.

A very effective way of dealing with this situation is to do something that both literally and symbolically marks the leaving of work and the entering into a more relaxed state. The types of transition activities that men have chosen vary considerably; vigorous physical activity; gardening; a massage; meditation; a relaxing glass of wine either alone or with a partner; a hot bath; a short nap; listening to some favorite music or doing some fun reading. Here is how one man told his wife about wanting to make the transition from work to home:

Honey, I know I'm pretty grouchy in the evenings and difficult to live with. I get all revved up at work and I'm just beat by the time I get home. As soon as I get in the door we get into a conversation and I feel overwhelmed. It just feels like more pressure. I think it would really help if I had some time alone after I got here, just to relax and unwind, without having to talk to you or anyone else. What I'd like to do is still come home at five, but I'd like you to pretend that I'm not here until quarter after six. If the phone rings, either don't answer it or say I'm not home if it's for me. I'm not sure what I'll do in that time, maybe go jogging or take a nap or just sit in our room. I'm pretty sure that if I can get that time to myself, I'll be much better company the rest of the evening.

In looking for transition activities, consider those things that are both pleasurable and relaxing for you. Perhaps one of the activities you chose in Exercise 6–3 will make for a good transition.

You may at first run into some resistance from your lover or children; they may believe that you're just taking more time away from them or that your new activities will upset the household routine. And they may be right. It will help if you carefully explain the reasons for what you're doing. If you choose your transition activities with care and stick with them, it probably won't be long before both you and those you live with agree that you're doing the right thing.

You should also be aware of periods of unusually high stress. All of us experience such times: the busy season at work, the days before final exams, working on a project with a deadline, and so on. Many men simply shrug their shoulders during such periods and stoically try to accept their burden, usually not realizing that they are causing others around them much unhappiness. Accepting such high levels of tension without doing anything to relieve them takes its toll, and many men are quite difficult to live with during such periods.

Although you may not be able to do much to change the pressure-producing situation, you probably can deal with it in a way that creates less tension in you. Taking a few minutes every hour or two to do something relaxing can be helpful; you will probably find that although you have "lost" a few minutes of work time, the increased productivity brought about by your more relaxed state will more than make up for it. Some men find a few minutes of physical exercise every hour or two helpful, others enjoy a quiet moment alone taking a walk or fantasizing, and some achieve good results from lying down and doing some deep breathing for a few moments. Transition activities are particularly useful during periods of high stress. The most important point is that you recognize that you are under a lot of pressure and make some plans to help you relax.

As surprising as it may sound after all we have said, physical contact with your partner, with or without sex, can be very soothing during times of high stress, providing that the cause of the stress is not the relationship and that you follow a few simple suggestions. Be aware that since you are under a great deal of tension, sex may not be "as usual." You may respond differently from when you are more relaxed. As long as you put no pressure on yourself to have an erection or to go on to sex or to have intercourse, there's no reason to avoid touching or sex, should you desire either. Being cuddled or made love to can be wonderful ways of making you feel cared for and relieving your tensions. But this is only true when the touching and sex do not add extra pressure. If they do, they are best avoided.

Following the suggestions in this chapter should help you be more relaxed in sex. However, there may still be times when you are tense. Men tend to try to ignore the tension and push on. We hope you now realize that such a procedure will rarely result in good sex. The best thing to do when you feel tense is to stop what you're doing and see if there are some ways of getting more comfortable. As we said earlier, telling your partner about your feelings is usually quite helpful. You should also check to see if sex is really what you want to be doing. If you get more comfortable, feel free to resume your sexual activities. If the tension remains, it's probably best not to continue with sex but to do something else that feels more comfortable. There will be plenty of opportunities for sex in the future.

10

Masturbation: From Self-Abuse to Pleasure and Self-Help

You may be wondering why a book like this includes a
chapter on masturbation. After all, you're an adult
and, whether you masturbate or not, probably don't
think that any comment or instruction regarding this
practice is necessary. Or perhaps you've never masturbated and don't have any interest in the subject.

There are two important reasons for dealing with
masturbation. First, it is one of the best ways of enhancing your sexuality and overcoming any sexual difficulties you may be experiencing. This is especially
true for men without partners. Second, masturbation
as practiced by many men is not as pleasurable as it
might be and, moreover, is accompanied by feelings of
guilt or shame. Overcoming some of these negative
feelings enables you better to enjoy your autoerotic
practices.

Following Kinsey, we define masturbation as "self-
stimulation which is deliberate and designed to effect
erotic arousal." Note that neither erection nor orgasm
is mentioned. Also note that, by definition, masturbation refers only to self-stimulation. Your partner may

play with your penis exactly the way you do yourself but by virtue of the fact that she and not you is doing it, it is not masturbation.

Although the overwhelming majority of men have masturbated at some time in their lives, it is something few feel good about. Even with the recent openness about sexuality and the greater tolerance for sexual expression, masturbation is the most difficult subject for people to discuss. In his study *Sexual Behavior in the 1970s,* Morton Hunt sums it up this way:

> *Most persons who masturbate remain more or less guilt-ridden about it, and nearly all of them are extremely secretive about their masturbating and would be horribly embarrassed to have anyone know the truth.*

For most men it is easier to admit to lying, cheating, or even to having sex problems than to acknowledge that they sometimes play with their penises.

The younger generation is only slightly better off. A recent nationwide study of teenagers by Robert Sorenson reported that of the boys who masturbated only 17 percent said they "never" felt guilty, anxious, or concerned about it, while 45 percent "often" or "sometimes" did have such feelings about it. Sorenson concluded:

> *There seems to be no sex practice discussed in this study about which young people feel more defensive or private than masturbation. . . . Self-esteem, embarrassment, and personal disgust seem to be the major inhibiting factors.*

The amazing thing about these results is that all the youngsters studied were brought up during the "sexual revolution"; all were born several years *after* Kinsey had clearly demonstrated the widespread prevalence of masturbation among men and convincingly argued that it produced no ill effects whatever.

There are many good reasons for our concern and anxiety about masturbation. The practice has been condemned, usually severely, throughout Western history, and not until Kinsey did anyone of importance have anything good to say about it. Jewish religious leaders considered it a grave sin since it was a deliberate waste of sperm that should have been used to add to the population. Christian authorities were no more lenient, calling masturbation immoral and unnatural.

In the middle of the eighteenth century, scientists and physicians joined in the attack against what was variously called "the solitary vice," "self-abuse," and "self-pollution." Masturbation came to be viewed, with absolutely no evidence whatever, as the cause of everything evil. As Kinsey and his colleagues put it:

Every conceivable ill from pimples to insanity, including stooped shoulders, loss of weight, fatigue, insomnia, general weakness . . . loss of manly vigor, weak eyes, digestive upsets, stomach ulcers, impotence, feeble-mindedness, genital cancer, and the rest, was ascribed to masturbation. . . . Patients [in mental institutions] were observed to engage in frequent masturbation, and this seemed sufficient proof that the insanity was a product of the sexual behavior. Since the lives of university scholars were not so easily observed, it was not so generally known that masturbation occurred quite as frequently among them.

If you think that all this happened hundreds of years ago and has nothing to do with you, you may be interested in what follows, taken from a popular book called *What a Boy Should Know,* written by two physicians in 1909 and widely read for many years after.

Whenever unnatural emissions are produced . . . the body becomes "slack." A boy will not feel so vigorous and springy; he will be more easily tired; he will not have so good "an eye" for games. He will probably look pale and pasty, and he is lucky if he escapes indigestion and getting his bowels confined, both of which will probably give him spots and pimples on his face. . . .
The effect of self-abuse on a boy's character al-

*ways tends to weaken it, and, in fact, to make him
untrustworthy, unreliable, and probably even dishon-
est.*

If you're not as "springy" as you once were, or if
you're looking "pale and pasty," now you know why.

The *Boy Scout Manual,* probably read by millions of
children and parents, until 1945 warned about the
evils of masturbation, and as late as 1940 a candidate
could be rejected at the United States Naval Academy
if it were discovered that he masturbated.

Even if you were born after 1945, what do you
think your parents had learned about masturbation? Is
it any wonder that you got all sorts of messages that
there was something terribly wrong about it?

When scientific authority first joined religious authority in attacking masturbation, punishment for offend-
ers was relatively mild. The main objective was simply
to stop the evil habit, often with the aid of patent medicines. But since education regarding the grave consequences of self-stimulation and patent medicines
proved ineffective, punishment became harsher and
harsher until, by the mid-nineteenth century, a perse-
cution of sadistic proportions had been inaugurated.

Some of the more extreme remedies involved tying
boys' hands to their bedposts or chaining them to walls
when they slept; putting a wire ring through the foreskin of the penis or wearing a spiked ring on the penis,
both procedures making erection and stimulation extremely painful; the wearing of straitjacketlike re-
straints to keep the hands away from forbidden terri-
tory; and, in a few cases, even castration and surgical
removal of the penis. These bizarre and barbaric practices quickly peaked and declined, but vestiges remained until the Second World War.

The belief that masturbation caused gross mental
and physical abnormalities such as epilepsy and insanity declined toward the end of the last century.
But it was quickly replaced by a new set of beliefs that
did little to ease the anxiety that most people had
about masturbation. The conviction grew that masturbation was a common cause of neurotic disorders and

marital sexual problems, a view shared by Freud. Thanks to Freud and others, however, a more liberal attitude toward self-stimulation in children arose; it was accepted as a normal, if somewhat repellent, childish habit. Provided, of course, that it was not done "to excess." Since "excess" was never defined—was it once a day? a week? a year? or what?—no one could ever be sure he wasn't doing it too much.

And, the new views maintained, what was legitimate and normal for children was "infantile" and "immature" when done by adults. There must be something seriously wrong with someone past adolescence who resorted to self-stimulation rather than engaging in "normal, healthy heterosexual relations." Some defect of character was obviously indicated since masturbation was clearly a poor substitute for "the real thing." These views were hardly designed to set anyone's mind at ease. An adult who masturbated was compelled to think of himself as somehow neurotic or socially inept, unable to find a partner with whom he could have sex the way it was supposed to be done.

The something-must-be-wrong-with-you-if-you-masturbate school suffered its greatest setback by the work of Kinsey and his coworkers who, in their massive study of male sexuality, reported not only that 92 percent of men had masturbated at some time in their lives, many of them while they were married, but that no detrimental effects whatsoever were to be found, regardless of masturbatory frequency. Kinsey went even further, claiming that the problem with masturbation lay not in the act itself but in the anxiety and guilt fostered by the traditional teachings.

The record does include thousands of cases of boys living in continual conflict, oftentimes disturbed over the effect of such behavior [masturbation] on their ultimate sexual capacities, occasionally attempting suicide—as a result of the teachings concerning masturbation. For the boys who have not been too disturbed psychically, masturbation has, however, provided a regular sexual outlet which has alleviated nervous tensions; and the record is clear in many cases that these boys have on the whole lived more balanced lives than the boys who have been more restrained in their sexual activities.

Kinsey's data and arguments definitely helped undermine the traditional views of masturbation and helped usher in a more tolerant attitude. Many men took some personal comfort from his statistics and some therapists and physicians reconsidered their views. Masturbation started gaining a small measure of respectability. In 1968, Wardell Pomeroy, a former Kinsey associate and well-known sex expert, published *Boys and Sex,* in which he encouraged his readers to masturbate as much as they wanted. The book was highly regarded by professionals and undoubtedly had some influence. And in the 1970s best-sellers like *The Sensuous Woman* and *The Sensuous Man* sang the praises of self-stimulation.

While masturbation clearly has come out of the closet, it would be a mistake to assume that it is therefore widely accepted. The newer views still represent a minority opinion. Kinsey's work is less than thirty years old, while the myths and misinformation attached to masturbation have been around for almost two thousand years. Things may be better, but how much?

Not a great deal. Masters and Johnson report that the men they studied held fairly traditional views regarding masturbation, *all* of them believing that "excessive" self-stimulation might lead to physical or mental abnormality, although none of them could explain how frequently "excessive" was. We have already noted the findings of a study of teenagers that demonstrated the defensiveness and concern they felt about masturbating. One particularly interesting aspect of that study is that none of the subjects believed the old stories about the emotional and physical damage that was allegedly caused by masturbation, yet they were still concerned about the practice. They felt badly about it even though they knew that it could lead to no harm. How could this be so?

It is well to remember that many authorities have not accepted the newer views of masturbation. Many, if not most, physicians, therapists, religious leaders, educators, and parents still believe, and convey to the people they deal with, that there is something wrong with playing with yourself, although they are no longer able to say just *what* is wrong with it. Then, too, there are still many who believe that masturbation is sinful. A recently issued proclamation on sexual matters by the Vatican repeats the old, familiar line: masturbation is "an intrinsically and seriously disordered act."

What is certainly a source of great confusion to many people is that many authorities speak and write with a forked tongue, taking on the one hand a very liberal attitude regarding masturbation (it's normal and healthy) while at the same time conveying the impression that at best it's a necessary evil and there is really something strange about anyone who is doing it.

David Reuben provides a fine example of this procedure. Here are some quotations from his *Everything You Always Wanted to Know about Sex,* a book that sold millions of copies:

> The only thing harmful about masturbation is the guilt that is drummed into children who admit masturbating. [*This is the tolerant stance: masturbation is fine. Now watch how he undermines it.*]
>
> . . . masturbation is fun. Certainly not as much fun as full-fledged sexual intercourse, *but the next thing to it. That is exactly what masturbation is,* a substitute form of gratification when sexual intercourse is impossible.
>
> [*In answer to a question regarding when masturbation is desirable, he mentions it is fine for those too young for partner sex and that it may be helpful for nonorgasmic women. He is then asked if there are other situations where self-stimulation is desirable.*] In those who cannot obtain sexual satisfaction in any other way. *Men and women in prison, very old people, and often the blind are restricted in their sexual outlets.*

What the good doctor—along with so many others who talk and write about sex—is saying is that masturbation is fine . . . for children, the aged, the infirm, and the incarcerated. Anyone else doing it just doesn't have what it takes to have the real thing—"heterosexual intercourse"—and is therefore forced to settle for this poor substitute. This is simply a continuation of the view espoused since the beginning of this century that self-stimulation in adults is immature and indicates some deficiency.

Men's attitudes about their own masturbatory activities strongly reflect the unhappy legacy we have been discussing. It is usually experienced as a necessary evil, useful for relieving sexual tension. Very few feel good about masturbating and even fewer talk about it. Even men who brag about all their other sexual activities never seem to say anything, boastful or otherwise, about their autoerotic practices.

When I started masturbating at the age of thirteen, there was a kind of openness about it with my boyfriends. We sometimes masturbated together in what I later learned were called "circle jerks," with the one who came first or shot the farthest being acclaimed hero of the day. And we often joked about it. But as we turned our attention to girls, the jokes and circle jerks ceased. I continued masturbating fairly regularly even when involved in a sexual relationship but never talked about it to anyone. I was always concerned that one of my partners would find out about it and sometimes had to invent strange excuses for what I was doing in there, the bathroom. One time, a woman I was living with walked in on me unexpectedly and there I was with my hand on my erect penis. I turned twelve different shades of purple and hastily concocted the weirdest story about having a sore spot on my penis which I was trying to examine. I don't know why I was so ashamed of playing with myself but I clearly felt that it was wrong and disgraceful. I was shocked when she said that it was OK with her if I was masturbating and she would like to watch. I immediately lost my erection and sexual desire. But we talked about it and that broke the ice for me. I lost most of my negative feelings about masturbation and have since been open about it with my partners. I'm certainly happy that she walked in on me.

Shame is the feeling that most often accompanies masturbation in adult men, shame that they should have to resort to this "childish" substitute. If they really had it together, they think, they would be doing something sexual with a partner. The very fact of playing with oneself conveys a sense that, at least on this one occasion, they weren't good enough or clever enough or masculine enough to get a partner with whom they could have "real sex."

Because of these feelings, and also because men have had little permission and practice in being sensual, many men do not derive as much pleasure as they could from masturbating. It is usually done very quickly, the whole object being to achieve orgasm and get it over with. Masturbating this way presents some problems. It develops a habit of coming quickly, which may carry over to sex with a partner. And it also reinforces our tendency to ignore bodily sensations more subtle than orgasm and reinforces our inability to linger over and prolong pleasure.

If men have such negative feelings about self-stimulation, and if it's not as enjoyable for them as it might be, why then do they continue to do it? Basically because it feels good. Even when done hurriedly and without much concentration on the sensations prior to orgasm, it still feels good.

There are also other reasons. Masturbation can be a source of comfort. Hunt reported that a number of his respondents said the urge to masturbate was often aroused by feelings of loneliness. The fantasies that so often accompany masturbation in men are another important motivating factor. The fantasies are not only fun but, as Hunt points out, they "can partially satisfy the psychological need for variety; it enables people to do, in fantasy, sexual things they do not ordinarily have the chance to do, or with partners they have no access to."

But you don't really need a reason for masturbating other than the fact that you want to do it. Sometimes you may be feeling sexy and also want to be alone (yes, *want* to be alone, not *have* to be alone). You may not want to deal with another person at the time, and there's no reason why you should have to. After all, dealing with a partner requires energy and consideration, and it is ludicrous to assume that you are going to want to expend such energy and give such consideration every time you feel sexy. Sometimes you just don't want to be concerned with someone else's needs and desires. And must you be? You can decide to have a fine time with yourself—not as a substitute or replacement for something better, but just because that's what you want. Sometimes masturbation simply fits your needs and desires better than anything else.

Now that we've said you need no reasons for masturbating, we'd like to turn around and give you some reasons. Masturbation, done systematically and in accordance with a few simple rules, has definite therapeutic benefits. You can use it to learn more about your body and its requirements, and to acquire skills useful in sex with a partner. We have found masturbation exercises very helpful in developing ejaculatory control and in dealing with erection problems. And you can learn a lot about yourself with these exercises even if you do not have a specific problem and are primarily interested in enhancing your sex life.

You may be wondering why masturbation exercises are so helpful or why they should be done in preference to partner exercises. While we have nothing against partner exercises and include many later in the book, masturbation exercises have a particular advantage. Namely, that it is easier to experiment with new things when you don't have to concern yourself with how someone else is feeling about what you're doing. In the long run, of course, you are probably going to want to use your new skills and understanding with a partner, but it is much easier to develop the skills without her distracting influence. Focusing, for example, is difficult for many men to learn with their partners present. Once they get the hang of it on their own, it is then much easier to transfer the skills to situations that involve their partners.

Of course, we can't guarantee that you'll feel good about masturbating. The negative ideas about masturbation that we discussed earlier are still very influential for many of us, since they were pounded into us, sometimes literally, as children and adults. You may find yourself feeling somewhat uneasy as you do, or even consider doing, masturbation exercises. You may feel guilty about doing something which you were told was sinful; ashamed that you are playing with yourself rather than getting it on with a partner as a "real man" should; or worried about what your partner or potential partners would think if they knew what you were doing. Or there may just be a vague kind of discomfort which has no particular content other than that you are doing something which isn't nice.

Unless your negative feelings about self-stimulation are tremendously strong, we suggest you try it. While it is asking a bit too much to expect your negative feelings about masturbation to disappear altogether, many men have found that doing it regularly under therapeutic advice in itself eased their discomfort. Another way of feeling better about self-stimulation is to talk about it to a partner or friend. We realize that not everyone will want to do this, but those who have done it invariably reported that it made them feel much more comfortable.

Before getting on to the concept of focusing and our basic masturbation exercise, we need to talk about how you masturbate. Most men masturbate by stroking up and down the shaft and head of the penis with one hand, although there is much variation with regard to how much of the shaft and head is included in the stroking, how firmly the penis is held, and the rapidity of the movements. We call this method of stroking the penis with one hand the usual way of masturbating.

Some men masturbate in other ways; for example, by squeezing the penis rather than stroking it, by rubbing it between both hands, or while lying face down and rubbing the penis against the bed or floor. These ways, if practiced exclusively, can lead to problems.

Larry, a man in his late twenties who had problems maintaining erections and ejaculating with a partner, had always masturbated by rubbing his whole body vigorously against his bed. He had never stroked his penis. The types of stimulation he got with partners were so different from what he did by himself that he did not experience them as arousing and often lost his erection or failed to ejaculate.

We certainly don't want to create any problems where none existed previously, so if you masturbate in some of the atypical ways but don't think they are causing you any difficulties, all well and good; stick with what you do. But if you are experiencing some problems with partners, we encourage you to expand your options by masturbating in what we are calling the usual way. How much pressure to use can only be determined by experience. The only thing to be concerned about is if you are squeezing your penis to a pulp; that's probably too much pressure. By asking you to try the stroking method we are not saying you should give up your old ways entirely. We are suggesting you expand possibilities, not limit them. Use the new method in doing the exercise and use your way at other times.

Focusing

In the exercise that follows and in others throughout the book, you are going to be asked to focus on your bodily sensations. Since most men have been trained not to pay attention to such things, it may not be easy at first. But it is well worth doing. Focusing has the effect of amplifying sensations, making their impact more powerful. It is also useful in determining the kinds of stimulation you best like. Focusing will assist you in discovering preferences that may not be obvious to you now.

Focusing basically means paying attention. It is a relatively passive attending to what is happening in a particular part of your body. You have already done some focusing in Exercise 9–1 when you attended to the tensest parts and your breathing. That is all that focusing is. It is more passive and gentle than the mode we men are more accustomed to, wherein we grit our teeth and forcefully concentrate on something. No forcing, no gritting of teeth, no pushing and shoving.

Men often get frustrated when their minds wander during focusing. There is no way of preventing your attention from skipping around. If you've ever meditated, you know this. The mind is like a drunken monkey, always jumping from one thing to another. You can't control this activity and, fortunately, you don't have to. When you do an exercise that asks you to focus, start by putting your attention to the part of the body that is prescribed. When you are aware that your mind has drifted off, simply bring your attention back to the part you want to focus on. Try to avoid getting into an argument with yourself and fighting the distracting thoughts.

Focusing is an intuitive process, not an intellectual one. You need to attend to sensations but there is no need to label, analyze, or think about them. You may find yourself engaging in some intellectual activities —"What should I call this feeling?" "Why do I feel more here than there?" Simply recognize that these are distractions and return your attention to the sensations.

A common problem with focusing concerns the expectations you have about what you "should" be feeling. Many men expect bells-ringing-and-bombs-bursting sensations and, when these are not forthcoming, think that there is nothing worth attending to. The sensations you do feel are unlikely to be earthshaking, sensational, or anything of the sort. They are just, well, sensations. They may seem trivial. Sometimes they may even feel uncomfortable or negative. Whatever is there is there, and that's what you should focus on. As your ability to focus improves, you may be surprised how interesting these little sensations become.

The following suggestions apply to Exercise 10–1 and all subsequent masturbation and partner exercises.

1. Make sure you have at least ten minutes more than the time specified in the exercise. All of it should

be private, uninterrupted time. The extra minutes can be used to relax, to get into a sexual mood, and to prevent any rushing or pressure. Since the importance of having plenty of time and not being rushed cannot be overemphasized, do whatever you need to ensure that you will not be interrupted or distracted.

2. Set the scene the way you like it. The time you take to do the exercises is your gift to yourself; make it as enjoyable as possible. Make the room light or dark, as you prefer, and make any other arrangements you want, such as candles or incense. Some men prefer music, which is fine so long as it is not so powerful that it interferes with your focusing. Some men have found that the best gift they can give themselves is to put a lock on the bedroom door.

3. Make sure your conditions are met. This is much easier in masturbation than in partner sex since you don't have to concern yourself about a partner, but check your emotional and physical states to determine if things are the way they should be to maximize the chances of an enjoyable experience.

4. You should be fairly relaxed before starting an exercise. Use what you learned in the last chapter to help you get there. Some days it's difficult to get relaxed no matter what you do. At such times, it's probably best not to do sexual exercises. Wait until you are more comfortable. It will do you no good to do the assignments when you are tense.

5. It can be helpful to get into a sexual frame of mind before beginning an exercise. Erection is not important but feeling sexy is. You might want to recall a good sexual experience, construct a fantasy, or look at some arousing pictures or literature. Do whatever you want to help yourself become aroused.

6. In the masturbation exercises, do not immediately go for your penis. Spend a few minutes touching and stroking other parts of your body that are enjoyable to touch.

EXERCISE 10–1: MASTURBATION
WITH FOCUSING
Time Required: 15 minutes

The goals of this exercise are to practice focusing on the sensations in your penis as you play with it and to discover what types of stroking feel best. Neither erection nor orgasm is necessary.

After you are feeling aroused, start stroking your penis slowly and gently, putting your attention in your penis so that you are aware of the sensations produced by the touching. Unless you have problems lasting as long as you like, use a lubricant (see the note on lubricants at the end of this chapter). If you do not have good ejaculatory control, do not use lubrication at this time.

Regardless of how soft or hard your penis is, there are sensations in it of which you can be aware. Your penis is richly supplied with nerve endings that produce sensation whenever they are stimulated. The sensations may differ depending on how excited you are, how hard or soft your penis is, and what kinds of touching you are doing. It's up to you to discover what these sensations are.

Take your time. This is not a test of speed. There is nothing to accomplish and nothing to finish. Just play and enjoy. Keep focusing and experiment with different strokes (for example, stroking the length of the entire shaft and head, just the shaft, just the head, circular motions), different pressures and different speeds (but not too fast). See what you like and go with it.

Continue playing with your penis in this manner for 15 minutes. If you find yourself close to orgasm before time is up, stop masturbating and wait a minute or two until the urge to ejaculate subsides, then resume stroking. If this does not help, read Chapter 15 now and then return to this exercise. If you want to come after 15 minutes, do so, but keep going slowly and keep focusing. Remember, there's no need to climax; do so only if you want to.

This exercise should be done at least five times. Before going on to the masturbation exercises in Chapters 15 or 18, you should feel comfortable focusing on the physical sensations and able to return your attention to them when you find your mind has wandered.

POSSIBLE PROBLEMS

1. You don't feel any sensations in your penis, or you do but they don't seem very interesting. If you do not experience any sensations, it either means that you are not focusing properly or that there has been severe nerve damage. Since the latter is so rare and so devastating in its implications, we

suggest you reread the section on focusing and try again. If the sensations seem dull and uninspiring, that's probably because you were expecting something of a cosmic nature. See if you can just attend to what is there and worry less about whether it feels as oceanic as you thought it would.

2. Your mind keeps wandering. Of course it does. That's what minds do. This is not a problem. Just keep bringing your attention back to the sensation in your penis.

3. You have difficulty with the exercise because you are tense or in a hurry. It is very important that you only do the exercise when you have sufficient uninterrupted time. Don't be like the man who always started to do it 15 minutes before a friend came to pick him up to go to work. Of course he couldn't relax; he kept wondering when his friend was going to knock on the door. Make sure you are comfortably relaxed before starting.

Some men discover new and interesting sensations in their genitals the first few times they do this exercise. For most, however, it takes longer. Whether it happens quickly or not, we hope you'll continue with the exercise. There are sensations in your body when it is being touched, and they are a large part of the raw material from which a state of arousal is built. Focusing helps enhance their power and enables you to feel more pleasure from what is happening to your body.

You may find that this exercise helps you to discover some new places and new ways of touching that feel good. There is probably more feeling in your penis than you knew. We hope you will enjoy pleasuring yourself in these new ways and that you'll soon share your discoveries with your partner. We imagine she'd be happy to learn how to give you the most pleasure.

A Note on Lubrication

Most men find that using a lubricant on their hand when they masturbate reduces irritating friction and enhances their pleasure. Since lubrication amplifies the sensations in the penis, it also makes focusing easier.

It is difficult to recommend lubricants since preferences vary considerably from person to person. Some men prefer petroleum jelly (Vaseline) since it is not quickly absorbed by the skin and need not be replenished during one masturbation session. But others find it "greasy and gunky." It usually needs to be washed off with soap and water. Hand or body lotion (such as Intensive Care or Jergens Lotion) is favored by others. Since lotion is absorbed rather quickly, however, you may need to squirt it on several times in a session. Massage oil, KY jelly, and Albolene also have large numbers of supporters.

Perhaps the best thing to do is start with whatever lubricant is available in your home. If it doesn't please you, try something else. Lubricants, like so much else in sex, are largely a matter of individual taste. There is at least one with the consistency, absorbability, and odor that will satisfy you.

11

Virginity and
Sexual Abstinence

Because of the influence of the fantasy model of sex, discussions of virginity and celibacy are rare. It is widely assumed that all men have had sex and want to keep on getting as much as they can. Like almost everything else in the fantasy model, these assumptions are erroneous.

Virginity

It seems that there are many more male virgins than is generally believed, and that they cover a fairly broad age range. A survey of college students commissioned by *Playboy* found that 26 percent of the men had not had sex with a partner. Covering a much broader age range, a *Psychology Today* survey reported that 22 percent of the male respondents were virgins. Since it is difficult for a man over the age of eighteen to admit to being a virgin, it is likely that these figures are lower than they should be. We have talked to many men in their thirties and forties, and even to a few in their fifties, who have never had sex. It

177

appears, then, that male virginity is real and widespread.

We all start out as sexual virgins but this status isn't considered a problem until either we start feeling pressure from others to have sex or we want to have it but our attempts are unsuccessful.

There is tremendous pressure on men to be sexual. Virginity is seen as an unnecessary evil, to be eliminated as early as possible. There is little compassion or understanding for those who haven't had sex or who don't want it. Here is what *Playboy* had to say about the subject in an unsigned article reporting the results of the college survey we cited earlier: "It is actually possible to go through four years of higher education without getting laid, though why you'd want to is beyond us. Fortunately, the odds are against it." The pressure comes not only from sources like *Playboy*, where you would expect it, but from places closer to home as well. Here is what a nineteen-year-old college student told us:

I'm starting to doubt myself because I haven't had sex. The thing is that I like girls and I spend time with them. But I'm really involved with my studies and playing ball, and I don't want to take the time to have a big-time relationship. Just picking up some chick to have sex with doesn't do it for me. I'm fairly content doing my thing and not having sex. But everybody seems to think I'm strange, and now I'm starting to wonder. The girls I know don't seem to understand where I'm at, and several have asked if I like guys more than girls. Of course I like guys, but I don't want to screw them. Some of my male friends know I'm a virgin. They keep trying to help me get laid, coming up with suggestions all the time. They don't understand when I say that I'm OK where I am. And even my father is on this trip. He never says anything directly, but whenever we talk he throws in little jokes or quips about it being good for a guy to have fun and sow his oats. I think he'd be prouder than hell if I told him I fucked some girl.

Other young men we talked to have reported similar stories. These men are not interested in partner sex or don't feel ready for it, but the questions and concerns of their friends and relatives affect them and they begin to doubt their position. It's hard to feel good about yourself when society at large and those closest to you view your state as a vile affliction in need of immediate cure.

If you were surprised by our citing pressure from parents as a factor contributing to the uneasiness of virgins, we should say that we were also surprised. While we have no way of knowing how widespread such pressure is, it is clear in some cases that parents, especially fathers, try very hard to get their sons interested in sex. We have never been able to interview any of these fathers, but from what we have pieced together from the stories their sons told it seems that they view sexual activity as an index of the normality of their boys. Sex with a woman, they seem to think, is a sign that the boy is a real man, or that he isn't homosexual, or an assurance that he won't get overly involved in drugs or alcohol. Such fathers don't understand that sexual activity in itself isn't proof of anything and that pressuring a boy to have sex before he is ready can only result in increased strain in the family and perhaps some serious problems for the boy.

Our views on virginity stem from our beliefs that the importance of sex has been greatly exaggerated in recent times and that people should be allowed to blossom sexually in their own good time. We believe that pressure to have sex is almost always destructive. It pushes people into situations they may not be ready to deal with and, more importantly, deflects them from following their own intuition and good sense.

Having sex is certainly not necessary for a good life, and the idea that one should have had sex by a certain age is ridiculous. We know we are swimming against the societal current, but we want to lend whatever support we can to those boys and men who are reasonably content with their virgin status and want to remain there, either for a while or permanently.

If you fit in this category, you already know it's not easy and we would be doing you a disservice if we told you otherwise. Virginity in males over the age of nineteen is now the exception rather than the norm. Virginity in those over twenty-three or twenty-five is considered by many to be odd and ungentlemanly. Almost any position that is statistically unusual is difficult to maintain because people tend to dislike and ridicule what is different. Others may wonder about you and perhaps make fun of you, and some will do all they can to change your status because, for reasons unclear even to them, your virginity bothers them.

Despite this, we hope you can maintain your integrity and wait until you feel the time is right. If being in love or being married is what you want before having sex, we support your waiting until your conditions are fulfilled. If you think that partner sex just isn't for you, we hope you can feel good about that position. You may want to rely on masturbation for sexual pleasure, or you may not, but your attitude is not an unreasonable or unhealthy one, despite the attempts of *Playboy* and others to convince you of the opposite.

Virginity can also be a problem when it is unwanted by the man himself. Many virgins find themselves in this position. They want to have sex but nothing seems to work.

There are many reasons why a man who wants sex doesn't get it. Several of the longtime virgins we talked with had more of a social than a sexual problem. They were quite shy, fearful of asking a woman out and of making a physical advance. For some of these men, it seemed that if they could somehow get together with a woman and get past the first kiss, they might not have too much trouble. But there's little hope for sex when they can barely talk to a woman.

Many men, virgins and nonvirgins alike, have not developed good social skills. The problem has been largely unrecognized until recently, for it was widely assumed that almost all men knew how to meet women and initiate relationships. A few institutions, such as the Human Sexuality Program, University of California, San Francisco, now offer social skills groups and workshops. Some assertiveness training courses also deal with the development of social skills. Although we know of only two books on the subject, both are good: Eileen Gambrill and Cheryl Richey's *It's Up to You*, and Phillip Zimbardo's *Shyness*.

A large obstacle for many virgins is their fear of what sex might lead to. Although we have no way of knowing if the male virgins we saw in therapy are representative of all males who have trouble losing their virginity, we were very impressed by their fear of involvement with women. It's as if they believed that having sex would lead to entrapment by the woman. They would have to stay with her, marry her, and do her bidding until the end of time. They would lose all rights, autonomy, and personal space. Since they deeply believe that sex would lead to such dire consequences, it's no wonder they have so much trouble getting into it.

While many therapists would undoubtedly argue that the only solution for such fears would be prolonged psychotherapy, we believe differently. Twenty-one of the twenty-five virgins we worked with got involved in sex after only relatively brief courses of therapy, even though most of them had been trying unsuccessfully for over five years. It wasn't easy for any of them, but those who got what they wanted agreed it was worth the effort.

Another obstacle for many virgins is the heavy performance pressure they put on themselves. Some have tried to have sex a number of times, but the demands to perform have been so great that they caused erection failure every time. Trying again doesn't help because nothing is done to decrease the pressure. Such men should read the chapters on erection problems and scrupulously follow the suggestions in Chapter 12 for sex with a new partner.

Another issue facing those who want to lose their virginity is their feeling of almost hopeless backwardness. They believe their peers are experienced and that women expect a man to know what he's doing. Often these beliefs and expectations are realistic. A man without sexual experience with partners is by virtue of that fact a beginner and has some things to learn.

But there is also another side, one that may give you some cause for optimism. Most women are not as con-

cerned with experience and performance as men think
they are. Although it is true that women tend to
expect a man in his late twenties or older to be sexually experienced, many are not offended or put off
when they find out otherwise. The women we talked
to who initiated a man in the ways of sex quite enjoyed
the experience. As one of them said:

> To tell the truth, I was shocked when he told me he
> never had intercourse before. I didn't think a man
> could reach the age of thirty-three without having sex.
> But the shock quickly died down and I thought, why
> not? I had the time of my life. It was fantastic being
> the teacher and breaking him in. He was so apprecia-
> tive and I got everything I wanted.

Some men who have had difficulty losing their virginity decide that going to a prostitute would help.
While there are no statistics that bear on the success
of such attempts, they are not without danger. Prosti-
tutes with hearts of gold are far more common in literature than in reality and we have talked with several
men who, after they failed with a prostitute, felt worse
than ever about themselves and couldn't bring themselves to attempt sex again for months or years.

A good way of dealing with involuntary virginity is
brief treatment with a therapist experienced in working with men on sexual issues (of whom there are
very few). Another way is using this book. Much of
the material and many of the exercises are the same
as those we use in our therapy work with virgins.

If you have not yet had sex with a partner but
think you want to, you should ask yourself why you
want to change. What would sex add to your life? Then
ask yourself what obstacles are in the way of having
sex and what prices you would have to pay to overcome them. You can be certain that there are obstacles
and prices. You can probably count on being rejected,
embarrassed, afraid, and awkward. There may be
other costs that only you can determine. When you
have listed the prices, try to see or feel yourself paying
them. Imagine yourself being rejected, fumbling with
the woman because of your lack of experience, facing

the fears of involvement or not doing well at sex, or any other costs you came up with. Now that you have faced the worst, ask yourself if you're willing to pay the fare.

If you can answer yes, you are ready to go on, reading the sections and doing the exercises that seem appropriate. If you're not sure, you can proceed anyway and, as you get further into things, perhaps you'll be clearer about your answer. If it's not worth the price, maybe you can stop pushing yourself to have sex and start concentrating on what is important to you. As we said earlier, there is no dishonor in not being sexual.

So, if you want to leave your virginity behind you, there is hope. You may have to confront some of your worst fears, and you may want to get some professional help with this, but there's a good chance that you can get into sex in a way that will be right for you. Make sure that your conditions are met and that you follow the suggestions in Chapter 12 for sex with a new partner. We hope you enjoy the experience. Whatever does or doesn't happen, whether or not it goes the way you think it should, it can be fun. And if it doesn't go precisely the way you hoped, there will be many other opportunities.

Abstinence

We use abstinence and celibacy to mean a voluntary and temporary withdrawal from sexual activity with partners. Since it is generally thought that men always want sex, abstinence is not something one is likely to hear men talk about, at least not favorably. We include this brief discussion because we have talked to a number of men who were considering abstinence but were concerned over what it implied about them as men. We have also talked to a much smaller group of men who have practiced celibacy for varying periods of time with gratifying results.

There are any number of reasons why a man might

choose to refrain from sexual activity for relatively long periods of time. Preoccupation with extended projects is one. You might be so involved with an activity—writing a book or musical score, studying for an important exam, spiritual concerns, etc.—that is so demanding and satisfying that there is little time for, and interest in, sex.

Another reason is that, while there may not be an obvious preoccupation with other matters, there is simply little sexual interest or energy. Many men try to ignore their lack of interest or, worse, get concerned about it and try to prove it groundless by engaging in lots of sex. We men simply haven't had much permission to be uninterested and uninvolved in sex. But such times occur for many of us, sometimes lasting for months or longer. While the reasons for the disinterest may not be clear, there is certainly nothing abnormal about it. Probably the best thing to do is honor your feelings and get on with the rest of your life.

Deep depression is one of the more obvious factors that can lead to a loss of sexual interest. The loss of a loved one or a serious setback in one's education or job can result in sexual apathy for some time. Some men get concerned about this and try to have sex anyway, often with negative results. It's best to wait until time heals the wounds and the interest reappears.

Even in the presence of sexual desire, there are times when abstinence can be beneficial. This is true when sex would get in the way of important processes and decisions. A not uncommon example of this occurs when a man decides it's time to rethink his romantic involvements. He has not been satisfied with them, perhaps feeling as one man did that "It's like I've had the same lousy relationship with eight different women." He doesn't want to spend the rest of his life in similar involvements. He needs time away from relationships to sort out his feelings, to determine why he continues in the same negative paths and how he can get more of what he wants.

Sexual involvement may not only impede his learning but it may also lure him back into what he is trying to escape. It might be best for him to avoid sexual activity until he is clearer about what he is looking for and how he can get it.

Abstinence can be useful in many situations, where a man wants to get to know himself better and come to some new understanding about where he is going. It can be a time of learning and growing, and it need not be as horrendously difficult as many men might think.

One of us went through a period of eight months of celibacy a few years ago and found the experience relatively painless and also quite gratifying.

It was generally a good time for me. I spent lots of time by myself, part of which was devoted to thinking about past relationships. I also spent time with friends, enjoying their company and sharing many of my feelings with them.

The people who knew I wasn't having sex acted a bit strangely, continuously asking how I could do it. It was as if they thought I were performing some miraculous feat. Men were much more surprised than women. Actually, it wasn't very difficult. At times I was lonely, but it wasn't as difficult as I had anticipated. Sometimes I was aware of missing something, but it usually wasn't sex. What I missed most was sleeping next to someone and the cuddling and playing around in bed. I got lots of hugs from my friends, but nothing could replace the warm sense of snuggling with a lover in bed. And that was really the worst of it.

Often I felt intense relief when alone. I didn't have to concern myself with anyone else's needs or feelings. Many times it felt very good to know that I didn't have to share my bed with someone. It was my bed and I could take it all up and do anything I wanted to there.

To say I learned a lot is a cliché but nonetheless true. I learned about myself and relationships and, surprisingly, about myself and sex. I realized for the first time how often I had not gotten what I wanted in sex because I had been so busy trying to be nice and considerate. And I saw how the resentment I had accumulated during such occasions spilled over into other parts of my relationships. Another important thing I learned was that my need for solitude was much greater than I had ever imagined. I enjoyed my own company and needed some quiet time each day to be with me. This turned out to be quite useful in later relationships: I could get more of my alone time when I wanted it, thus making it easier for me to really be with my partner when I was with her.

Some of the men who've practiced abstinence have reported similar stories, but for others the experience was somewhat different. None of the ones we've talked to regretted their experience; in fact, all thought it quite worthwhile.

We are not trying to sell celibacy any more than we are trying to sell sex. But we do offer our support to those who think that a period of abstinence would be useful. It can be an important experience. Certain problems are encountered by those who undertake such a project, and we want to mention them. A consuming sexual hunger, surprisingly, is not usually one of them, especially since abstinence need not rule out masturbation.

One problem is that of loneliness. Since abstinence rules out what is usually called a romantic or primary relationship, you are not going to get many of the things that occur in such relationships. You may have to manage with much less physical affection, companionship, and the special kinds of communication and closeness that you are accustomed to. Your closest friends may be able to make up for some of it, but not all. You will be deprived of some of your pleasures and you will feel lonely at times.

Another problem is the meaning that you and those close to you put on your behavior. You may find yourself wondering if there is something wrong with you, especially when you realize that staying away from sex isn't terribly difficult. And, as the example given above indicates, your friends may wonder along with you. Sex has been so oversold that many people can't even conceive of not having it regularly. So you'll probably have to put up with some questions and astonishment.

A last issue concerns what happens when you decide to become sexually involved again. Some men, but not all, reported that getting back into sex after a long period of abstinence was a bit awkward. This is hardly an insurmountable obstacle but there can be feelings of strangeness and embarrassment. Following our suggestions in the next chapter for sex with a new partner can alleviate whatever slight difficulties there are in this area.

If you're willing to handle these issues and if a period of celibacy seems like it might be right for you, why not? And don't worry. No matter how long you stay in that state, you won't forget how to "do it."

12

Dealing with a Partner

Relationships come in an almost infinite variety and there are countless ways of expressing and dealing with relationship issues. Our focus here is relatively narrow. We restrict ourselves to those issues and problems that play a significant role in the development and maintenance of a satisfactory sexual relationship.

Although the chapter is divided into sections, we see it as a unit and believe you will profit from reading all of it, even those sections in which you have only minimal interest.

The ideas and suggestions presented here are effective but they have limitations. They work best in a caring and supportive atmosphere, or at least one that is not overflowing with hostility. If the relationship is in serious trouble—if bitterness and anger are the norm or if the partners can barely be civil to one another—the relationship, not sex, is what needs attention. While good sex is sometimes possible in bad relationships, the combination is much rarer than most of us believe. This chapter is no substitute for the competent professional help that is usually required to resolve the problems in seriously disturbed relationships.

Talking about Sex

Talking to a partner about sex is one of the most difficult things to do. Even though there have been many changes in sexual attitudes and behavior in the last few decades, it probably isn't much easier to talk about sex now than it was twenty years ago. We have heard from people with broad sexual experience, some of whom considered themselves swingers and had had sex in every conceivable way with almost everyone in town, but it was evident that they had problems discussing their sexual thoughts, feelings, and behavior with their partners. We have also talked to many young men and women who were brought up during the sexual revolution. While most of them started their sexual careers at a much earlier age than their parents and are much freer in their thoughts and activities, they aren't much more comfortable discussing sex with their partners. Doing it is obviously much easier than talking about it.

A few years ago we heard the following on a radio program devoted to the new sexuality. The speaker recounted an interview he had done with a young man about a recent sexual experience.

INTERVIEWER: Did you know the woman well?
MAN: No, I met her that night.
I: How was the experience?
M: Fine.
I: Did you have an orgasm?
M: Yeh.
I: Did she have one?
M: Gee, I'm not sure. . . . I guess so.
I: But you're not sure. Is there a way you could have found out?
M: Hmmm. . . . I don't know.
I: You could have asked her, couldn't you?
M: Asked her? I hardly knew her name!

There is no doubt that the inability to talk about sex is one of the main reasons why sex is not as good as it could be. In earlier chapters, we asked you to talk about sex or at least consider doing so, and much of the rest of the book is also about talking about sex. Since we consider sexual communication so important, we want to say some general things about the subject here and also to deal with some of the objections that men have raised about it.

In saying that talking is important, we do not mean that sex should be primarily a cerebral affair, with long analytical discussions before and after every experience. There are many times when talking is unnecessary or distracting. Talking about sex is a useful option you should cultivate if you want to enhance your sexuality, an option to be used when appropriate.

When is talking appropriate? It's difficult to give general rules but we offer some examples. If you're with a new partner, it's relevant to do something about contraception. How can this be done without words? Another example is when your partner initiates sex and you aren't in the mood. How can you let her know your feelings? Suppose you like a particular type of stimulation or activity and your nonverbal attempts to indicate this to your partner have failed. How can you let her know what you like? Perhaps your partner did or said something that annoyed or angered you. How can you deal with this situation without talking?

Given, then, that there may be some good reasons for talking about sex, let's look at some of the common objections men raise.

One is simply that they would rather communicate nonverbally. In response to this, we say that nonverbal communication is one level of communication and an important one. Not everything has to be spoken; many times it is relevant and effective to indicate your desires or feelings without using words. As a supplement to verbal communication, acts and gestures are fine. As a substitute, they don't quite make it. The man who has sex with his partner every day is shocked when she complains that he never tells her he loves her. Isn't his lovemaking a way of saying that he loves her? It may be, but only on one level, and she also wants to hear it at the verbal level.

Nonverbal communication is important. Use it where it works. And recognize its limitations.

A second objection to talking about sex is that it interferes with spontaneity. A view of spontaneity as something that precludes the use of words strikes us as unnecessarily restrictive and quite unreasonable. Words can be as spontaneous as actions and, besides, where is it written that sex should be spontaneous?

The issue of spontaneity and exclusive preferences for nonverbal communication are in most cases merely screens for the fact that people have great difficulty talking about sex. Rather than admitting the difficulty, they find reasons why talking is unnecessary or a hindrance. This would be fine if they could have the kind of sex they want without using words. The problem is that they usually can't.

We begin with the premise that talking about sex is quite difficult. Rather than trying to sidestep the issue, we prefer to bring it out in the open and then find ways of dealing with it.

One of the reasons why sex talk is so difficult is that there are very few good models. Neither the kinds of sources we examined in Chapters 3 and 4 nor more academic treatments of sex demonstrate much in the way of how human beings can discuss sex. This glaring omission reinforces a myth we all learned—even if you have sex, it's not nice to talk about it. Given this lack of permission to talk and the lack of models for how to do it, it's not surprising that most of us are not very good at it.

Another reason for difficulty in talking is that it can produce a powerful kind of intimacy. Verbally expressing your joy, anxiety, preferences, dislikes, and other feelings is a way of sharing yourself. This holds great promise but also great threat, since we are all at least somewhat ambivalent about the prospect of closeness. How much easier to let two more or less disconnected bodies go through the mechanics of what we call making love.

Man is the only animal that communicates with words. This does not mean that all talk is noble, meaningful, or even interesting. But in certain situations, like sex, talking can open the doors to real sharing between people.

Talk is also threatening in other ways. If you clearly say what you like and want, you are displaying yourself in a very personal way and exposing your vulnerability, since your partner may reject your requests or disagree with your opinions. It's then difficult to say that you didn't really mean what you said; such tactics work much better with nonverbal communications, most of which are subject to many interpretations and therefore are easier to explain away if you run into resistance.

Being clear verbally also seems selfish to many people. It's considered fine to be suggestive, for example, loudly complaining about how much your back hurts in the hope that your partner will offer to give you a massage, or rolling around in a way that your penis innocently ends up close to your partner's mouth. But to come right out and ask her to rub your back or suck your penis, well, that's something else. We can only repeat what we said about selfishness in Chapter 6: it's not such a bad habit. As long as you are willing to give as well as take, you have every right to ask for precisely what you want. It may be difficult at first, but it grows on you.

The last threatening aspect of communication to be discussed involves the fear of criticizing others. People worry about making their partners feel bad. After all, how would she take it if you told her you wish she'd brush her teeth before sex, or that she holds your penis too tightly, or that you'd like her to take a more active part in the lovemaking? Not only might she feel bad, thus perhaps forcing you to deal with your guilt about that, but she might turn around and criticize you.

Many people don't want to rock the boat by saying anything that is or might be construed as negative or critical. Mutual protection societies get formed in relationships, where each partner protects the other, and therefore himself, from disquieting communications. Which may sound very nice, what with all that protection, but which usually means that neither is getting what he or she wants aside from the protection.

This is a nice little game, but the rewards are meager. It's impossible for negative feelings not to exist in relationships. Your partner is going to say and do many things that adversely affect you, and you are going to do the same to her. The two of you can decide not to deal with the negative feelings generated by such occurrences, as discussed above, or you can decide that you are both free to express negative feelings in an attempt to clear the air and get more of what both of you want. Needless to say, we prefer the second alternative because it does result in greater contentment in the long run and also prevents the piling up of resentment. Keeping resentment to a minimal level is important; hostile relationships are often nothing more than the effects of resentment piled so high that it eventually got completely out of control. Putting the pieces back together after that happens is difficult.

There is no doubt that complaining or expressing negative emotions is difficult. But we believe it is something that needs to happen fairly frequently if you want your relationships to stay alive and healthy. The crucial point in expressing complaints is not to blame your partner; just let her know how what she says or does affects you, as in this example:

> "Martha, it really bothers me that you keep talking about your ex-husband so much. I feel like I'm always being compared to him, especially sexually. It's hard for me to get fully involved in sex with you, because I'm wondering if George had some better way of doing it or if he gave you more pleasure than I do. I'd feel much better if you stopped making these comparisons."

It is true, of course, that if you make such statements, your partner will probably feel free to do the same. Which means that you'll have to hear some things you'd rather not. That can be excruciatingly painful at times, but the anticipation is often worse than the reality. It can be lived with and, more importantly, can enrich both your relationship and your sexual patterns.

We want to emphasize that there are many levels of communication and that no one is suggesting that Shakespearian odes are necessary. Understanding this point is important because the concept of communication sounds very serious and frightening to so many people. It can be quite simple and go no further than your level of comfort.

Acts and gestures are one level of communication, and words form another level. But the verbal level itself consists of a number of different levels. These differ in many ways, but the ones we want to discuss have to do with the length, complexity, and difficulty of the messages sent. Our preference is always for the shortest, simplest, and most comfortable messages. Many therapists and educators take the opposite approach, asking their clients or students to talk in ways that are too demanding or threatening. The following example indicates some of the differences between the two approaches.

An intern presented a case that involved a sixty-five-year-old man with erection problems. Because it was obvious that the man made many probably incorrect assumptions about what his wife felt and wanted, he was asked to go home and check out all of his assumptions with his wife. That's a tall order for anyone, but it was worse in this case because the man had never talked to anyone about sex. Although he and his wife had a generally warm and supportive relationship, sex had never been discussed. It seemed highly unlikely to us that the man would even try to carry out the assignment. We predicted also that he would not carry out any further assignments and would become resistant to any suggestions from the therapist, because she had asked for far too much. Unfortunately, we were proved right.

The intern wanted to know whether we thought communication was necessary. We did, but it had to be built around the fact that this man had never talked about sex. It had to be short, simple, and something he felt he could say. Without going into great detail about the case here, we only want to say that two simple messages were worked out that met these criteria. One of them was, when she had stimulated him to erection and was starting to get ready for intercourse (which she thought he wanted): "This feels good. Don't stop." The other, to be given after he ejaculated, was: "What can I do for you?" These brief statements were all that were needed to accomplish what the therapist had tried to obtain through a much more difficult, and in this case impossible, route.

Most of the examples in the book are at a low level of complexity. Short and simple are what work best most of the time. Long speeches are usually not necessary.

You should also choose messages that are most comfortable for you or, if there's no way you can be comfortable saying what you want to say, messages that are the least uncomfortable. You may find that the talk-and-listen format presented below is a useful way of making you more relaxed.

There are of course times when long and somewhat complex messages are required. The problem is that they are often not heard or understood. You might want to check out what you do when someone talks to you at length about a complex issue. If you're like most people, you try to listen but get easily distracted, mainly because you begin formulating your response. So you're busy writing your speech while she's talking, and guess what she's doing when you're talking?

The following exercise is useful for minimizing this type of distraction. It can be used any time you have something important to say, especially if it can't be said in a sentence or two. It's very valuable for saying things that have been or might be misunderstood.

EXERCISE 12-1: TALK AND LISTEN
Time Required: 5 to 10 minutes; 15 minutes maximum

When you have something important to communicate to your lover, tell her so and ask for the amount of time you think you need to get your message across. The time need not be right now; you can set an appointment for doing it later. It is important that you agree on a time when you are both reasonably relaxed and free from any interruptions.

For your talk-and-listen session, sit facing your partner and tell her what you want to say in as simple and direct a way as possible. You might want to go over your thoughts beforehand to make sure they are clear and concise. Stick to one main point and be as specific as possible.

Your partner should understand before you begin that her job is only to listen and understand. She is not to interrupt you unless she needs clarification. She is not to defend herself, answer you, or comfort you.

Let her know when you are finished. She is then to tell you in a sentence or two what she understood your main point to be (e.g., "I hear that you're very angry with me because I didn't want to have sex the last four times you initiated; you think that means I don't care about you"). If you think she has correctly understood you, tell her so. If not, correct her and have her give you her new understanding. Continue in this way until you are satisfied that she understands. Try not to be picky, however. Understanding means only that she can correctly summarize your main point, not that she can repeat verbatim all that you said.

If she wants to reply to what you said, use the same format and try to understand what she has to say. It's usually best to take at least a few minutes between your statement and hers.

Some of the people to whom we've suggested this exercise have reported that it also worked quite well in nonsexual areas, with friends, colleagues, and children. It's truly amazing how often we aren't understood and how often we don't understand others. The feeling of being understood is a powerful one and in itself can bring people closer together.

You need to realize, however, that understanding is not the same as compliance or agreement. Your partner will probably understand you better if you use the talk-and-listen format, but that doesn't necessarily mean that she will agree with you or comply with any requests you make. She may not, for example, apologize for rejecting your last four advances, or feel any different about the next four, but at least she will understand what meaning you are attributing to her actions. If she chooses to tell you what's going on with her, you may better understand what the rejections really mean. And that, though perhaps not exactly what you wished for, may still be something.

Though communication is an important art to cultivate and can make your sex life more enjoyable, it is not a panacea and it has limitations. One of them has already been mentioned—communicating won't always get you what you want. You need to guard against the unrealistic expectation that just because your partner understands your desires, she will agree with them or fulfill them.

Communication is also limited because it may conflict with the equally important right of privacy. Despite what some of the therapy gurus have been preaching, there is no such thing as complete openness or honesty, nor should there be. You have the right to keep private many of your thoughts and feelings, and so does your partner. These rights should never be surrendered. Further, there are times when it is best to keep one's mouth shut. We have seen permanent damage done to relationships when, for example, a man told his partner about an affair he had or when a woman told her partner that the conception of their child was not the "accident" he thought it was. There is no guarantee that talking is going to produce joy and goodwill. There is simply no substitute for common sense and good judgment in this or any other area. You need to consider the possible consequences of what you say. In most cases, the consideration can be brief because the consequences are not serious. Other issues are potentially more volatile, however, and you should take into account the value of discussing them.

Another limit of communication has to do with its results. If understanding and/or change are not forthcoming the first few times a subject is discussed, further repetition will probably be futile. If your messages are clear and there is no change, then something is getting in the way. The possibilities are many, including that some other issue, like control, is really at stake, or your partner cannot hear the message the way you are sending it, or, even if she can hear and understand, she cannot do what you want. You may want to shift the discussion to these other issues.

Endless repetition is not only purposeless, but it is also destructive since it makes communication sterile and undermines the value of any discussion. Patience is one thing; useless perseverance is something else. It is disappointing, frustrating, and puts a strain on the relationship.

Contraception

Contraception is a subject boys and men used to think about but in recent years have learned is none of their business. It wasn't many years ago that the condom or rubber was the primary means of preventing conception. While it would be ridiculous to say that all men took birth control seriously, it was true that they were at least aware that it had something to do with them. Males carried condoms in their wallets or the glove compartments of their cars, practiced putting them on, and traded jokes with friends about their uses and problems (wearing one in sex was like taking a shower in a raincoat, it was said). Boys were often admonished by their fathers, coaches, and friends that while sex was fine, they should take care not to get a girl "in trouble."

Times have obviously changed. Since the advent of the birth-control pill and the IUD, the idea has developed that contraception is almost exclusively a female affair. Family-planning agencies have focused their energy almost entirely on women, sometimes treating the rare male who entered their portals as an unwanted intruder. Unfortunately, some women themselves have also contributed to the illusion that birth control has nothing to do with men. Carrying a good idea to ridiculous extremes, they claim that women must be totally responsible for their bodies and have reacted with shock or hostility to the suggestion that a man could be interested or involved in contraceptive decisions and practice. Another factor is the media, which have managed to convey the impression that all women are either taking pills or are equipped with an IUD.

Not surprisingly, men have gotten the message and many indicate no interest in, or concern about, contraception. Why should they, given their impression that women have taken care of the subject? This lack of interest is then taken by some women and by many workers in the family-planning field as proof that men

are only interested in sex and care not at all about
women and the consequences of sex—an interesting
example of a self-fulfilling prophecy in action.

The consequences of excluding men from birth-control planning and participation have been serious. There
have been needless arguments and bitterness over who
should have taken precautions, numerous broken relationships, and countless unnecessary abortions. Despite
the pill and IUD, the rate of unwanted pregnancies
has not been reduced; in fact, it has substantially increased in the teenage population.

The involvement of men in contraception will not
solve all these problems. But it can make a difference.
Perhaps most importantly from your point of view, it
can make your sex life a bit more enjoyable.

The fear of pregnancy is one of the factors that make
sexual partners uneasy. Even the suspicion that contraception isn't being used, or used effectively, is enough
to make them less comfortable than they would otherwise be. While it is true that the woman will bear the
brunt of responsibility for a pregnancy or abortion, the
man usually finds that, like it or not, he is also involved. Abortions are hassles and unwanted children
are disasters.

Birth control is a much more complex subject than
most people realize. There are many reasons why people do or do not effectively use contraceptive methods.
It is difficult for many women who, though they know
they will bear the main responsibility for any unwanted
consequences of sex, have also been taught that having
children is necessary to their feminine identity. Women
experience many such conflicts over the use of contraception, and hence many are not effective contraceptive
users.

We believe that women should not have to take sole
responsibility for preventing conception, any more than
men should have to take sole responsibility for sexual
satisfaction. Sex involves man and woman, and so does
contraception. Sharing the responsibility for birth control can lead to increased comfort about sex, since
both partners know they are doing the best they can
to preclude consequences neither wants. It is also a

special kind of intimacy which can bring the lovers closer together.

Joint participation in contraception also means more effective contraception. Several studies have clearly indicated that the man's attitude toward contraception is an important factor in how effectively it is used. Should your partner have conflicts about contraception, it will help her and the relationship if she knows she can count on your understanding and support. Should she be using a method inconsistently, you can use one over which you have control and also initiate discussions aimed at finding one both of you are comfortable with.

We hope you won't make the mistake often made by family-planning personnel of equating male participation in birth control with the wearing of a condom. Being involved has nothing to do with who ingests, puts in, or puts on a contraceptive. Being involved means only that you share and participate, and there are many ways of doing this.

One good way is simply to ask before the first time you have sex with a partner if she has a contraceptive. If not, you can use a condom if that feels right, or you can suggest engaging in activities other than intercourse until a decision about contraception is made. Another way, if your partner is using the pill or diaphragm, is to offer to pay all or part of the cost. If she needs to see a doctor to get a contraceptive, you can offer to accompany her. Both of you can discuss the various methods and choose the one that seems best. You can listen to any conflicts she has about birth control and do whatever is possible to help her deal with them.

The following story shows how one man participates in contraceptive issues.

One of my first sexual experiences resulted in pregnancy and I resolved that I would do all in my power to prevent that from ever happening again. I've never liked rubbers. I don't care what anyone says—they do dull sensation. So I've always relied on my partner's using something, but I've always been involved. Before having sex with a new partner, I ask if she has anything. Usually they do. But several times they didn't and, surprisingly, I was the one who refused to have intercourse. I just told them that intercourse without birth control is not something I'm willing to do, and I suggested other sexual activities. It always worked out fine.

I like participating in contraception. I talk to my partners about the method they use and, if there's a relationship of any duration, I always pay some of the cost. Most of the women I've been with in the last few years used a diaphragm, and I've bought the cream. Several have showed me how to put it in but, even though I've tried a number of times, I'm not very good at it. But we laugh at my bumbling attempts and that becomes part of our being together. I don't find that inserting the diaphragm interferes with our sex. It's just part of what we're doing and I prefer to have it put in when I'm there. I don't like it when the woman goes off to the bathroom to put it in. It makes me feel excluded. I like to hold her, touch her, or talk to her when she's doing it. It feels nice and close.

A few women have been surprised by my interest in contraception. They later told me that their first reaction was some suspicion at why I was minding their business. But this initial reaction has always given way to appreciation. Because of my interest and participation, my lovers have shared some things with me that they haven't with other men—their feelings and conflicts about conception and contraception, as well as their thoughts and feelings about sex. I think I've also been open about my feelings. My interest in birth control has served me well. I never worry about pregnancy, I feel comfortable with my partners, and I really enjoy them.

While this is not the place for a lengthy discussion of various contraceptive methods, a few words are in order. The pill and IUD have received the most publicity because they are the favorites of most family-planning personnel and appeal to those who like to be up on the latest technological advances. Both, however, have dangerous side effects which need to be considered. And here as elsewhere, there is a great deal to be said for the simple methods. Both the diaphragm and the condom, when used properly with spermicidal jelly or foam, are very nearly as effective, and neither has worrisome side effects.

If you are certain that you never want to have children, or more children, you might want to consider a vasectomy. It is a relatively inexpensive and safe surgical procedure which in no way decreases sexual interest or has any other negative side effects. The only problem with vasectomies is that they must be considered permanent; usually they cannot be reversed. Talk to your doctor if you have any questions about this procedure.

Successful contraception is simply the effective use of whatever method you and your partner choose. Pick a method that makes the most sense and feels most comfortable to use. Then there will be less temptation to take chances with it and, should one partner weaken, the other can be there to give support and implement its use.

Sexual Choices and Saying No to Sex

Every sexual feeling and invitation opens the door to a number of alternative actions, some of which will be more satisfying to you and your partner than others. Many men are not aware of all the possibilities and hence end up either not getting their needs met as well as possible or having trouble with their partners. This section is intended to make you more aware of your choices and help you exercise them.

One choice that men have difficulty making is that of refusing to engage in sex at a particular time. This is felt by many to be unmanly since a man should be interested and able all the time, especially if he gets a direct sexual invitation from a woman. Aside from being silly (no one is always interested in anything), this piece of mythology is harmful. For many men, being able to say no to sex is a prerequisite for being able to say yes to it. Sex is best when they are confident of their ability to refuse to engage in it. When they have sex, it's because they want to, not because they have to.

The man who can't say no to sex is always at the mercy of his partner's wishes, or what he thinks to be her wishes. This is a very uncomfortable situation for him, one that leads to deception and argument. If he can't refuse her directly, he may pretend to be angry or tired or busy so that she won't approach him. Or he may start a fight, correctly believing that this will dampen her interest. Even without these strategies, the situation is not good because he feels compelled to have sex when he is uninterested or his conditions are not met.

Let's look further at this situation. Suppose your partner indicates a desire for sex and you find that you have no sexual interest at all (remembering that interest refers to how you feel rather than what your penis is doing). You don't have to try to get in the mood or resort to deception. You can simply tell her that you are not interested. The telling should be done with words rather than gestures. Otherwise, she is liable to misunderstand what you are communicating.

What are the best words to use? The best approach to the subject is probably to ask yourself how you would like her to reject your sexual invitations. Word for word, what would you want her to say? Try using the same wording in your rejections. Rejections are almost as hard to give as to get. The first time you give them directly, you will probably be awkward, but you'll feel better about them as you get more practice.

Before you tell your partner that you're uninterested in sex, however, you should consider if you want any contact at all with her. Do you want to be alone, not having anything to do with her? If so, it's probably best to say that clearly ("I'm sorry, honey, but I just want to be alone now"). She may be disappointed and hurt, but at least there won't be any misunderstanding and she will know what you want.

You may find, however, that although your sexual interest is lacking, you do want some contact with

her. You may want to cuddle, talk, take a walk, or do
something else with her. Even though her desire
may have been for sex, she may be willing to settle for
something else. Unfortunately, these other alternatives
often do not get mentioned or acted on because a hassle develops over the sexual invitation and rejection.
Such hassles can be precluded in most cases if you
are clear about how you feel and what you are interested in. The following example is but one of many
possible responses when your partner asks for sex and
you are not interested.

> I really don't feel like sex tonight. I've been feeling
> down since I found out that I didn't get the promotion
> at work. I don't want to lead you on but if you're will-
> ing, I'd like to lie here with you and talk.

If lying together and talking should lead to some
sexual interest on your part, you are free to make
another decision. If not, you and your partner may
still enjoy each other. What you're doing may not
be totally satisfying to her if she was really set on
sex, but at least it's something, a way of being together. And it avoids the horrible arguments that can
occur when she feels that you have no interest in her
at all.

We do not mean to overplay the being together part.
Contact is important in relationships, and so is being
alone. You have a right to be alone when you want
to. Be as clear as you can about what you want at any
given time regarding contact and sex, and let her know.
We can't emphasize it sufficiently: feeling comfortable
rejecting sex and togetherness is crucial to a good relationship and good sex.

While it looks ridiculous on paper, many men act as
if they believe it is wrong ever to frustrate or disappoint their partners, and this obviously hampers their
ability to say no. There's not much to be said about
this idea other than that it's impossible to attain. Every
relationship involves rejections, frustrations, and disappointments. All you can do is accept their inevitability. Make them as honest and clear as possible.

You can only give what you can give. And that is usually sufficient.

Another area of difficulty arises when you aren't sure what you want. You're not exactly turned-on but not exactly turned-off, either. Suppose, given these feelings, your partner initiates physical contact. Many men hesitate to respond to their partners' touch for fear of leading them on. This issue has been discussed in the chapter on touching. All that needs to be said here is that there is no reason to hesitate (and that's true of your initiating physical contact as well). If you are concerned about misleading her, you might want to say something like: "I'm not sure what I'm in the mood for. Let's see what happens." Start doing what you want and see how you feel. You may be content with the touching and, if your partner is also content, there's no problem. If you both get turned-on and want to continue to sex, there's also no problem.

Many men have trouble with the situation where their partners want to go on to sex and they don't. This is similar to the situation previously discussed, where your partner initiates sex and you aren't in the mood. Let's assume you and your partner have been cuddling and she indicates she'd like sex. Take a minute to consider exactly what you'd like. If you're absolutely not in the mood for any kind of sexual activity, tell her. But perhaps you're interested in something sexual, but not what you think she wants. If your sexual encounters almost always include intercourse, you can still have sex this time without intercourse. If you're not interested in intercourse, but would be willing to do something else, let her know. Don't assume that sex has to include any particular activities or follow any particular pattern. You have choices. Another way of telling your partner what you want is to say, "I'm not interested in anything for myself but I'd like to do something for you." These kinds of statements let your partner know clearly what she can expect from you and prevent the building up of inappropriate expectations. She will usually appreciate your clarity and your willingness to do what you can.

Several myths stand in the way of applying these alternatives—those that state that a man should always want sex, that sex should always include intercourse, and that sex must always be reciprocal, with both partners simultaneously being involved to the same extent. We have discussed the first two in other places, but the third requires more attention.

The sexual model we learn emphasizes simultaneity. Intercourse is the paragon of the model, since with it both partners are doing the same thing together. If both experience orgasm, everything is perfect. (Fortunately, however, the emphasis on simultaneous orgasm has decreased in recent years.) In other sexual activities, too, many believe that both participants must be busy at the same time. Thus, in oral sex, the 69 position is very popular.

There is nothing wrong with simultaneous sex as long as you realize that it is an option, one that has both advantages and disadvantages. Nonsimultaneous sex is another possibility, one that is appropriate to situations where one partner is more interested in sex than the other. We explore this subject further in the section on working out disagreements. Here we want to add that an advantage of nonsimultaneous sex is that it can result in much stronger physical sensations. Since you are not busy both giving and receiving, you can give directions to her on how best to please you and can devote all your attention to focusing on the pleasurable sensations. We have suggested to many couples that they try oral sex with one partner taking the active and the other the passive role, rather than using their customary 69 format. More than 75 percent of them reported that the nonsimultaneous way was more enjoyable.

There is one more situation we want to discuss here, and that concerns when you want something sexual for yourself but don't want to give anything at the same time. This is just the opposite of the example we explored earlier, when you are willing to do something for your partner but don't care for anything for yourself. Suppose you'd like a quickie, or would like your partner to use her mouth all over you, or don't have any preferences other than wanting to be on the receiv-

ing end of a sexual experience. This is difficult for
many men to handle because it sounds so selfish. We
are wary because we have heard so much from women
and the women's movement about how selfish men are.
But when you think about it, why shouldn't you be able
to get what you're willing to give to your partner at
other times? There's nothing selfish about that at all. A
simple request is all that's needed—"I'd like to just lie
here while you make love to me," or "I know we've
got to leave in ten minutes, but you're turning me on
and I want you before we go."

There are many possible responses to any sexual
situation. Consult your feelings about what you want,
then work it out with your partner. Most times there
will be an option to please both of you.

The First Sexual
Experiences with a Partner

The first time a couple has sex together is a poignant
moment. Two people come together to share an experience and themselves, often in conflict or confusion
within themselves, and with differing goals and expectations. Each hopes for at least a tolerable experience
and fears a humiliating one, each yearns for acceptance (though this yearning may be ambivalent) and
fears something less. Both are concerned that they will
not pass the test; that their bodies, behaviors, or personalities will be compared to some superior standard
and be found wanting.

Men have what they consider to be special concerns
about first experiences. Since they believe they are totally or primarily responsible for the management and
outcome of the sexual encounter, they wonder if they
can get the woman ready, get and maintain their
erections, and provide the kind of ecstasy they assume
their partners desire. In short, they hope their performances will be, if not fantastic, at least passable.

What men often don't recognize is that their partners

go through very similar types of questioning and ago-
nizing. The woman wonders if the man will find her
body attractive, if she'll be able to please him, and if
the man will find sufficient interest and pleasure to want
to return.

It's only logical that people should be uneasy when
they have sex with someone new. Even in these days of
instant sex and instant intimacy, sex still means something special to most people. It's not something you do
with just anyone. In sex you allow a unique access to
yourself—to your nudity, to the feel and smell of your
body and its fluids. And it can go even further. You
may allow access to your emotions, at least to your
interest and excitement. In doing so, you run the risk
that this may be the start of real contact with the other
person, a kind of intimacy, with all the possibilities and
dangers that intimacy implies.

Because of the tension that so often accompanies
first-time experiences, they are often unsatisfactory.
Many men do not get or maintain erections in such
situations or ejaculate more quickly than they like, and
then feel bad about these "failures." Other men function adequately but don't get enjoyment from the sex.
Many women do not have orgasms the first time they
have sex with a partner, a fact for which many men
blame themselves.

It doesn't have to be this way. First-time situations
are unique and there is no way of dissipating all the
strangeness and tension involved. But the experiences
can be more comfortable and enjoyable, with fewer
"failures" and bad feelings.

Saying how to make them better is simple—wait
until you are comfortable with her and all your conditions are met—but difficult for many men to practice
because this approach flies in the face of the prevailing
notion of instant sex. What will the woman think if
the man doesn't make sexual advances almost as soon
as he has met her? Men think that the woman will feel
disappointed, angry, undesirable, or will conclude that
the man isn't interested in women or sex. In fact, most
women are quite willing to delay sex until they have
spent a significant amount of time with their new part-

ners and have gotten to know them. Many women actually experience some turmoil over what to do about sex with new partners. They are torn between their own desires and what they think the man wants, as illustrated by this quote from a woman with whom we talked:

> I wish all men were taught the kinds of things you're saying about not getting into sex right away. Often when I'm with someone I'm just getting to know, I'm in a quandary as to what to do. I want to get to know him better. I'd like some physical contact but I'm not really comfortable having sex at the beginning. But I'm supposed to be liberated and I worry that if I don't agree to sex he might feel rejected or get angry. I don't want to hurt him or lose him, but at the same time I wish we didn't have to fuck until we knew each other better and I really wanted to have sex with him.

Many men and women feel this way and go through a lot of difficulty trying to figure out what to do, often making decisions that do not reflect their feelings. How much better it would be if they could just tell their partners how they feel. With only a few word changes, the above quotation could be said to a new partner, probably with little chance of misunderstanding or negative consequences.

There may be times, of course, when a woman you hardly know will want sex immediately. Should you find yourself in such a situation, remember that you don't have to go along with her plans if they don't fit yours. You can tell her how you feel ("I'd like to get to know you better but I'm not ready to go to bed with you now") and see if anything can be worked out.

This suggestion strikes some men as ridiculous, but we know of only a few cases where it didn't work out well. The exceptions all involved men who presented themselves as the greatest lovers since Casanova. One man, thinking about an evening that ended quite badly, remembered that

> I really came on like Hot Pants Harry when I met her at the bar. I must have given the impression that

I would drive her through the ceiling with ecstasy. I can see why she got mad when I said I wasn't in the mood for sex when we got to her place.

If you don't present yourself as a stud, you won't be in danger of being accused of false advertising.

A second factor that leads to quick sex is spending too much time together at the beginning. We continue to be surprised at how frequently men initiate sex with a new partner, not because they wanted to but because they couldn't think of anything else to do. Here is how Sam, who chronically got sexually involved on the first date with a partner, described his experiences.

Typically I take the woman to dinner or a show, then for a few drinks. Then to my place. We talk a little and then I make my move. You asked if I really wanted sex all those times. The honest answer is no, at least not most of the times. Sometimes I wish I hadn't brought her home. But there she is. How can you deal with that gracefully? I just can't say it's time for her to go. What would she think? Last week there was a weird situation with the woman I met at my cousin's. I definitely knew what I wanted from her when we got home. I wanted a back massage—my back was killing me from helping my cousin move—but how can you ask for a massage on the first date?

Although Sam felt he didn't know the woman well enough to ask for a back-rub, he was willing to have intercourse with her and share her bed for a night. Which is quite interesting, when you think about it: for many people, sex has become less personal and intimate than a massage or conversation.

If you can't tell your partner that you're tired and want to go home, that your back is sore and you'd like a massage, that you don't feel ready to have sex with her, or any similar feelings, sex is probably not going to be very satisfying. If you're not comfortable telling her any of these things, what is sex with her going to do for you?

We use the idea of minimal contact to deal with new partners. Rather than trying to rush a new woman into bed or making a date for Saturday night at your place or hers—a situation that almost begs for a sexual advance—we suggest a few coffee dates first so you can determine just what is your interest and level of comfort. A coffee date need not have anything to do with coffee. It is merely a time-limited get-together during which no physical contact other than a handshake or hug is permitted. The woman should be informed of the time limit when the date is arranged, and the limit should be adhered to no matter what happens. Examples of coffee dates are short walks, giving her a ride someplace, sharing a drink or meal.

Minimal contact allows you to find out how you feel about a woman in small doses, giving you time to make satisfying decisions for yourself and ease any discomfort you may experience. If your interest in her continues and you are comfortable, you can arrange longer get-togethers and do what you want.

We have suggested coffee dates to both men and women and almost everyone who tried them reported that they produced a great sense of relief. They were able to get to know others without feeling pressured to fill up vast amounts of time or have sex with people they didn't care for or feel comfortable with. You might be surprised by the number of times we heard stories like the following.

I was pissed that I had agreed to do the coffee date thing. As soon as I met Jennie at the party I knew we would hit it off just fine. She was so lovely, so warm, those beautiful eyes. . . . I was sure I could take her to bed that night and love it. But I kept our agreement and asked her for lunch the next day. I don't know what happened but she was a different person. She was still lovely, but we really didn't have much to say to each other. I kept looking at her eyes, trying to rekindle what I felt the night before, but it just wasn't there. She didn't even seem very warm anymore. I'm not putting her down. She's an OK person, but I can see that she's not what I need. I wonder how I got so worked up about her at the party. I think I'll vote for coffee dates now. When I think of what might have happened had I gone to bed with her that night, it makes my skin crawl. There's nothing worse than realizing you're not interested in a woman after you've

had sex with her. It's so hard to leave gracefully and
my feelings are so bad that they wipe out any good
feelings that might have happened during sex.

Now for some specific suggestions for sex with a
new partner.

1. Get to know her and give her the opportunity to
know you. Give yourself time to determine if you really
want sex with her.

The only possible problem is that she might misinterpret your lack of sexual attention as meaning that
you don't like her or find her desirable. Women are so
accustomed to men making sexual overtures as soon as
they meet that they may wonder what's going on even
though they really prefer to delay sex. A simple explanation is all that's required.

This is lovely but I think I should be going now. I
like you and am very turned-on to you but I'd prefer
not having sex until I know you a little better. Then
I'm sure it'll be good for both of us.

2. Be sensual with her before you even think of
doing anything sexual. Hold hands, hug, kiss, snuggle,
or do anything else that feels good. The chapter on
touching may give you some ideas. Do what feels comfortable and stop when you feel anxious or when you
want to stop. If you have concerns that you are being
a tease or leading her on, talk to her about them.

3. Do what is necessary to feel comfortable with her
and get your conditions met. You might want to talk to
her about any concerns you have about being with her,
about what she expects in a relationship or sex. You
might also want to talk about the types of physical contact you enjoy. This need not be a serious "There's
something I want to talk to you about" event. A
simple "I really like it when you touch me like that" is
fine. Establish a habit of discussing your preferences
with her; it will serve you well.

If you're feeling adventurous, you might want to
discuss the types of sexual activities you enjoy. Here's
what one man told us about discussing sex long before
he and his partner went to bed:

It was a new experience for me. Susan and I had gone out four or five times and were strongly attracted to each other. But she said she wasn't ready for sex. It's funny how I can accept that from women but how difficult it was for me to tell them the same thing. Anyway, one day out of the blue she asked what I liked in sex. This took me totally by surprise and it took a few minutes before I could say anything. But I did state some of my preferences and she did the same. That conversation really turned me on and I was looking forward to doing it with her. We didn't get to bed the next two times we were together, however. We continued our sex talk and I got more relaxed about it. The next time we got it on and it was very nice. There was a whole new quality to it. I just felt so cozy with her. Getting to know her was part of the reason and so was the sex talk. I felt that I had already come clean with her, she knew what I wanted and liked. And since I knew what turned her on, I didn't have to try to figure it out.

I learned a lesson from her and I'm grateful. That was several years ago and since then I've usually put off having sex with a new woman until we've spent some time together and we've talked some about sex. I'm happy to say that I'm now the one who initiates this talk.

4. Consider a session or two of massage before having sex. Massage is a good way of getting comfortable with your partner and will also tell you how ready you are for sex. If you're not comfortable in the massage, that's a good warning that some of your conditions are not being met. The massage can be done informally ("I'd like to give you a back-rub") or by using the more formalized instructions given in Exercise 8–3.

You might also want to consider *sleeping* with her, which can be a nice and cozy way of getting more comfortable with her. We know this sounds a bit old-fashioned, but it has worked very well for the men who've tried it. It's possible, of course, that sleeping together might lead to sex, which is fine if that's what feels right at the time. But make sure your conditions are met and that sex is what you want. If not, just sleep.

5. When your conditions are met, when you are

comfortable, and when you are feeling aroused, feel free to engage in whatever sexual activities you like. Try to remember what we said about sexual choices. Intercourse is not required. If you have had erection or ejaculation problems in the past, it is best not to have intercourse the first few times you are with a new partner. Do other things that feel good to both of you.

6. Give feedback about your experiences with her. Feel free to tell her—before, during, and after sexual encounters—what you liked and didn't like, and encourage her to do the same. This eliminates guesswork and misunderstandings, thus helping both of you to know each other better.

7. Express your feelings when appropriate. If you have feelings that get in the way of your sexual responsiveness or, for that matter, your ability to relate to her in any way, you would probably do well to discuss them with her. It will help her to know you and it may also totally or partially resolve some of the difficulties.

8. Don't do anything you don't want to do. If she suggests that you have sex on the front lawn or that her dog join in your sexual activities, and if such things simply aren't your style, let her know immediately. Take care of yourself.

Following these suggestions will allow you to begin sexual activity with a new partner with a maximum of comfort and a minimum of stress. They will not all be easy to follow, but you now have the skills to at least begin. In later chapters, we supplement this list with other ideas for men who have erectile or ejaculation problems.

Changing Sexual Patterns in Relationships

Many men suddenly or gradually find that they are not content with the sexual patterns in their relationships. The sources of the dissatisfaction vary: too little (or too much) sex; insufficient variation in practices and positions; not enough initiation or participation by the partner; not enough excitement; and so on. Sometimes the precise nature of the discontent is not clear; the man just knows that sex doesn't feel as good or as interesting as it once did.

The best way to begin with this problem is to discuss it with your partner. It is not important whether you know precisely what is bothering you or what changes you want. The feeling of discontent is sufficient basis for a discussion, during which clarity may develop. Some men have been surprised to find that their partners feel exactly the way they did, but whether or not this is true, a talk is beneficial for putting forth your thoughts and feelings, and preparing for change.

The initial conversation about the subject is important and will strongly influence subsequent events. We suggest that you use the talk-and-listen format given earlier in this chapter and that you spend a few minutes beforehand deciding what it is you want to say. Your message needs to be clean and clear, and it should not imply that something is wrong with your partner. Like this:

(A) Mary, I've been thinking that our sex life isn't as exciting as it was when we first met. I'd like to talk with you about it and see if we can make some changes that will make sex better for both of us.

Not like this:

(B) Mary, having sex with you sure hasn't been any fun lately. I'm going to tell you some things I want you to do to correct the situation.

The man in example A is clearly stating his dissatisfaction and expressing a desire that they both try to work it out. The man in example B is headed for trouble. He's telling his partner that it's all her fault (which very rarely is the case) and putting her on the defensive. Her reaction will probably be such as to make impossible any improvement in their sexual situation.

Be as specific as possible about your complaints. Talk about how you feel dissatisfied and, if you know, what changes you'd like. Ask for your lover's reactions and ideas. Make sure she understands this is a joint venture. Everything need not, and probably cannot, be done in one discussion. Terminate the discussion when one of you gets tired or when progress ceases, and give yourself some time to think over what has been said. Then you can talk again.

The result of your talks should be specific plans for how change is to be effected. Without specific plans, there is an excellent chance that the changes will not come to fruition. Consideration should also be given to possible sources of resistance to the change and ways of dealing with them.

Charlie wanted his wife to initiate sex more often. He had told her about this in the past and, while she always agreed to initiate more, she rarely followed through. There was good reason for this. If she did initiate when Charlie wasn't in the mood, he became angry. She would feel free to initiate only if she knew that she wouldn't have to deal with his anger. With a little help from a therapist, they worked it out so that Charlie got practice turning down her sexual invitations without getting angry. As he became more comfortable saying no, she felt freer to initiate when she was in the mood.

Of all the sources that one might consult regarding possible changes, the best are your fantasies and past experiences. What kinds of sexual attitudes, events, and practices have you thought about, fantasized about, or dreamed about? Surely some of these could be carried out in reality. What about your past experiences? What factors made sex better with other partners or with this partner at other times? Can some of these factors be reinstituted now?

While on the subject of fantasies, we want to add that the sharing of sexual fantasies, whether or not they are carried out, is exciting to many couples. You might want to try this if your partner is willing. But take it slowly until you are comfortable with this type of sharing.

Keep in mind that change is rarely easy and don't expect too much too soon. Your partner may well be willing to initiate sex, or have oral sex, or meet some of your other wishes, but she may not always remember to do what you want or do it in quite the way you want. Patience is required, and so is support. Let her know that you know she's willing and is trying. And give feedback so she'll know how she's doing.

You will go a long way to ensuring that your desires are met if you reinforce what you like and correct what you don't like, as long as the corrections are given in a supportive and nonblaming way. If your lover rarely initiates sex, make sure you tell her how much you enjoyed it when she does initiate. If she has a lot to learn about sucking your penis, give her directions and let her know when it feels good.

If you have trouble working out the changes you like, be sure to read the section later in this chapter on working out disagreements.

Sexual Boredom in Long-Term Relationships

Wanting to relieve boredom in a sexual relationship is a specific example of making changes in a relationship and is therefore closely related to the previous section. But sexual boredom is an interesting phenomenon in its own right.

While many people assume that boredom is inevitable in long-term relationships, we believe that this is just another bit of mythology. Sex is not the same after ten, twenty, or thirty years with the same partner, but it need not be boring or unsatisfactory. The mystery may be gone since the partners know each other well after a number of years, but the increased comfort, trust, cooperation, and knowledge of one another that comes with being together for so long can more than compensate for its absence. For some people, sex gets better as the years go by, while for others it stays at the same high level for many, many years.

Why, then, do so many others complain that sex gets boring after a few years? The people complaining of boredom to whom we have talked can be loosely grouped into three categories, each with a different reason for the boredom.

The first group consists of those who have maintained a rigidly narrow pattern of sexual activity since they began. Sex is programmed down to the last detail and always proceeds according to plan. It's no wonder that they are bored.

Changing the routine can be helpful to people in this group. Having sex at different times, in different places, and in different ways can introduce the kind of variety that will relieve the boredom. You need to talk to your partner about the changes you want or about the idea of making changes. Specific ideas for change can come out of your discussion, from your fantasies, or perhaps from some of the exercises in this book. If you want still more ideas, you might consult some pornographic films or literature and also Alex Comfort's *The Joy of Sex*.

The notion of introducing variety into sexual relationships suffering from boredom is not new and has, in our opinion, been somewhat overdone in recent years. It can be beneficial, but only with the people who are bored because of a lack of variety. Most of the people who complain of boredom, however, do not fit into that group. They fall into two other categories and it is highly unlikely that sexual variety will do anything for them.

The second category of people who complain of sexual boredom consists of those in relationships with little feeling left in them. Some of these people engage in varied sexual techniques and activities but the boredom persists because there is no feeling between the partners (or worse, there is lots of feeling, all negative). Since all the positions and techniques in the world can't substitute for feelings of caring, attraction, and passion, this situation is more difficult to work with than the first type of boredom.

Our position is not very optimistic. Unless a way can be found to rekindle the interest, caring, or love that once existed, it may not be possible to relieve the sexual malaise. This is not to say that the relationship must resume its early form or that it must in any sense become ideal. But some feelings must be awakened if sex is to be different. This is sometimes possible and sometimes not. We do not believe that a book is the best way of dealing with this situation. Professional help is required in most cases.

The last category of sexually bored people consists of those whose expectations exceed reality. While they complain of boredom, on questioning it usually turns out that they are not so much bored as dissatisfied because sex no longer is—or never was—what they thought it ought to be. People in this group, like those in the preceding one, have often tried various ways of increasing their sexual enjoyment. They have read all the books, seen all the movies, attended all the workshops. Nothing helps, at least not for long, because what they are after is unattainable. Rather than exploring the reasonableness of their expectations, however, they continue to look for the method that will fulfill their fantasies.

This issue is a large one and, because the values of sex have been so exaggerated in recent years, one to which we are all subject to some degree. We discuss it in greater detail in Chapter 22. For now it is enough to say that dissatisfaction and boredom are inevitable for those who cling to superhuman expectations. What needs changing are the expectations rather than the behaviors. Our chapter on sex and aging will be useful for those who have unrealistic expectations about sex in the later years.

Sex does not have to get boring in long-term relationships, unless the opposite of boredom is defined in terms of the excitement that characterizes adolescence or fantasy. Sex does not get boring for those who retain some affection for their partners, have realistic expectations about sex, do not do what they don't want to do, and who feel free to have sex in ways, places, times, and positions that feel right to them at the moment. In fact, a number of people have told us that sex became really good for them only after they had been together for more than ten years and that since then it had kept improving. Sex was no longer characterized by youthful passion and awkwardness, but it sure was fun.

Working Out
Disagreements

Disagreements are an inevitable part of every relationship. Many can be easily and satisfactorily negotiated, but not all. Some people delude themselves into thinking that all differences can be ironed out. Such, alas, is not the case. Some differences cannot be resolved in a given relationship, and for others the amount of effort required, as well as the amount of ill will generated, makes the price too high.

One extremely common type of disagreement revolves around the amount of contact and sharing in the relationship. Usually it is the woman who desires more attention and communication. Without them, she may withdraw sexually. We deal with this situation in greater detail in the next chapter. We mention it here because so many times sexual disagreements are the result of this more basic conflict.

Two other common disagreements have to do with the frequency of sex and types of sexual activity. While many people still believe that it is always the man who wants sex more often and who is eager to try variations, this isn't necessarily so. In fact, in our experience we have found that there are just as many relationships in which the reverse is true.

With either of these types of conflict, the first thing to do is to determine precisely what you or your partner wants. This can be more difficult than it sounds. A desire for more frequent sex sounds deceptively simple: "I (or she) just want to do it more often." But what is "it"—touching, oral or manual sex, intercourse, orgasm, or something else? The it has to be pinpointed; its precise nature makes a difference as to whether or not it can be fulfilled. The partner less inclined to have more sex may be willing to increase the amount of physical contact or sexual activity other than intercourse, but may not be willing to have intercourse more often.

Another way of looking at the same issue is to ask what would it mean for the requester to get what he is asking. Is he primarily interested in the physical act itself or its symbolic meaning? If it's the meaning rather than the act that's important, the issue can often be resolved without increasing the amount or variety of sex.

For example, a woman may ask for more sex because only during sex does she feel loved; it's the only time her partner pays any attention to her. While an obvious solution is to increase the amount of sex, a better response in some respects would have the partner start paying attention and showing love in other ways. Another example is a man who wants his partner to swallow his semen because he feels this would show her complete acceptance of him. In some cases like this, the women were willing to have the men come in their mouths. But the majority of such situations were worked out in other ways, more acceptable to both partners.

Here again we emphasize the importance of understanding clearly what the disagreement is about. More sex, oral sex, anal sex, more active participation, and similar requests are not specific or clear enough. Exactly what is it that you or your partner wants? And what would it mean to you to get it or not get it?

The symbolic meanings of sex are many, and we deal with some of them in Chapter 22. For now, just be sure you know what you want and what you and your partner are disagreeing about.

Of course there are situations where one partner simply has a greater desire for sex than the other.

We recall one man who claimed he wanted sex at least once a day, every day, while his partner was satisfied with once a week. Sex was this man's only way of showing his wife he cared for her. But even after he learned to express his love in words and nonsexual touching, he still wanted sex more often than she did. The discrepancy in desire was resolved in several ways, only one of which will be mentioned here. We suggested masturbation as a sexual supplement for him but that didn't appeal to him because it didn't include his partner. Whereupon she said that she would be happy to hold and stroke him while he masturbated. He wasn't exactly thrilled by the idea but finally tried it. This practice soon became a regular part of their sexual repertoire.

The compromise this couple worked out is something that others who have different preferences regarding frequency might want to try. The main obstacle to its implementation is the myth that in sex each partner does something to the other but no one does anything to himself. It's a powerful myth, but when you think about it there's no good reason for it. While masturbating this way is not as exciting to many people as other forms of sex, it is an alternative that allows for sexual satisfaction with some participation by the partner.

If you and your partner understand each other's position and no agreement seems possible, you both need to consider how important the matter is to you. Is it really vital that you have sex more often or that she suck you or initiate sex? If it's not terribly important, you might want to drop the subject. It may not be worth the hassle. Even if it is important, consider what the chances for resolution are. If your partner is adamant, or if it seems that a change will create considerable ill will in the relationship, ask yourself if it's worth it. Since you're not going to get everything you want, it pays to put your energy into those issues that are most important and that have a reasonable likelihood of being resolved in a way that does not involve serious negative side effects.

If you want to continue with trying to make changes, here are some ideas:

1. Let your partner know how important the issue is to you and how willing you are to try to find a mutually agreeable solution.
2. Ask what her objections are.
3. Taking her objections seriously, see if you can suggest ways of dealing with them, or offer to work with her toward this end.
4. Offer her something in return, something she wants but you have so far been unwilling to grant.

The following story illustrates how these suggestions worked in one case.

George had never had anal intercourse and wanted very much to try it with a woman he was seeing. She refused. Although the relationship was generally sound, fights soon developed over this conflict. We suggested that George ask his partner why she was so opposed to the idea, and that he do nothing but listen while she talked. Her objections were that the whole idea seemed dirty to her and that she feared it would be painful. George asked if she would be willing to keep an open mind on the subject and to see if something could be worked out. She agreed after exacting a promise that he would not push her. A discussion with us and some reading helped free her from the idea that anal lovemaking was shameful. We told her that while this kind of sexual activity might be uncomfortable at first, if she wanted to try it lubrication and the relaxation of the pelvic muscles would help. We suggested that, since she would be doing this for George's enjoyment, she should ask for something for herself. There was something she wanted—a whole evening of George pleasuring her, "just spending a whole lot of time lavishing physical affection on me" —but George had refused to do it because it involved so much time. The trade was made. She got her evening of loving and enjoyed it. George got what he wanted but the results were not what he had expected.

"It was weird. It just wasn't anything like I thought it would be. I mean, it was OK, but nothing special. God, to think I got so hassled about it."

There is one situation you need to look out for. If a disagreement assumes major proportions and can neither be resolved nor dropped, and is causing real problems in the relationship, the chances are excellent that sex is not what you are disagreeing about. Something more fundamental is probably at stake. Get some help before it wrecks the relationship.

13

Some Things You Should Know about Women

Although men and women spend much of their lives in each other's company, many think and act as if the opposite sex were an alien species. Throughout history—in jokes, folktales, songs, and literature—men have bemoaned their inability to understand women. Even the great Freud, after decades of inquiry, finally threw up his hands in despair, crying, "What do women want?"

Female sexuality has been a particularly vexing area for men, who have believed and vainly tried to reconcile many outlandish and contradictory ideas about how women related to sex. From the wanton slut of the fantasy model, who can never seem to get enough of sex, to the prim Victorian lady for whom any sex, or any thought of it, would have been far more than enough, we have gone from one extreme to the other, never quite knowing which to trust.

Ignorance breeds doubt and fear, and to these emotions must be added others—envy and anger. Men have often thought that women had it too easy in sex. Women didn't have to *do* anything. They could, if need be, just lie there and spread their legs. Men, on the other hand, had to do all the work; at the very least, they have to achieve erection. The woman got to lie back and evaluate the man's prowess. It just didn't seem fair.

Since the natural order seemed weighted in favor of women, men used their physical and political power to tip the scales their way. Men defined how women should feel and behave sexually, and it wasn't long before women started acting the way men said they should, even to the point in Victorian times of denying that they were sexual at all. But the uncertainties and fears remained.

It would be presumptuous to assume that in one chapter we can clear up issues that have perplexed millions of men over hundreds of years, but we are going to try at least to shed some light on the topic of female sexuality. This chapter is divided into two parts. The first discusses what women say they want in sex and the second deals with some of the anatomical and physiological aspects of female sexuality. The order reflects our priorities: what women say they like is more important than where the parts are and what they do.

We want to emphasize that this chapter is in no way intended as a blueprint for satisfying a woman. There is tremendous variation among women, as there is among men. Nothing is true of all women. This point was underscored powerfully in the preparation of the chapter. A number of women—colleagues, friends, clients—read it and made comments. There is hardly a point in the chapter that was not disputed by at least one of them. The intention of the chapter, then, is to serve as a basis for thought and discussion. Even if your partner disagrees with everything we say, if she lets you know how she differs from what we say and explains what is true for her, then this chapter will have served its purpose.

What Women Want in Sex

Female sexuality, as we said above, has traditionally been defined by men. Male authorities—religious, literary, medical, scientific—decided what women were like sexually and what they wanted. Only rarely were women themselves consulted about the matter. When a woman was courageous enough to try to define her own sexuality, no one paid much attention because it didn't seem that a woman would know what she was talking about. It was easy to pass her off as unfeminine, a castrating bitch, or a threat to the established order of things and continue in the delusion that men knew what was best.

This pattern is in the process of change. Women are now studying female sexuality and there is more societal permission for them to explore their own sexual feelings, styles, and preferences. But it is a mistake to think that the tenacious hold of male-dominated ideas has been broken. Many if not most women still find it difficult to assert themselves sexually. Many of them are struggling to do just this, but it isn't easy. One of the most powerful lessons many women learned was that they should defer to men in sex; they certainly shouldn't say or do anything that might be taken as a reproach or criticism. This obviously makes it difficult for them to assert their own sexual desires, especially if the man takes any suggestions as an insult.

In order to find out what women had to say about sex, we decided to ask them. Bernie Zilbergeld and Lynn Stanton did a study in which over four hundred women responded to a questionnaire asking what they liked and didn't like in sex. Most of the material and all of the quotations in this section are from that study.

To get the maximum benefit from the material to be presented, you should do the following exercise before reading further.

EXERCISE 13–1: WHAT YOU THINK WOMEN WANT IN SEX
Time Required: 30 to 40 minutes

Make a list of the kinds of things you think women (your partner, a potential partner, or women in general) want in sex, in terms of attitudes, behaviors, techniques, or anything else. Make another list of the things they don't want. Be as specific as possible in both lists.

You might want to keep your lists handy as you read the rest of the chapter and compare your responses with what is presented. When you find a discrepancy, ask yourself what is the basis for your information. Did a partner say or do something that led to your belief, did you hear it from others, read it in a book, or are you guessing? We do not mean to imply that you are wrong if you disagree with what we say. As we mentioned earlier, many women disagree with many of our statements. We only want you to make sure that you have good reason for disagreeing. If you believe that a certain point is not true for your partner but aren't sure why you believe this, why not check it out with her?

We were pleased to discover that most of what the women said was congruent with our own thinking and with the approaches we were successfully using to help men enhance their sexuality. This convergence seems to point to the possibility of a more realistic and human expression of sexuality. To be sure, women want more from men, but what they want has nothing to do with bigger penises, harder or more frequent erections, perfect performances, or mind-blowing orgasms. They want more of the kinds of things many men are now realizing that they want to give—equal treatment, understanding, sensitivity, communication, and a greater sharing of themselves. Another way of saying the same thing: women want more of what men have not been allowed to give because of the rigid ordering of human qualities into male and female categories. They want men to be more fully human, more fully themselves, so that women can be who they are.

Before going on, we want to mention that we are not saying that women are right and men are wrong, nor that women are paragons of sexual wisdom. Women's sexual training is at least as unrealistic and cruel as men's, and in many cases much worse. As a result, many women have problems with sex. They are in conflict over what is right for them, or can't get their minds and bodies to operate in harmony. Many of our respondents candidly admitted their problems and confusions. And more than a few said that the reason they hoped for a change in men was that this would make it easier for them to change.

If there is any one point which summarizes what women want from men it is a greater sharing of themselves. This issue extends far beyond the area of sexual activity but often affects it since a woman who thinks her man is not giving enough in other areas may well be angry or inhibited in bed. There is no doubt that this is the greatest complaint women have about men: that they do not give enough of their time, attention, feelings, and understanding.

> He says he loves me but you'd never know it from the way he acts. We never do any touching, talking, or anything else. He doesn't have time for me because he's so busy with all the "important" things like his job, working on his stupid boat, paying bills and caring for the lawn, and watching a zillion football games on TV. I want more of him. I don't care if the lawn never gets mowed.

A common pattern in contemporary relationships is that the woman makes requests for more contact, which the man often interprets as meaning that she's asking for more than he's able or willing to give. Whereupon he retreats further into his other activities, which makes the woman angry and more demanding. Which makes the man withdraw even further, ad infinitum. In this pattern, it is not the man's aggressiveness that upsets the woman, but his passivity and withdrawal, his lack of responsiveness in expressing his feelings toward her.

Another common pattern, better known than the first because of the widespread publicity given to it by the women's movement, involved a domineering man lording it over his partner. He doesn't respect his partner as an equal and feels free to tell her how to live her life, free to criticize and belittle her, and, in general, not to take her seriously. Curiously, this pattern is more similar to the one discussed above than may seem apparent at first glance. Both involve women not getting what they want (and this is usually also true for the men) because their men refuse to give.

Many of the points that follow are only elaborations of these two patterns. And, unfortunately, we don't have any easy solutions. Women have been trained to focus more on relationships than have men, who learned more about dealing with things like jobs, ideas, and games. Relationship patterns and problems are often merely logical outgrowths of the different socialization patterns. Many times, however, compromises are possible, providing there is some genuine affection between the partners and an ability to listen to what is being requested by the other. Often what is being asked is much less demanding and threatening than what was imagined. In most relationships, there is no reason why the man (or woman, if that be the case) can't have time to work on his boat, while the woman (or man) also gets some of the contact she (or he) desires. We hope that what follows will be of value in helping you hear what some women say they want.

The days are long gone, if they ever existed, when women wanted nothing from sex and submitted to it only to please their men. Women like men who are interested in what they want. They view sex as a cooperative venture between equals and expect to be taken seriously. The man who is concerned only with his own needs and satisfaction is held in contempt.

I like a partner who can be sensitive to my needs while still being true to his own satisfaction. I like to have my requests listened to and to not be forced into doing things I don't like. In short, I like an equal relationship rather than a one-sided one.

What I hate most is when a man is concerned with his own needs to a degree that leaves no room for mine. It feels like a denseness on his part, an unwillingness to listen to me. It makes me feel like I have to struggle to be an equal person in the sexual interaction, and often that I am simply unable to have an impact on him. The behaviors range from near-rape (insisting on intercourse when I don't want it) . . . to

berating me for being oversexed when I want sex and
he's not in the mood.

In general, women seem much less performance-
oriented in sex than men. Sex for them is a process of
shared contact and communication rather than a mad
scramble to achieve certain goals.

The important things are sharing and mutual pleasure. The sharing of minds, bodies, and souls is where
it's at for me.

Men get so busy pursuing performance goals that they
forget sensuality, playfulness, the pleasure of taking
one's time during a sexual encounter, doing things
like exploring fantasies, experimenting with different
things, and taking the time to stop in the middle of
lovemaking for a sip of wine and some talk.

Women tend to have a fairly differentiated view of
sex. Each part is important, to be appreciated for its
own sake, whether or not it leads to something else.
What is usually called foreplay is not something they
see only as a prelude to something better. It is valuable
in its own right, and women like men who are sensual
enough to enjoy this aspect of lovemaking.

I like sensual men. A man who will spend as much
time kissing my neck (if he and I are both enjoying
it) as my breasts can turn lovemaking into a slow,
delicious exploration and discovery of each other.

I enjoy a man who enjoys all forms of foreplay for
their own sake and who doesn't have to have intercourse every time.

Expressions of physical affection are extremely important to most women, and not only sexual touching. They want to touch and be touched at times
when sex isn't possible or desirable, as well as times
when sex may be a result of the touching. Women
who are only touched when their partners want sex
are not content.

Affection is what I crave. Touching is important *all* the time.

I get so angry when a man thinks that all touching must lead to sex. I want to be able to touch, and want him to touch me, just as a way of saying, "I like you," or "I care for you," without having to end up in bed.

The hugging, kissing, and stroking called foreplay comprise one example of the physical affection women like. The uniting of genitals is another, but one that is distrusted by women unless it is preceded and followed by other kinds. They resent feeling that they are nothing but receptacles for the man's sperm, useful until he has ejaculated and then discarded like yesterday's newspaper. Afterplay, therefore, is another type of affection that most women like.

I like a man to hold me after intercourse. There doesn't have to be a lot of conversation, just a few tender words, some physical intimacy, some contact that tells me that the closeness is still there even after the orgasm is over.

I resent a man who, after orgasm, jumps up and says "Now on to the important events of the day."

Another aspect of the affectionate, sensual approach that appeals to so many women is a slow, unhurried attitude.

I like him to move slowly—to kiss me, fondle my body, to allow me to pleasure his body through kissing and stroking—and to take time to try different things, to be able to stop for a while and start again. I like sex to be a slow, sensuous experience.

I like a man who is relaxed and unhurried during sex. When a man rushes, I assume that he is caught up in himself and his feelings and that it is not a sharing experience.

This should not be taken to mean that every sexual act must go on for hours or that women are against quickies. It is true that some women have learned to distrust quickies because they think they are being used without regard for their own needs. Despite this, however, most women do like or can learn to like quick sexual encounters provided that they feel cared for and respected and that this is not the only type of sex they get. A moral we draw from this is that quickies work best in the context of a caring relationship, where both partners trust the other and know without question that they are valued and appreciated. A quickie at the beginning of a relationship, however, is a good way of leaving the woman feeling used and abused, and may end the relationship before it gets off the ground.

Gentleness and sensitivity are greatly admired by women. Women usually do not like feeling that they are in a football game when having sex.

Being gentle is a virtue.

Perhaps what saddens me the most is the way that some men feel they must act in order to fulfill their masculine role. This includes gruffness, a lack of tenderness (such as hugging and soft body stroking), and poor expression of emotion.

Again, this should not be construed to mean that women are not sometimes interested in rough sex. Many are, but usually only in the context of a relationship where they feel respected and cared for. Rough handling outside that context—despite what Harold Robbins and other such experts have to say about it—leaves most women feeling abused and thinking that the man is an insensitive clod.

We realize that we haven't said much about orgasms so far. Surprisingly, the women who responded to the questionnaire didn't have much to say about this topic. Women want orgasms, there is no doubt about that, but they tend to view them somewhat differently than men do. While most men can barely conceive of a sexual experience without an orgasm for them, women are more flexible. They don't see orgasm as necessary every time. Sex can be good even without orgasm.

It follows then that for many women orgasm is not the main reason they engage in sex. They have sex because it's a way of sharing themselves and a pleasurable experience. They want the option of being able to have an orgasm, but don't want to focus on it to the point where everything becomes only a means toward this end.

> I don't want to feel that I have to climax every time. I want to be able to get what I need to have an orgasm when I want one, but that isn't every time I have sex. I want to be able to enjoy just doing what feels good, without worrying how it should end.

Women do not like being pressured to have orgasms. Being sensitive to their needs is valued, as is the willingness to give them the kinds of stimulation they want (which may or may not be intercourse). Trying to make them come so that you'll feel like a good lover is not.

> If I haven't climaxed but feel warm and happy and sleepy and tell my partner I want to sleep, it makes me *angry* if he insists I must have an orgasm. That says, "I'm meeting my male ego needs and to hell with you."

In conformity with the idea that women are more interested in an experience than a performance, the more technical aspects of sex that concern so many men received little attention. Not one woman mentioned penis size as being important and only a very small number said anything about the ability to last a long time. This is not to say that a woman won't feel cheated or frustrated if you ejaculate in twenty seconds every time you are with her—she probably will —but only that this is not the most important consideration for most women. If you are relating in ways that are satisfying to both of you, learning to last longer is a simple matter.

Many women complained about rigid, mechanical

patterns on the part of their lovers, where technique was emphasized over personal expression, playfulness, and passion. They don't like to feel that the man is doing something *to* them; they want the man to be *with* them, sharing the experience.

> I am not interested in sexual performance. I am interested in sexual expression on a one-to-one basis without a driving manual for instruction and reference.

> A mechanical approach is the biggest turn-off for me. I'm treated as a machine or Barbie Doll, to be touched, diddled, rubbed, or sucked in certain parts according to what worked for the last girl or what he read in a book. No emotional communication, no joy, just engineering designed to do the job as effectively as possible so he can get on with what he really wants to do.

Part of the complaints about rigidity dealt with the man's unwillingness to experiment. We were a bit surprised by this because we have so often heard this complaint from men about women. A number of women said their lovers were quite resistant to trying new places, times, positions, and activities. Some said that their partners refused to have intercourse in any but the missionary position, some that their partners would have sex only late at night, while others complained that while their men wanted oral sex from them, they refused to reciprocate.

> For all their talk, men seem to be more inhibited than women.

> Many women expressed a desire for less seriousness and more playfulness in sex.

> I like for men to regard sex as a fun thing, not as something real heavy.

> Most of all I love playfulness and rule-breaking in lovemaking. Nothing sacred or orderly or sequential, just experimenting and the shared closeness that it brings.

Reading these comments reinforced an impression we developed in our work with men, in and out of therapy—namely, that many men regard sex as a very serious undertaking, with no levity permitted. The issue here is of course our old friend performance. When you're trying to get the job done, to perform well, humor and playfulness are experienced as distractions. On the other hand, when you are having an experience without much regard for where it ought to go, you can do whatever feels right at the moment, be it laughing, crying, talking, fucking, nibbling, cuddling, or something else.

In line with their desire for a sharing experience, the women requested more communication about sex. They wanted men to be more open about their feelings and preferences, and they liked men to ask about their partners' preferences. All in all, women want an atmosphere of openness in talking about sex, where each partner is free to say what he or she likes and dislikes, how he or she is feeling, and to verbalize anything of relevance to the process. Several women were clear that when this atmosphere prevails, orgasms are not a problem. They can say what they want and, when they get it, orgasms usually occur.

Communication plays a huge part in satisfaction and enjoyment. One good thing men can do is give me feedback on what they want and don't want, encourage me to do the same, and do all this not only with body language but also by verbalizing.

When I feel OK about saying what I want, and if he can go along with these things, I don't have to worry about orgasm.

A number of women stated that they need the man to voice his preferences in order for them to feel free to voice their own.

I like for men to tell me what feels good to them and what they like for me to do sexually. It not only helps me know what to do but it also makes it easier for me to tell them what I like.

This is sometimes difficult for men to understand since they know they're relatively uneasy and unskilled in communication and assume that women are much better at it. While this is often true, the problem for women is that they learned that a man should take the lead sexually. For a woman to say what she wanted, to make suggestions—this was taboo unless the man took the lead. Which is precisely what the women in this survey said.

It is vital that men recognize the tremendous influence they wield over how much and what their partners are willing to say. Women want to share their thoughts and feelings, as well as their bodies, with men, but they need support and encouragement.

> My least favorite thing is men who make it hard for me to talk to them, in bed or out. I don't think men realize how hard they can make it to share information in bed—simply by being unresponsive, or disinterested, or overtly hostile. And then they wonder why we can't get into a good place together. Even after all these years, I still find it's hard to discuss what I need and want—emotionally, sexually, and in terms of the relationship—unless the man listens actively and is supportive.

This should come as no surprise. All of us need interest and support if we are to say what's important to us, particularly in areas that are difficult to talk about. No one wants to talk to someone who looks as if he'd much rather be somewhere else.

Most of the women were also very clear about wanting to know more about their partners' feelings. Because men characteristically do not say what they feel and think, sexually or otherwise, women often feel left out. One of their most fervent desires is to be included more often, to hear what's happening with their men. And this includes the bad feelings as well as the good ones.

> I really like for a man to tell me how he's feeling (anxious, uncomfortable, distracted, etc.) instead of "pushing on."

I appreciate it when he's able to stop the lovemaking because he's getting tense, and talk or play or get a sandwich and let me in on what's happening with him. It makes whatever he's experiencing as a problem just a part of our sharing, and it gives me permission to do the same.

There is an important message here about what a man can do when he feels uncomfortable in sex or is having a problem. Too often a man will try to hide his feelings or problem, vainly attempting to override the feelings by pushing on. The woman usually senses that something is amiss but can't figure out exactly what it is, a situation hardly conducive to an enjoyable experience. Or she may misinterpret his reticence to mean that the man doesn't like her or that she did something wrong. She wants to know what is happening for him. Sharing feelings with her will be received as a gift.

This is especially important if you are having problems. Time and again we have listened to men tell us that women yelled or berated them for losing an erection or coming too fast. We don't want to say such things never happen because we know they sometimes do. But in those cases where we have been able to hear the woman's side of it, her anger was triggered not by the event itself but by the man's reaction to it —blaming her; refusing to continue the experience; or withdrawing into a sulky isolation, leaving her feeling alone and helpless.

So if you are having trouble, don't withdraw. Let her know what's going on with you, and see what the two of you want to do next. It sounds almost too simple to be true, but listen to what the women said.

The only time that men's sexual problems become real problems is when the man uses it as a way of distancing himself from me by withdrawing or berating himself, refusing to accept my acceptance of the situation.

I'm annoyed and uncomfortable when a man is experiencing problems with the erection and works at it so intently that I begin to feel used. It's like the erection is so damn important that nothing else matters. I would rather not have intercourse if he is apprehensive about losing his erection or coming too quickly. I really like for him to stop when this occurs and to tell me how he's feeling, to share the experience with me rather than making the situation uncomfortable for both of us.

We close this section on what women want in sex with three statements that seem to sum up most of the main points.

We want men, not supermen; lovers, not beasts; and intelligent, warm companions, not Hollywood handsomes stroking their egos at our expense.

I like a man who feels free to be vulnerable, to give up his masculine stereotype, who can be gentle and sensitive and passive, as well as aggressive. A man who allows me to do the same. A man who can relinquish control of the lovemaking and allow it to be a shared experience. A man who can tolerate imperfections in himself, his penis, and me. . . . A man who appreciates and enjoys women's bodies—even the not-so-perfect ones.

Actually, the things I respond most to in men are qualities which are traditionally considered feminine: tenderness, gentleness, caring, touching, and sensitivity to emotions.

We have presented what 416 women said they wanted in sex. We wonder how the woman or women you relate to feel about what our sample said. We invite you to find out.

Female Sexual Anatomy and Response

While no one denies that there are differences between male and female sexual anatomy and physiology, most modern sex researchers and therapists have been

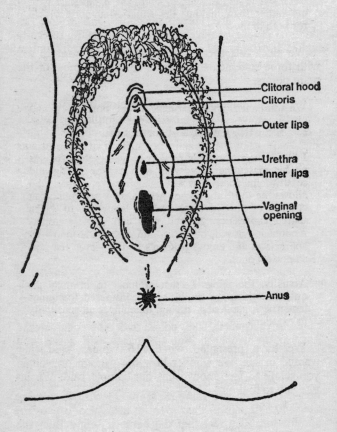

Clitoral hood
Clitoris
Outer lips
Urethra
Inner lips
Vaginal opening
Anus

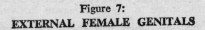

Figure 7:
EXTERNAL FEMALE GENITALS

more impressed with the similarities than the differences. Men and women are not as different as was once thought.

The similarities are evident at the very beginning of life. During the first six to eight weeks of life, male and female fetuses are indistinguishable and follow an identical course of development. The fetus is basically female in that it will develop female sex organs unless something external is added. The something external is the hormone androgen, which stimulates the development of male sex organs.

Male and female sex organs develop from the same basic structures. To take but one example, a structure called the genital tubercle becomes the clitoris in girls and the head of the penis in boys. Both of these organs are richly supplied with nerve endings sensitive to touch and both are capable of expansion. In this sense, it is proper to think of the penis and clitoris as counterparts. The similarities between males and females go beyond just these two organs. Almost every part of the male sexual anatomy has a counterpart in an organ or tissue in women which has similar origins and functions.

Despite our common beginning, however, our genitals end up looking quite dissimilar. The external genitals of a woman are illustrated in Figure 7. Of course, all women do not look the same. Just as men's genitals differ in placement, size, color, and other characteristics, so do women's. But the figure will serve well enough for our purposes.

Let's start at the top with the clitoris, a unique organ. Its uniqueness lies in the fact that it has no function other than providing pleasure. Men have nothing quite like it, since their penises are also organs of elimination. The fact that the penis is larger than the clitoris does not mean much. The smaller organ has about as many nerve endings, so it is very sensitive to stimulation.

The importance of the clitoris was not fully appreciated until the work of Kinsey and Masters and Johnson. Before them, it was commonly believed that the vagina was *the* sexual organ in women. Not only should they have orgasms with penile thrusting in the vagina but, should they need some warming up first, that was done by finger thrusting in the vagina. A number of factors helped undermine the idea of vaginal supremacy. One was the finding that when women masturbate, they usually stimulate the area around the clitoris and rarely insert anything into the vagina. Another important factor was that many women who are not orgasmic in intercourse do have orgasms when they or their partners stimulate the clitoral area.

The clitoris rarely gets direct stimulation during intercourse. As you can see in Figure 7, it is quite difficult for a penis to be in the vagina and touching the clitoris at the same time. To accomplish this in most positions you would need an L-shaped penis, and you just don't see many of them anymore. The clitoris does receive indirect stimulation from penile thrusting in intercourse. As the penis moves in and out of the vagina, it tugs on the vaginal lips. Since the lips are attached to the clitoral hood, thrusting does affect the clitoris. However, this stimulation is indirect and insufficient to produce orgasm in many women.

The clitoris can also be stimulated in a more direct fashion by rubbing it against the man's pubic bone. This can be accomplished in the female superior position if the woman leans forward far enough. It can also be achieved in other positions—for example, the male superior—if the couple makes a special effort to do so. In older marriage manuals this practice was called "riding high," meaning that the man should position his pubic bone so that it pressed against his lover's clitoral area. While pubic-bone clitoral stimulation is possible, such contact is often difficult to maintain during intercourse. And, even if maintained, the stimulation it affords is not always sufficient to allow the woman to have an orgasm.

The outer lips of the vagina are covered with pubic hair. The inner lips are closer to the vaginal opening and are usually closed. When the woman spreads her legs or is aroused, they part, exposing the urethra and vaginal opening. Both the outer and inner lips are sensi-

tive to the touch in many women, although such stimulation in itself is unlikely to produce orgasm.

Since we have made statements about what is and is
not likely to lead to orgasm in women, we should add
an important qualification. Erogenous zones and orgasms are largely the result of conditioning, and while
what we are saying seems true of most women, there
are others who do not conform to these ideas. There
are women who can have orgasms through breast stimulation alone, and there are others who are orgasmic
through stimulation of areas other than the clitoris,
vagina, or breasts. It's important to remember that
there are many individual differences.

While often thought of as a hole, the vagina is actually a potential rather than a real space. In the unaroused
state its walls are relaxed and touch each other. When
sexually excited, the walls balloon out, forming an actual space. This space will form itself to fit snugly
around whatever object is inside of it, from the small-
est penis to a baby's head.

While the erotic sensitivity of the vagina differs from
woman to woman, it is true that the outer third of the
vagina (the part closest to the entrance) contains the
most nerve endings and probably the only nerves in it
that are sensitive to touch. The inner two-thirds are, in
many women, quite insensitive to touch and, in fact,
minor surgery has been performed in this area without
the use of anesthetics. However, the inner two-thirds
are sensitive to pressure and stretch in many women,
and the thrusting and distention that occur during intercourse can be very pleasurable for them.

Fashions change quickly in the sex field, and although it seems not too long ago that women who had
little feeling in their vaginas were being called neurotic
and in need of psychoanalysis, more recently we seem
to be in the grip of what Germaine Greer has called a
"veritable clitoromania." Some radical feminists and sex
authorities talk as if the vagina were of no importance
whatever to the woman, being a source of pleasure only
for the man. We have more than once observed talks on
female sexuality that so overstressed the importance of

the clitoris (no doubt in reaction to the previous under-estimation of its role) that women with little feeling there, or those who achieved orgasms with penile thrusting in the vagina, asked if something was wrong with them.

Since the vagina will accommodate itself to any size penis, some well-meaning people have argued that women have no preferences regarding penis size and that there is no size difference among erect penises, anyway. Yet the fact is that penises do differ in size, whether hard or soft, and there's no point pretending otherwise. And while most women don't have strong size preferences, it would be folly to think that they have no preferences at all. Of the questionnaire respondents we talked to, some said they liked long, thin penises, others favored short, thick ones, and others had still different choices. But they didn't put these preferences on the questionnaire. Why not? Simply because choices regarding penis size are just not that important to them. We call such preferences druthers. A druther is an ideal, something you'd like if you could have anything you wanted. But it's not necessary or even a high priority.

Perhaps you can think of some of your druthers. If you could have anything you wanted in a woman, you might like a certain kind of smile, nose, hair, behind, breasts, or whatever. But since this world is far from perfect, you easily accept your lover without such qualities. And this is precisely the way the overwhelming majority of women feel about penis size. Even if they have a preference (and not all women do), they can easily live without it. Certainly they are not going to let it dictate their choice of a man.

That's the good news. Now for the bad. Although we have never in our personal lives or work encountered a woman who was so obsessed with penis size that she let it run her sex life, we are sure that a few such women must exist somewhere. Just as there are a few men who absolutely will not have sex with a woman unless her breasts can fill a 38D bra, there are probably a few women who won't be satisfied with anything less than a twelve-inch penis. Should it be your misfortune to run into one of these women, the only rea-

sonable suggestion we can make is that you get away
as quickly as possible. Being that concerned about a
physical characteristic over which no one can have any
control is not a good sign. Besides, if you don't have
the requisite number of inches there is nothing you can
do about it. Better to spend your time with one of the
millions of women who couldn't care less about such
things.

We want to discuss briefly some of the physiological
changes that occur as a woman goes through a sexual
experience. This discussion parallels the one on men
in Chapter 7. For the reasons mentioned there, we do
not use Masters and Johnson's concept of the sexual
response cycle in this discussion. For women as for
men, there are many different ways of having a sexual
experience.

The main changes that occur for both women and
men are the result of vasocongestion, the accumulation of blood in various parts of the body. Muscular
tension increases and other changes also occur. Orgasm reverses the blood flow and releases the tension,
but these phenomena occur even without orgasm,
though more slowly.

A sexual response begins when the woman re-
ceives some kind of sexual stimulation, which can be
almost anything—touch, smell, fantasy, or sight. An
increased volume of blood is pumped into various parts
of her body, increasing their size and sensitivity to
stimulation. The pelvis is not the only area so affected.
While women's reactions differ considerably, usually the
breasts, lips, and ear lobes are sensitized.

Vaginal lubrication begins soon after blood starts
flowing into the pelvic region. The lubrication is produced by the vaginal walls in a process similar to sweat-
ing. Lubrication does not mean, as once thought, that
the woman is ready for penetration or close to orgasm.
It only signifies that she is beginning to become aroused.
The amount of lubrication varies from woman to woman and from time to time in the same woman. Some
women lubricate so freely that it seems to flow out of
the vagina while others produce only a sparse amount.

The flow of blood to the sexual tissues causes them

to enlarge. The breasts, clitoris, and inner and outer vaginal lips puff up. The vagina starts expanding and lengthening at the same time. As stimulation continues, the outer two-thirds of the vagina narrows, creating what Masters and Johnson call the "orgasmic platform." Some men and women have taken this narrowing of the vaginal opening as a sign that the woman is not aroused; in fact, it signifies the opposite.

The clitoris, as mentioned, expands as more blood flows into it, in a process quite similar to penile erection. The clitoris always increases in diameter but only in some women does it also get longer. As stimulation continues, the clitoris retracts under its hood. It may no longer be visible and is often difficult to find. Many are the times that men have gone in search of it, wondering where on earth it went. There's no need to look for it because you probably won't find it in any case. Even though not visible, however, the clitoris still responds to stimulation of the area around it.

Increased muscular tension may be evident—in the face, hands, thighs, abdomen, or almost any place. There may also be involuntary contractions or spasms in the pelvis, buttocks, and elsewhere. Other changes include increased blood pressure, heart rate, and respiration rate.

As with men, all these changes are reversible. If the woman is distracted or stops to talk to her partner or starts doing something which is less stimulating for her, her excitement level will drop, accompanied by physical changes reflecting the lesser degree of arousal. This is nothing to get concerned about. A reinstatement of the conditions and activities that led to the higher level of arousal will probably have the same effect again.

But let's stay with the woman in a high state of arousal and discuss what would happen if, for whatever reason, she didn't have an orgasm. Women's orgasms have received so much publicity in recent years that it is easy to think that not having one would be disastrous. In reality, it is no different from what happens to a man who doesn't have an orgasm in a sexual encounter. There may be a feeling of frustration or disappointment or there may not. It depends on many factors, not the least important of which is how the woman feels about her partner and their sexual relationship. If she generally can get what she wants and knows that the man is willing to do what she desires, it's usually no big thing if she doesn't have an orgasm. On the other hand, if she feels that the man cares only about his own satisfaction and isn't willing to do anything for her, the lack of orgasm can be a serious matter.

This discussion refers only to occasional lack of orgasm. If the lack of orgasm is the norm, the woman may lose interest in sex altogether.

If you and your partner are satisfied with your sexual activities, each knowing you usually get what you want, there's no reason why every encounter should end in orgasm. Your sexual experiences can be interrupted or terminated at any point without undue physical or emotional damage to either party. The important thing is that neither of you puts pressure on yourself or the other to have orgasms, for doing so can create a situation that is quite difficult to live with, much more so than an occasional lack of orgasm.

Orgasms in men and women are quite similar, the main difference being that women do not ejaculate. In both men and women, orgasm is a reflex that releases the muscular tension and reverses the flow of blood to the pelvic area.

It is important to know that women require stimulation not only up to the point of orgasm but throughout the orgasm as well. In this, they differ from men. Once men reach the point of inevitability, orgasm will occur even if stimulation ceases. In a woman, however, if stimulation is interrupted a second before the onset of orgasm or in the midst of it, the excitement may decline rapidly, resulting in no orgasm or a truncated one.

In many women orgasm is accompanied by contractions of the pelvic musculature, contractions which you may feel if your finger or penis is in the vagina. While Masters and Johnson and other authorities define female orgasm in terms of these contractions (meaning no orgasm without the contractions), it seems to us that such a definition is unreasonably narrow. Irving Singer, in his book *The Goals of Human Sexuality,* argues persuasively that orgasms without contractions are not only possible but the norm for many women. Some women with whom we've discussed this issue agree. Orgasms, like everything else in sex, follow no absolute pattern. There may be evident pelvic contractions or there may not. Only your partner knows if she has had an orgasm.

Traditional thought had it that men's and women's experience of orgasm differed greatly. Men's orgasms were more explosive and short-lived while women's, though less powerful, were more prolonged. It is difficult to know what to make of this information. When men and women talk about their orgasms, the most impressive feature is the tremendous variation among individuals, and among different orgasms in the same individual. The only research study we know of in this area found that neither physicians, psychologists, nor medical students could correctly differentiate between written descriptions of male and female orgasms.

The next logical issue to examine is multiple orgasms. People scoffed when Kinsey reported in 1953 that 14 percent of the women he interviewed said that they could have two, three, or even more orgasms during one sexual encounter. It was not so easy to scoff when Masters and Johnson demonstrated that women in their laboratory could indeed have more than one orgasm in a relatively short period of time with continued stimulation.

Most men do not seem to have this ability. They experience a period after ejaculation during which no amount of stimulation will produce either erection or ejaculation. Whether or not such a refractory period is necessary is something that cannot be answered at this time. We believe, and there is some research evidence to support the idea, that at least some men can learn to have multiple orgasms similar to women's. Whatever the merits of this viewpoint, the present situation is that very few men have multiple orgasms while a number of women can and do.

But even with women the picture is not clear. While many authorities write and speak as if it had been conclusively proved that all women are capable of multiple orgasms, such proof does not exist. It is simply not known how widespread the ability to have multiple orgasms is.

What is unfortunately clear is that the emphasis on multiple orgasms, by the media and some experts, has created a great deal of confusion and feelings of inadequacy. Many women feel deficient if they have only one orgasm and many men wonder what is wrong with them if their partners are not multiply orgasmic. Imagine what a woman who rarely or never has orgasms might think of herself.

A vast confusion has been created between what may be possible and what should be done. Just because a woman is capable of having several orgasms is no reason that she must have several. But because of all the anxiety surrounding sex, whenever an authority announces that people are capable of something or other, a lot of us take it to mean that there's something wrong with us if we can't or aren't doing it.

If your partner likes to have several orgasms, that's nice, but no nicer and no more proof of anything than if she has only one or none on a particular occasion. The only reason for having more than one orgasm is that it feels good at the time—unless, of course, you or she is training for the orgasm olympics. If your partner desires continued stimulation to have another orgasm, you are free to decide whether or not you want to participate in the process. Try to avoid the compulsion to participate when you don't want to. Also avoid the notion that all her orgasms should come through intercourse.

The last orgasm issue we discuss is the means by which a woman is orgasmic—the old clitoral-vaginal controversy. The old idea, formulated by Freud and his followers, and still very influential, is that women should have orgasms by means of a penis thrusting in their vaginas. This should happen without any simultaneous clitoral stimulation (what Lonnie Barbach calls "Look ma, no hands" orgasms). This notion plays a large role in the fantasy model of sex where every woman is capable of orgasm via intercourse. Orgasms derived from hand or mouth stimulation, or from intercourse plus hand stimulation, are considered by the adherents of this idea to be immature or infantile.

The truth is that many women do not have "no hands" orgasms. In a recent work that looks at this issue, *The Hite Report*, it was reported that only about 30 percent of women consistently achieve vaginal orgasms (meaning through intercourse). The women who are orgasmic through means other than intercourse are no more neurotic, frigid, or hostile toward men than women who have vaginal orgasms. Most of them are perfectly normal and healthy; they just don't have orgasms by means of a thrusting penis.

This wouldn't be a problem were it not for the fact that it differs so widely from the model we learned.

My first sexual experiences fit my model of sex: we did the foreplay thing and, when the woman was ready, we inserted my penis and fucked away until both of us had orgasms. This was the way it was supposed to be. Then I got involved with a woman who liked intercourse but never had orgasms with it. She wanted me to play with her clitoris before or after intercourse in order for her to come. At first I was shocked by what I thought was her problem. Then I thought that I could make her come in intercourse if we had longer sessions of foreplay, used different positions, and a number of other techniques. All of which failed. Then I thought that something was wrong with me. If only I knew the right things to do, I could get her to come "the right way." For almost a year I vacillated between thinking that something was wrong with her and something was wrong with me. Finally, with a lot of help from her, I started to realize that nothing was wrong with either of us. The problem lay in my model of sex, which was far too limited. Not too long ago, many years after our sexual relationship had ended, I talked to her about this issue and we had a good laugh about it. She told me that she finally had managed to have a few orgasms in intercourse but that they took too much effort and were not worth the trouble.

The main point here is simply that there is nothing wrong with women who do not have orgasms the "right way." There is, in fact, no right way. It is our models that are in need of correction, for they are narrow and limited, far too restrictive to encompass the variety of human sexual experience.

The last part of a sexual experience is basically the same in men and women. It is simply a return to the unaroused state. The swelling in the genitals and other areas decreases as blood flows away from them, the muscles become relaxed, and the organs and tissues return to their normal positions. This process occurs more quickly if there has been an orgasm than if there has not. Sometimes, if there has been a very high level of arousal and no orgasm, the return to the unaroused state can take a considerable amount of time and there may be some discomfort. Masturbating to orgasm can bring relief, if it is desired.

Men and women display divergent tendencies immediately after sex. Many men have a tendency either to go to sleep or to leap into some other activity, whereas many women like to cuddle, talk, and in other ways continue the experience of being together. Our speculation is that these differences are rooted in socialization practices rather than in physiological differences. The time after sex can be difficult for men to handle since there is no longer any agenda or format. There is no task to be done, no goal to be reached, and nothing to be accomplished. We men are not trained to deal comfortably with such situations. There's just you and this other person and nothing in particular to do except relate.

If you are interested in pursuing this, perhaps the best thing to do is tell your partner what you're feeling. Tell her you feel like jumping up and making a sandwich, or turning on the TV, or taking a walk, or whatever—tell her and don't do it. Resist the urge to do something and stay with her. Kiss, hug, talk, listen. It may be uncomfortable if you've never done it before, but try to stick it out for a few times and see if you don't start feeling more comfortable. We've worked with a number of men on this issue and almost all have found that they quickly become more comfortable with this kind of intimacy. They were soon participating for their own satisfaction, not just to please their partners.

Now that you have read about what women say they like and how they function, you may be wondering, "How does this apply to my partner? How should I act with her?" Many men ask these questions and we have a simple answer. Namely, that we don't have the foggiest notion.

We can only repeat what we have already said several times—there are tremendous individual variations. What is arousing for one woman may be repugnant to another.

> When I was in high school, the word was that blowing in a girl's ear and putting your tongue in there was a good way to get her hot. So, not knowing what else to do, I always did the ear thing. Some girls obviously liked it. But others didn't, and one said that it was a complete turn-off.

What is true about ears and blowing in them is true for every other part of the body and every other technique—some women will like it and some won't.

Take women's breasts, for example. Most men seem to be turned-on by breasts; by seeing them, touching them, kissing them. And they assume that women will be very aroused by such actions. There is no question that this assumption is true for many women. But just how common is women's sensitivity to breast stimulation? Probably not as common as most men think. Kinsey reported that most women were only moderately aroused by having their breasts stimulated. Lonnie Barbach, who has probably worked with more women on sexual issues than any other therapist, estimates that about 60 percent of them get a lot of pleasure from having their breasts touched, while the rest either get only a small amount of pleasure from it or are relatively indifferent to such caresses.

This presents an interesting problem, one that is especially evident in new relationships but also present in many older ones as well. The man, we have been

taught, should somehow know what his partner likes.
But how can he manage this if women are different?
Reading all the books in the world won't help since his
women may have different tastes than those discussed
in the books. Besides, even the books differ. Lots of
experience is often thought to be a panacea, but it
isn't. What worked for the last partner, or even the last
twenty partners, may not be what the present partner
wants. It would be nice to think that the woman will
come to the rescue, clearly letting her partner know
what she wants. It sometimes happens this way, but
rarely. As we saw in our discussion of the questionnaire study, many women are uncomfortable stating
their preferences, particularly in a new relationship.
What, then, is a man to do?

There are several possibilities. You can just do
whatever you want, either not caring about her or figuring that if she wants something different, she'll say
so. However, it should be clear from what we presented earlier in the chapter that this option is bound
to create problems. Women are less and less willing
to put up with it.

Another alternative, used by many men, is to play
Sherlock Holmes and attempt, using whatever clues
are available, to figure out what would please her. The
problem with this method is that it only works well
when your partner gives frequent, clear, and relatively
consistent clues. Otherwise, you are going to be working very hard trying to decipher all of her nonverbal
communications. You will make many errors and put a
tremendous amount of pressure on yourself.

Our own bias, one that agrees with what many
women want and that has worked very well with the
men who have used it under our direction, is for open
communication. Since your life will be much easier if
you know what pleases her, ask her or somehow give
her permission to tell you, perhaps by voicing your
own preferences. As we noted earlier, this permission
is very important to many women.

The first time I had sex with Carla I asked, "What
would you like?" Not exactly eloquent or brilliant, but

it produced some interesting results. She told me what she wanted and we had a very nice time. A few days later she said that since she had orgasms through oral or manual stimulation but not with intercourse, she never indicated her needs the first few times she was with a man. Only after they knew each other better and were more comfortable sexually would she say what she wanted. But my simple question had allowed her to express what she wanted the first time we were together sexually. She appreciated my interest and I must say that I was quite proud of myself.

The power of a few words is well illustrated by this example. Asking, however, should not be confused with demanding. By asking your partner what she likes, you are giving her the opportunity to express herself if she so desires. Be aware that she may not choose to answer, at least not then. For many women, being asked what they want by a man is such a new idea that they need some time to get accustomed to it. It is also possible that she hasn't given much thought to her preferences. If you get no response, feel free to do whatever you want. Do not push her to answer. If you indicate your interest and willingness to listen, you are doing all that can reasonably be expected. The chances are good that she will get around to telling you when she is ready, or the next time you ask in a gentle and nondemanding way.

If initiating this type of discussion is very difficult for you, you might find it easier by making use of an external prop. This chapter is such a prop. Asking her to read it, followed by a discussion of the points she agrees and disagrees with, can be valuable.

14

On Not Lasting
Long Enough

Lack of ejaculatory control, usually called premature ejaculation, is one of the most common sexual complaints among American men. Although the phenomenon itself has been known for quite some time, it was not considered a major problem until very recently. As long as the woman's satisfaction and orgasm were not considered to be important, there was relatively little concern with how long a man could last. As long as he enjoyed himself, what was the problem? Just thirty years ago, Kinsey reported that 75 percent of the men he interviewed ejaculated within two minutes of beginning intercourse. While he recognized that this might be "inconvenient and unfortunate" from the point of view of their partners, he didn't consider such occurrences to be premature and seemed hard put to figure out what the problem might be.

Much has changed since Kinsey did his work. Although men are as performance-oriented as ever, perhaps even more so, the criteria of a good sexual performance have changed. It is no longer sufficient to "get a lot," although that is still important. The real test of a good performance these days is the ability to satisfy one's partner, usually defined as giving her at least one, but preferably more, good orgasms in intercourse.

With this change in definition of male sexual prowess has come first an interest, then a concern, and now almost an obsession with lasting longer. As might be expected, the people who write about sex have done their share to promote this obsession. In his *How to Get More out of Sex,* David Reuben unmercifully lambasts men who ejaculate quickly, implying that they are immature and accusing them of masturbating in the vagina. He warns that it is the man's job to keep his penis in his partner's vagina long enough to provide her with "satisfactory service." *The Sensuous Man* tells us that premature ejaculation is a "major disaster." It mentions the possibility of satisfying your partner through oral or manual play after you've had your orgasm, but then discounts the utility of this approach because "the two of you can't really get the most out of your sex life unless you can prolong your intercourse long enough for her to have an orgasm (or lots of orgasms)." And Gail Sheehy in her book *Passages* several times mentions the importance of the man withholding ejaculation long enough to bring his partner "through an ascending chain of orgasms."

Lasting a long time in intercourse seems to be a very important item. After all, who would want to be a major disaster? Or cheat their partners of ascending chains of orgasms?

Many men have been influenced by this type of thinking and have sought treatment to help them last longer. They are convinced that sex will be much better when they can have intercourse for longer periods of time. Their partners will become orgasmic or perhaps multiply orgasmic. And sex will just be better. Everyone will be happy and sated.

We're sorry to disappoint you, but it may not be that way at all. In order to explain this statement, we need to look more closely at what is meant by premature ejaculation. It is not a monolithic entity and, in fact, includes men of quite different ejaculatory behaviors.

There are men who ejaculate at the slightest provocation, sometimes even before touching their partners but more typically shortly after the commencement of any genital contact. Another group of men come as soon as their penises enter the vagina or within a few seconds of vaginal containment. Still other men can thrust for a few minutes before ejaculating, but they do not feel any sense of control over when they come.

The lack of ability consciously to control when ejaculation occurs is what characterizes all the men in the above categories. Ejaculations sort of sneak up on them; many report that "all of a sudden, it just happens." Sometimes they have some warning and realize they will soon come, but there's nothing they can do about it. Anything they do to hold off ejaculation only seems to speed it up.

These men are the ones who benefit most from learning ejaculatory control. All those we have worked with enjoyed sex more when they had acquired better voluntary control. Their own orgasms felt better—fuller or more complete, they said—and their partners appreciated the greater duration of intercourse, although many of the partners still did not become orgasmic through intercourse. For the types of men we have been talking about, then, it often is advisable to develop control over their ejaculatory processes.

However, there are many other men who want to last longer. They believe their partners would enjoy sex more or become orgasmic if only they (the men) could last longer. Which sounds reasonable and considerate until you realize that many of these men already have good ejaculatory control. Some of them are able, when they desire, to have intercourse for from ten to thirty minutes.

We'll never forget the man who called himself a premature ejaculator even though fairly regularly he lasted for forty-five minutes of vigorous thrusting. We know he lasted this long because his partner confirmed it. Actually, she had never been orgasmic in intercourse and had no desire to become so. She much preferred shorter intercourse because she sometimes

became so sore through almost an hour of thrusting
that she could barely sit down the next day. That had
little influence on the thinking of our client, who was
convinced that she would have orgasms if only he
could last an hour.

It is only natural to assume that a few minutes
longer might do the trick (more enjoyment, orgasms,
multiple orgasms) but this is often an illusion. If you
can already last for ten to fifteen minutes, or even
longer, the chances that your partner will become orgasmic or find more contentment if you last longer are
highly improbable.

If your partner is not orgasmic in the length of time
you usually last, it might be a good idea to talk to her
about what she wants. Perhaps she is orgasmic in other
ways and doesn't care about becoming so in intercourse. Much of the obsession with lasting longer is
due to the exaggerated importance most of us have
given to intercourse. Maybe she would prefer to get
what she wants through some other sexual activity.
Whatever her feelings in this regard, we hope you can
listen to her. Don't be like the man we cited in the example who thought he knew how things should be for
his lover. And remember that there is nothing inherently better about long-lasting sex than the shorter
variety. Sex that *has* to last a certain length of time,
especially long periods of time, can be very boring.
It can also give you a real pain in the crotch.

It is interesting that despite all the interest in premature ejaculation, there is no agreed-upon definition of what it is. Some people, like David Reuben,
think a man is premature unless he can thrust for five
to ten minutes. Others, following Masters and Johnson, define prematurity as the inability to satisfy the
woman 50 percent of the time in intercourse. Both of
these definitions have serious drawbacks.

The definition we use is quite simple and does away
with the term premature ejaculation. We are interested
in a man's ability to exercise voluntary control over
his ejaculatory process. This is not to say that anyone
can be in total control of such a bodily function. Rather, a man with good control is one who usually can

decide approximately when he will ejaculate. He usually can last a long time when he wants, and he also can come quickly if he so desires. His control of the process allows him to do what feels right at the moment.

Of course, a man without this type of control doesn't necessarily have a problem. If he and his partner are content, there is no reason for change. Only if you are dissatisfied with your lack of control should you follow the procedures in the next two chapters.

Most of the men we've worked with have been consistent in their lack of control. They've experienced it all their lives and with all partners. But there are many exceptions. Some have reasonably good control in some activities, like masturbation or when their partners stimulate them by hand, but not in others, usually intercourse. Some other men report having had good control at some time in their lives but having since lost the ability to delay ejaculation. Still others report good control with certain partners but not others. A great many men come very quickly the first time or times they have sex with a new partner. This is usually a transitory phenomenon, with control returning after the man is more comfortable with his new lover.

If your problem is situational—that is, if it occurs at some times but not others, with some partners but not others—you need to consider if your conditions are being met when you don't have control. The chances are that they are not, and you'll probably reap more benefit from working on them than from doing exercises to develop control. Or perhaps you can do both.

Just as there is no consensus about a definition for premature ejaculation, there is no agreement on what causes it. There has been speculation that men's socialization predisposes them to speedy ejaculations. It is true that men are taught to put a lot of value on speed. And many of our early sexual experiences, whether masturbating in the bathroom or having sex in the backseat of a car, carried the risk of discovery, so the quicker we got them over with the less the chance of being found out. While this type of thinking seems plausible, it doesn't explain why, given similar early experiences, some of us lack ejaculatory control while others have enough to spare.

Some in the psychoanalytic tradition have argued that coming quickly is a neurotic process, a manifestation of conflicts regarding women. They believe that such conflicts must be worked out before the man can learn to delay his ejaculations. However, since treatment based on this idea has not been notably successful, while more direct behavioral approaches have been, serious doubt is cast on the credibility of the whole argument. This, of course, does not rule out the possibility that some cases of premature ejaculation may be caused or maintained by internal or interpersonal conflicts. But even in such cases, the suggestions in the next two chapters, combined with the fulfilling of conditions, are usually all that is needed to resolve the difficulty.

Despite the fact that our understanding of what causes lack of ejaculatory control is inadequate, solutions to the problem do exist. The most widely employed remedies, however, are the ones with the least value. Every man who has come sooner than he wanted has tried to control his ejaculations, usually by gritting his teeth and will in an effort to hold them back. This method rarely works since it only creates tension, which in itself can trigger quick ejaculations.

Another popular method, still advocated by some authorities, attempts to decrease excitement by telling the man to "think of other things" while he is having sex. While this approach sometimes works, the price is tremendous since the man is asked not to experience his good feelings. What is the point of lasting longer or having sex at all if you are not allowed to enjoy it?

We have the same objection to the use of numbing ointments. These preparations, which can be purchased at most drugstores, partially anesthetize the penis. A numb penis, the theory goes, should last longer than one that feels more. These ointments sometimes work but often they do not. If you are considering using one of them, you might want to consider the costs. Not only do you sacrifice some enjoyment but, since you don't learn anything about controlling ejaculations, you become forever dependent upon the ointment.

Our thinking is that lasting longer should not involve the numbing of feeling. Rather, it should allow you to feel more, to enjoy and luxuriate in high levels of sexual excitement and sensation for as long as you like.

There are several methods that allow you to do just that. Two of them depend on the ability to control the muscles in the pelvis, the muscles developed by the Kegel exercise in Chapter 7. One technique requires that you relax these muscles when you feel close to orgasm, thus delaying ejaculation. The other technique is just the reverse, tightening the same muscles as you near ejaculation. They both work, but experimentation is necessary to determine exactly when to tense or relax the muscles. We will not say any more about these procedures but you might want to explore them on your own. You should first, however, practice the Kegel exercise until you are in good touch with the pelvic muscles.

Both of these methods, as well as the others that have been successful in developing ejaculatory control, have one point in common—training the man to pay attention to his feelings of sexual excitement. Unlike the think-of-something-else notion, the effective methods ask that you pay more attention to the good feelings. By attending to these feelings, you know when you are approaching ejaculation and can take some simple steps to delay it.

While we do not understand why some men have acquired good control with no conscious effort or training, it seems to be true that all, or at least most, men who have control make adjustments in their behavior when they feel close to orgasm. One of us, trying to determine how men controlled their ejaculations, observed that he always changed his manner of thrusting when he felt close to orgasm but didn't want it to happen yet. He then asked a number of other men with good control to observe their behavior to see if they made any adjustments to help them last longer. All of them, including several who before observing themselves adamantly denied making any adjustments, discovered that they did indeed make changes in their behavior. The type of changes made varied considerably: squeezing or relaxing the pelvic muscles, slowing the tempo, changing the depth of thrusting, or changing the type of thrusting (e.g., from in and out to circular motions).

The procedures in the next two chapters are designed to enable you to do what these men do. They somehow acquired their skills without any special training but, at the end of your training program, your skills will be the same as theirs.

Without realizing it, you have already successfully negotiated a very similar training process: when you learned to control your urinary function. When you were very small, you had no control over urination; it just happened when your bladder reached a certain degree of fullness. But then your parents let you know that this was not satisfactory and that you had to take charge of the situation. You gradually learned to recognize the sensations in your body announcing that you were about to urinate, and you could signal that you had to go to the bathroom. At this point your training was incomplete. You could tell if something was about to happen but you couldn't delay its occurrence.

As time went on, you completed your training. You not only knew when urination was imminent but you could also exert some control over when it happened. You might realize that you had to urinate, but if you were in the middle of an interesting game you could squeeze some muscles and wiggle around enough to hold it back, at least for a while.

All this is many years behind you, of course, and you probably have no memory of the experiences. The processes of control have been under automatic pilot for years and you may not be aware that you are doing anything to delay the onset of urination, just as some of the men we questioned didn't realize that they did anything to delay ejaculation. If you have any doubts about what we are saying, focus your attention in your crotch the next time you have to go to the bathroom but are in a situation that requires you to wait.

What you need to learn to control your ejaculations is not much different from what you learned then, and learned very successfully. And this time it will be much easier. Your body is better coordinated and your mind is far more developed, two factors that will help considerably.

Our approach in developing ejaculatory control is based on a simple technique developed in the 1950s by James Semans. The method consisted in the stimulation of the client's penis by his partner until he felt the sensations signaling that ejaculation was near. His partner stopped stimulation, resuming when the man no longer felt close to ejaculation. With practice, the man could enjoy more and more stimulation without ejaculating. Semans's method is the foundation of almost all of the successful procedures used by sex therapists today for developing ejaculatory control.

Masters and Johnson took Semans's stop-start method and added a squeeze; instead of merely stopping the stimulation of the penis, the woman squeezes it where the head and shaft join. We have used both the stop-start and the squeeze and found that they both give the same results. Since the squeeze is a bit more difficult to learn, we no longer use it.

Semans worked only with men who had cooperative partners, and Masters and Johnson argued that ejaculatory control could not be developed without such a partner. Fortunately, they were wrong. We have devised some methods that do not require a partner's participation and that have yielded the same impressive results as the partner exercises.

If you want to gain more control over your ejaculatory process so that you can enjoy intense sexual pleasure without immediately ejaculating, go on to the next two chapters. The training will of course involve conscious attention and effort at first. As time goes on, however, you will be less and less aware that you are monitoring your arousal level and making adjustments in your behavior. You will consciously forget about making adjustments and be free to enjoy fully your partner and yourself.

15

Starting to Develop
Ejaculatory Control

Ejaculatory control can be effectively learned either on your own or by doing exercises with a partner. We suggest that even if you want to do the partner exercises, you do at least the first masturbation exercise in this chapter before starting to work with her. The reason for this suggestion is that it is easier to learn the rudiments of control without her distracting presence. Once you have mastered the fundamentals, it will be easier to work with her.

If you absolutely don't want to do the masturbation exercises, you should at least read this chapter before turning to the partner exercises in the next chapter. Should you encounter problems in doing the partner exercises, it may be necessary for you to reconsider your stance regarding the masturbation exercises.

The first step in attaining ejaculatory control is learning to pay attention to your arousal level in a sexual situation so that you will know when you need to change your behavior to delay ejaculation.

Figure 8 (page 266), representing a hypothetical sexual experience, will help facilitate your understanding of arousal levels and the adjustments you need to

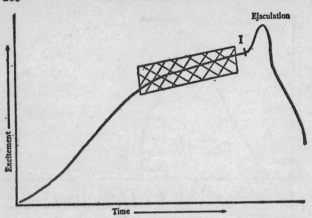

Figure 8: Male sexual response with ejaculatory control

make. The flat part of the curve, what Masters and Johnson refer to as the plateau phase, is usually experienced as very pleasurable. Men who can last as long as they like do so by spending as much time as they want at this level of excitement. Those who do not have ejaculatory control do not spend much time here. In fact, their arousal level does not seem to flatten out at all, going directly from zero to orgasm, as illustrated in Figure 9 (page 267). What is needed is a way of staying at the plateau level for longer periods of time, thus prolonging the pleasure and delaying the ejaculation.

Point I in Figure 8 stands for inevitability, shorthand for Masters and Johnson's sense of ejaculatory inevitability. This is the place, a few seconds before the ejaculate appears, where the man senses that ejaculation is about to occur and that there's nothing he can do about it. It will happen even if all stimulation ceases. The reason for this is, as we said in Chapter 7, that the internal sex organs have already begun contracting, starting the ejaculate on its way through the penis.

Before the point of inevitability there is an area (the shaded portion of the curve in Figure 8) where, if stimulation ceases, ejaculation will not occur. This means that you can enjoy high levels of arousal and,

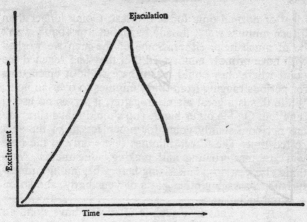

Figure 9: Male sexual response with ejaculatory control

providing you stop stimulation somewhere in this area, not ejaculate. There is no precise way of demarcating the point at which you should stop. Any time you are feeling very excited but not yet at inevitability is acceptable. With practice you will learn where you need to stop.

You will be asked to masturbate to a high level of excitement, stopping when you feel close to ejaculation, to learn more about where you should stop. You will undoubtedly make some "mistakes"—stopping too late to prevent ejaculation—on your way to discovering the boundaries of the stopping area.

Stopping stimulation, meaning complete cessation of stimulating the genitals, is simply a training procedure and will not always be necessary. After establishing good control using the stop-start method, you can learn to make more subtle adjustments that will allow you to control your ejaculations without stopping.

The following guidelines apply to all the exercises in this chapter:

1. Except where noted, each exercise requires fifteen minutes. We use fifteen minutes because it has produced good results, not because we think this is an

ideal or normal time for sex to last. Going longer than fifteen minutes won't do any harm but it probably won't be of much help, either. Some of the men we worked with have proudly announced that they had reached the point where they could masturbate without ejaculating for periods ranging from thirty minutes to over an hour. While this is a great attention-getter, it serves no useful function. On the other hand, you should make sure you are not consistently going for much less than the suggested time. The fifteen minutes refers only to the time you are masturbating and making adjustments. Anything else you do—fantasizing before beginning to masturbate, massaging other parts of your body, and so on —is not included.

2. If you want to ejaculate after you have done an exercise, you may, but it is best if you go slowly, focusing in your penis and being aware of the point of inevitability as you reach it and pass through it. Done this way, ejaculating after an exercise will be an integral part of your learning better ejaculatory control.

3. Since you want to develop new patterns of functioning, it is important to be consistent in your masturbatory practices. Once you start with the exercises, it is best not to alternate with your old ways of masturbating, for this would only impede your progress.

4. The exercises should be done at least three or four times a week. In general, the more frequently you do them, the sooner you will reach your goals.

5. At times you may find that you have difficulty getting an erection, either before starting an exercise or after stopping to allow your arousal level to decrease. This is not a cause for concern. If playing with your penis, accompanied by fantasy if you like, does not result in an erection in a few minutes, do not try to force it. Come back to the exercise later when you are in a sexier mood.

6. Do the exercises in the order in which they are presented. Two criteria should be satisfied before moving from one exercise to the next. First, you should be able to last the fifteen minutes with no more than two or three stops. Second, you should feel reasonably comfortable doing the exercise, confident that you can

delay ejaculation. If the next exercise gives you a lot of trouble and the situation does not improve after several attempts, go back to the previous one until you are more comfortable with it. We hope you won't be discouraged if you need to return to an exercise you've already done. It probably means only that you tried to move too quickly through the exercises, a mistake many men make. Remember that you're trying to learn to take your time. See if you can take your time doing this. The process should be a relaxed and comfortable one, without any pressure or hurry.

The last thing to be dealt with before getting to the exercises is what to do about sex with a partner. Since you are learning new habits, it is best if what you do with a partner does not undermine your learning, something which can happen if your sex with her is done in the old, fast way. There are several options. The first is simply not to have sex with anyone until you have completed all the exercises. Obviously, this is not an acceptable way for many men, but does fit for some who have no regular partners.

The other two alternatives consist of different ways of applying your learning to sex with a partner. One way is to have as much sex as you want with her, but not intercourse until you feel you have good control with manual and/or oral stimulation. The reason for excluding intercourse at the beginning is that for most men intercourse is the most difficult activity in which to maintain ejaculatory control. Read the section called Ejaculatory Control without Partner Exercises in the next chapter and follow the suggestions given there.

We have found that the method of not having intercourse until you have good control works best, but we know there are men who are unwilling to accept such a limitation on their activities. If you feel you must have intercourse, do so but be sure to follow the guidelines given in the next chapter. You will probably find that many times you don't have much control, but as long as you continue with the masturbation exercises and following the guidelines, it should develop in time.

Finally, the exercises.

The first exercise is the basic one in this series. You will use it to determine the point of ejaculatory inevitability, if you are not already familiar with it, and the points at which you must stop stimulation to prevent ejaculation. As we said earlier, there will probably be times when you stop too late. You may need to do this a few times to learn where you need to stop.

EXERCISE 15–1: STOP-START MASTURBATION

Step A: With a dry hand (no lotion or other lubrication) masturbate for fifteen minutes without ejaculating. Focus in your penis so you will know how aroused you are. When you are very excited and feel that you are approaching the point of inevitability, stop masturbating and do nothing but focus in your penis. The urge to ejaculate will subside in anywhere from thirty seconds to two or three minutes. You may also experience a partial or complete loss of erection; this is common and nothing to be concerned about. When the desire to ejaculate has subsided, resume masturbation. Stop time, the time when you are waiting for your excitement to abate, is included in the fifteen minutes.

You will probably have to stop a number of times when you first do the exercise. As you continue doing it, you will better learn when to stop and how long to wait, and the number of times you need to stop will decrease.

When you feel confident of your control and need only two or three stops during the fifteen minutes, go on to Step B.

Step B: This is exactly the same as Step A except that you now use a lubricant on your hand. You might want to reread the section on lubricants at the end of Chapter 10.

POSSIBLE PROBLEMS

1. You are practicing brinksmanship, stopping only a split second before reaching inevitability. Nothing useful is gained by this practice and it can cause problems. Waiting until the last second can increase anxiety, resulting in unnecessary ejaculations. You can stop any time you are feeling very good and excited.

2. You find that you need to stop again as soon as you resume masturbating. This means that you are not allowing sufficient time for the ejaculatory urge to diminish. Take longer stops.

3. You don't seem to be making any progress, i.e., you don't learn when to stop and the number of stops required doesn't diminish. This may mean that you are too tense while doing

the exercise. Do what you need to ensure that you are in a comfortable, reasonably relaxed mood before beginning. You might benefit from rereading Chapter 9.

You have taken the first steps toward developing voluntary control over your ejaculatory process and may be feeling like one man who said at this point, "By God, now I know I can handle the problem; I haven't felt this confident in years." You are ready to start making more subtle adjustments which will allow you to maintain ejaculatory control without stopping.

Many men think of sex in terms of a very rapid, in-and-out thrusting of the penis, whether it is thrusting in a vagina, hand, mouth, or whatever. It simply has not occurred to them that other ways are both possible and enjoyable. As we said before, men with good control rely on many other ways than just the quick in-and-out. They have found ways that are pleasurable but not so exciting as to bring on immediate ejaculation.

One man, almost legendary for his lengthy sexual encounters, shared his secret with us. Many years ago he considered himself to be a sexual flop because he came very quickly when he received any stimulation from a partner. He had no one from whom to get help, this being long before the advent of sex therapy, so he decided to experiment with different masturbation techniques. He discovered that by using a circular motion, employing the base of his penis as a fulcrum and moving the shaft and head in small circles, he had complete control of when he ejaculated. He then transferred his discovery to sex with partners. In intercourse, for example, instead of moving in and out of the vagina, he inserted his penis as far as possible and, moving his hips in a circular motion, moved it around the vagina. When he wanted to come, he started thrusting in and out. Both he and his partners were quite satisfied with the results.

We are not suggesting that you try to become a legend in your own time, but we hope you can learn from this story. There are types of stimulation that feel very good without bringing on ejaculation. The next exercise will give you an opportunity to discover some of the ways that work for you.

EXERCISE 15–2: MASTURBATING WITH SUBTLE ADJUSTMENTS

Focusing in your penis, masturbate for fifteen minutes without ejaculating and without stopping. When you reach high levels of excitement, make changes in your masturbatory behavior to decrease the arousal. Changes you can make include: slowing down the pace; changing the amount of pressure you are applying; varying the site of maximum stimulation, for example, by stimulating only the shaft of your penis rather than the head; changing the type of stroke, for example, using shorter strokes or circular motions. You might also want to try relaxing or tensing your pelvic muscles, as suggested in the last chapter. Needless to say, try one change at a time. Find out what works best for you, then stay with it and master it.

The more subtle types of adjustment need to be made a bit sooner than stopping. If you make them too late, you can always stop to prevent ejaculation. When you feel you are no longer close to ejaculation, you can resume the more arousing type of stimulation if you want.

POSSIBLE PROBLEM
Progress is more difficult now than with the stopping exercises. This is to be expected. Finding the changes that work best takes some time, as does determining just when to make the changes. Do not be afraid to make them very early; there's no rule that says you have to start sex with wild in-and-out thrusting.

Many men find that their new ways of moving are quite enjoyable and come to prefer them over their old ways. Going slower, making shorter thrusts, moving in circular ways, or squeezing the pelvic muscles just become part of the way they like to have sex. When this happens, lasting as long as they like is no longer an issue.

For many men, what has been presented so far will be sufficient to develop a high degree of ejaculatory control, and they will want to move on to partner sex. They should first, however, do the last exercise in this series, 15–5, which need be done only once. Other men, however, will not yet feel ready to move on and, for them, we suggest two fantasy exercises.

We have found that fantasy is an excellent means of making the transition from masturbation exercises to partner sex. Our use of fantasy might best be called role-rehearsal. Fantasizing a behavior under controlled conditions prepares you to carry out that behavior in your life and also reduces some of the anxiety you may feel about it. You will be asked to fantasize sexual situations while masturbating with the stop-start method, and later, while employing the more subtle means of delaying ejaculation. You will be in a much better position to have ejaculatory control with a partner after doing these exercises.

Some people find it easier to have clear fantasies or images than others. Most of us have some difficulty, at least initially, seeing distinct pictures in our minds. In general, the more you practice, the more vivid and lifelike the images get. Even if this does not occur—and we know that some men never develop clear images—the fantasy exercises can still work. Having fantasies that are less than clear, or having thoughts or feelings rather than pictures, will do as well.

What is most important, whether you have thoughts, feelings, or images, is that you be able really to imagine the scene or idea you are dealing with. You can help yourself get more fully into the fantasy by noticing details. If the scene you are working on is of your partner stimulating your penis with her hand, for example, ask yourself how firmly she is holding the penis. Is she using long or short strokes? What about the texture and temperature of her hand? What's going on in your penis as she touches it? When you fantasize intercourse, be aware of how your bodies fit together, the temperature, texture, and wetness of the vagina, and so forth. Any details that will help you feel more like you are really there will be useful.

EXERCISE 15–3: STOP-START MASTURBATION WITH FANTASY

Step A: Using the stop-start method, masturbate for fifteen minutes while fantasizing having sex with a partner. Start the fantasy with the first touch or kiss and go through all the steps that might occur in this imagined sexual event, or at least as many of them as you can comfortably get through in fifteen minutes. You probably won't get through an entire sexual event in one session. That's fine. Next time you do the exercise, start the fantasy where you left off the last time.

As part of the fantasy, see yourself needing to stop with your partner and doing so. When you stop in the fantasy, stop your masturbating. When the urge to ejaculate has subsided, resume the fantasy and the masturbation. Be sure to include some scenes of needing to stop during intercourse. Needing to stop can be dictated by two criteria: when you actually feel you need to stop to prevent ejaculation and at places in the fantasy where you feel you might need to stop in reality. Use both; just be sure to stop masturbating at the same time you stop in the fantasy.

Many men have trouble maintaining control with some of the fantasy scenes. The two places where they have the most trouble are when imagining entering the vagina and when thrusting becomes hard and fast. Since what gives you trouble in fantasy will tend to do the same in reality, you want to work with the scenes that are difficult. When you run into a difficult scene that does not get easier after several attempts, go to Step B.

Step B: Instead of masturbating to a fantasy of a whole sexual encounter, fantasize only the scene that gives you trouble. Make sure you are relaxed before beginning. Masturbate slowly, get into the fantasy as fully as possible while at the same time remaining aware of your level of excitement, and stop *before* you need to, both in the fantasy and in your masturbating. Go through the scene again and again until fifteen minutes are up. If at any time during the exercise you feel tense, discontinue it and do something to get more comfortable, then resume the exercise.

As you get more comfortable with this scene, you can shift to stopping when, rather than before, you need to. When you are comfortable and in control while fantasizing the difficult scene, return to Step A and incorporate this scene into the larger fantasy.

If you have trouble with more than one scene, work through all of them, one at a time, in the manner suggested above.

POSSIBLE PROBLEMS

1. You have difficulty staying with the fantasy, perhaps because of drifting into other thoughts and fantasies. When this happens, simply come back to the scene you were imagining. You will need to do this a number of times every session.

2. You don't stop in time to delay ejaculation because you

forget about your excitement level. It is, of course, essential that you remain aware of how aroused you are so that you can stop in time. This is difficult for some people, since it means you have to focus on both the fantasy and your arousal. You can try keeping most of your attention on how excited you are, even if this means less distinct images. A better way is to record the fantasy and play it while you masturbate. Since you won't have to put any effort into developing the fantasy, you can listen while putting your attention on your level of arousal.

3. You rush through the fantasy in an effort to complete it in one session. This exercise was not intended to be mastered in one session. The important thing is that it be carried out as suggested and without hurry. You need to get through all the possible scenes that might occur in a real sexual event, but there is no need to do so in one masturbation session. Speed is not only unimportant, but it can impede your progress.

When you have mastered that exercise, go on to the next one, which is quite similar.

EXERCISE 15–4: MASTURBATING WITH SUBTLE ADJUSTMENTS AND FANTASY

This exercise is identical to 15–3, with the exception that you now use the more subtle changes you discovered in Exercise 15–2 rather than stopping. Follow all other directions for 15–3. As you make adjustments in your masturbation, imagine yourself making them in the fantasy. Should any scenes cause you discomfort or make you feel that you are losing control, work through them using the suggestions in Step B of 15–3.

You should by now feel even more confident of your ability to exercise control over when you ejaculate. The next exercise sounds silly but is important, and you can have lots of fun with it. Whatever happens, it can be a good learning experience. It requires a minimum of time and need only be done once or twice.

EXERCISE 15–5: QUICKIE MASTURBATION WITH FOCUS

Focusing in your penis, masturbate and ejaculate as quickly as possible. Try to come even faster than you did before starting your training program. Keep focusing until you ejaculate.

If you do come fast, you can learn something about what makes for quick ejaculations. If you find it difficult to do, you will realize how far you've progressed. In either case, you win. And that is the point of the exercise, and of sex.

_____

You might have found the exercise difficult to do because you were afraid that it might undo all that you have learned. Fear not, it will only broaden your horizons. You can control your ejaculations so that you can last a long time. See if you can also control them so that you can last a short time. You now have options; use them.

To use a bad pun, you've come a long way, and are ready to use your newly acquired control with a partner.

16

Lasting Longer
with a Partner

In this chapter we present two basic approaches for developing ejaculatory control with a partner. The first thing you should decide is which best fits your situation and desires. Whichever you choose, it will help if you have read and understood Chapter 12, Dealing with a Partner, and have done at least some of the masturbation exercises in the last chapter.

One approach requires a partner who is willing to work with you on a series of exercises, 16–1 through 16–6. The general outline was developed by Semans, elaborated by Masters and Johnson and others, and has been widely employed. Its main drawback is the necessity of a cooperative partner with whom to do the exercises.

The second approach is not dependent on a cooperative partner and involve no exercises with a partner. It requires complete mastery of the masturbation exercises in the last chapter and the willingness to follow a set of guidelines when having sex with a lover. This approach, though not as well known as the partner exercise method, has yielded approximately the same results. It is presented first in this chapter so that those with partners can get a feel for it before making a decision about whether to do the partner exercises.

Ejaculatory Control without Partner Exercises

It is crucial that you have mastered the exercises in Chapter 15. You should be able to masturbate for fifteen minutes without ejaculating and without stopping. The more subtle adjustments should be sufficient for you to control your ejaculations. You should keep masturbating with subtle adjustments even after you no longer have trouble lasting as long as you want. When you start going out with someone with whom you might want to have sex, incorporate her into your masturbation fantasies.

It is also essential that you have done, and feel comfortable with, the assertiveness exercises in Chapters 6 and 12. The masturbation exercises and other training procedures will do you no good at all unless you are willing and able to get what you need in a sexual situation. The guidelines below assume that you already have some skill and confidence in asserting yourself. It won't always be easy, but if you have done all the preparatory work, you are ready to use your ejaculatory control with a lover.

Most of the principles you need to follow with a partner have already been given in the section on sex with a new partner in Chapter 12. They should be adhered to without exception. The suggestions below supplement that list.

1. Don't engage in intercourse until all your conditions are met and you are comfortable with her. This means that your first few experiences should not include intercourse. Let her play with your penis and make adjustments to allow you to delay ejaculation a reasonable length of time. This is a good way of checking your control with her. If you have trouble lasting with hand or mouth stimulation, you'll probably have more trouble with intercourse. Have intercourse only after you've established good control in other activities.

2. Stay focused in your penis during all sexual ac-

tivities with her and make adjustments early. It is important that you be able to indicate that you want to stop, should a stop be advisable.

3. Check your arousal level before vaginal insertion. If it is high, make some adjustments before entering her (e.g., stopping for a minute or so; squeezing your pelvic muscles). Don't start moving immediately after you have entered. Rest for a minute or so and be aware of your arousal level.

4. Go slowly in all your sexual activities, especially in intercourse. Take your time and experience all the sensations, making adjustments when necessary.

5. Don't expect things to work perfectly in the beginning. They won't. If you run into a problem that doesn't improve after a few experiences, you need not panic. You have the skills to work it out. Figure out as precisely as possible what the difficulty is: for example, "I have good control except when she starts moving wildly in intercourse." Then find an appropriate exercise to help you deal with it. In the example given, you could use a masturbation exercise, masturbating to a fantasy of her moving wildly in intercourse, going over the scene again and again while making adjustments to retain control. When you have mastered that, you can have intercourse with her again and now be more confident of your ability to control your ejaculations. If this isn't sufficient, you could ask her to move more slowly, at a pace at which you have good control. Then have her gradually increase the tempo. If you do this a few times, you will extend your control to cover the movements that at first gave you problems.

Remember that you can always ask her to slow down or stop if you feel you are losing control.

6. There will be times when you come fast, either because you lost control or because you wanted to. Don't apologize in either case. Enjoy yourself and do something for your partner if she so desires.

These principles should be carried out to the letter when you are starting to have sex with a new partner or trying to change sexual patterns with a familiar lover. These are the most anxious and trying times, so go slowly and follow the rules. As you become more comfortable with exercising your ejaculatory control with her, you will become less conscious of following the principles and they will become automatic.

That's really all there is to it. The program is simple but quite effective. Should it not work well for you, you should consider whether you have truly mastered the masturbation exercises and are following the guidelines. If you need to return to the exercises to learn the fundamentals better, do so. The same is true for the principles. They have to be followed. Do what is necessary to put them into effect. Should there still be difficulties, you have the option of doing the partner exercises.

Partner Exercises for Lasting Longer

Before undertaking the program, discuss it with your lover. She should read Chapter 13 and the exercises in this chapter so she will understand what is being asked of her. Discuss your feelings and her feelings about the project and work out any differences before starting.

Everything depends upon clear communication and understanding and, since you don't have a therapist to help you, you need to expend some effort to ensure that the two of you agree on what is going to happen. Your partner should understand that the exercises constitute a training program and will not be needed forever. Since how long they are needed is largely a function of how often they are done, you should reach an agreement about frequency. She should also understand that the exercises need to be executed exactly as described and that you are in total control when the exercises are being done—of the type of stimulation, of when to stop and when to resume. You should be very clear about your willingness to satisfy her manually or orally before or after doing an exercise. Problems often arise because the woman feels she is doing all the work and getting nothing in return. Do everything possible to prevent this from becoming an issue. There will probably be misunderstandings and differences of opinion over this and other matters. They need to be talked out and resolved as quickly as possible.

It is very important that you don't restrict the physical activities with your partner to these exercises. Allow time and space for holding, hugging, kissing, taking baths together, and any other mutually enjoyable expressions of physical affection.

Since the stop-start method is the one used in the exercises, your partner should clearly understand that she must stop immediately when you tell her to. You need to work out how you are going to let her know when to stop. Most men simply say "stop" or "now," but any language is fine as long as you both know what is meant. The language must be spoken; nonverbal messages do not work well in these exercises.

The following guidelines apply to all the exercises in this chapter unless otherwise indicated:

1. Both of you should read, discuss, and understand each exercise before you do it.
2. Do whatever is necessary to feel relaxed and comfortable before beginning an exercise.
3. Start a session with some hugging, holding, or a massage. Then go to the exercise.
4. During the exercise, keep focused on your aroused level rather than on your lover.
5. The goal in each exercise is to last for fifteen minutes, including stops, without ejaculating. You can come after fifteen minutes if you wish, but go slowly, be aware of your arousal level and the point of inevitability, and enjoy yourself.
6. You should feel confident that you will be able

to delay ejaculation by stopping, and need no more than two or three stops during a fifteen-minute period, before going on to the next exercise. If you have a lot of difficulty with the next exercise, and it doesn't get easier after a few experiences, return to the one before it and practice it until you have further developed your skills.

7. The more frequently you do the exercises, the better. Three times a week is the minimum.

EXERCISE 16–1:
PARTNER STIMULATION OF PENIS

Step A: Lie on your back and have your partner take a position sufficiently comfortable for her to last for fifteen minutes. You might want to try the position recommended by Masters and Johnson, illustrated in Figure 10 (page 283), but any position is acceptable as long as you both are comfortable. Your partner is to stimulate your penis with her unlubricated hand in ways that are most arousing to you; feel free to give her instructions on how to touch you. Keep focused in your penis and tell her when to stop. Allow sufficient time for the urge to ejaculate to diminish before asking her to resume stimulation. If you find that you need to stop again as soon as stimulation is resumed, try taking longer stops.

When you can last for fifteen minutes with no more than two or three stops and feel confident of your control, do Step B.

Step B: This is exactly the same as Step A except that your partner now uses lotion, oil, or some other lubricant on her hand.

POSSIBLE PROBLEM
You aren't stopping in time because you're attending to your partner rather than your level of excitement. You may find yourself wondering if she is enjoying herself, if her hand is getting tired, if she is bored. There is nothing wrong with considering these questions as long as you swing your attention back to your penis as soon as you become aware that your mind has wandered. You might also want to talk to your lover about your concerns. Maybe she *is* bored some of the time. Can it be OK with you that she is willing to do the exercises even though it's not exciting for her? However you work it out, the important thing is that you have the space to put your attention where it needs to be, on your arousal level.

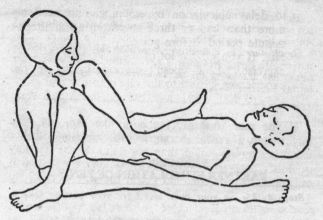

Figure 10:   Position for partner stimulation of penis
Adapted from *Human Sexual Inadequacy*,
by William H. Masters and Virginia E. Johnson, 1966.

Now that you feel comfortable delaying ejaculation by stopping with your partner, you're ready to use more subtle changes. The use of changes other than stopping is a departure from the approaches of Semans and Masters and Johnson who use, respectively, only the stop-start and squeeze methods. We have found that the employment of more subtle changes facilitates the development of ejaculatory control and is also more easily accepted by both the man and the woman. Hence, the following exercise.

EXERCISE 16–2: PARTNER STIMULATION OF PENIS WITH SUBTLE ADJUSTMENTS

Assume the same positions you used for the previous exercise and have your lover stimulate your penis in ways you like. Your goal is to last fifteen minutes without ejaculating and without stopping, by employing any changes you like in your and her behavior. Since types of changes to delay ejaculation other than stopping have been discussed several times, we assume you are familiar with them. Experiment and find out what works best with your partner. You will make some mistakes at first, but you may still be able to delay ejaculation by stopping. In time, you will learn how and when to use the other kinds of adjustments.

The first few times you do the exercise, your partner should not use lubrication on her hand. When you have good control, she can start using a lubricant.

Should there be difficult problems with this exercise that do not resolve themselves after a few sessions, consider spending some time mastering the subtle adjustments by yourself, following Exercise 15–2.

If you and your partner both like oral sex, you might want to repeat the above two exercises with her using her mouth rather than her hand. If she has any qualms whatever about doing this, don't try it; it will only lead to problems and get in the way of reaching your goals.

EXERCISE 16–3: PENIS IN VAGINA WITH NO MOVEMENT

Lie on your back and have your lover sit on your legs. She is to play with your penis until you have an erection. Then let her rub your penis gently around the outside of her vagina and in her pubic hair. Be aware of your arousal level and make any necessary adjustments. Take as long as you need to get accustomed to the idea of having your penis around her vagina. When you are feeling comfortable with this, and confident that you are in control of your ejaculatory process, then—and only then—should she slowly insert your penis. The two of you will then be in the position illustrated in Figure 11 (page 285). It is crucial, however, that there be no insertion until you are comfortable and in control. If it takes you more than one session to feel that way, that's fine.

Once your penis is safely ensconced in her, she is just to sit and you are just to focus. She should not make any movements except as we now explain. Without any stimulation, your erection may tend to go down. If this starts to happen, ask her either to contract her pelvic muscles a few times or to move slightly, just enough to keep your erection firm.

That's all you need to do for fifteen minutes. Focus in your penis and see how it feels to be surrounded by her vagina. You might become aware of the texture, temperature, and lubricity of the vagina. Be aware and get used to being there; it can be a very friendly place.

Should you feel that you are losing control, you can either ask her to get off or you can try relaxing or tensing your pelvic muscles.

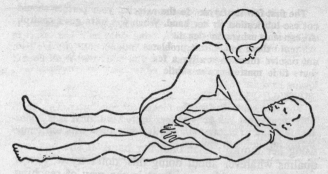

Figure 11: Female in superior position
Adapted from *Human Sexual Inadequacy*,
by William H. Masters and Virginia E. Johnson, 1966.

If you want to ejaculate after time is up, do so (we assume you have talked to your partner about this), but go slowly and be aware of the point of inevitability.

POSSIBLE PROBLEM

The first time or two you do the exercise, you get very excited and ejaculate. This is not a problem unless it continues to occur. If it does, you have several options. One is to go back to her stimulating you with her lubricated hand and get more comfortable with that. Another is to do a masturbation exercise accompanied by a fantasy of being inside her; follow the suggestions for Exercise 15–3, Step B. Still another possibility is to spend several sessions without fully entering her. Rub your penis around the outside of her vagina until that is comfortable, then put it in only a little way. Gradually increase the depth of penetration as you feel more confident and comfortable.

EXERCISE 16–4: PENIS IN VAGINA WITH MOVEMENT

Step A: This is similar to the previous exercise, except that your partner should thrust slowly, at your instructions as to how much and how fast. Use the subtle adjustments or stops to enable you to go for fifteen minutes without ejaculating. It is important that your partner not start thrusting to satisfy herself. That will come later. For now, you are in control of what kind and how much movement there is. Get comfortable with the pace before increasing it.

Step B: Both of you move slowly.

Step C: Gradually increase the pace, employing the subtle adjustments whenever you like, using stops as a last resort to prevent ejaculation. Continue in this fashion until you are both moving as much as you want. Keep in mind that it all doesn't have to happen in one session.

POSSIBLE PROBLEM

You lose control when the movement gets faster. This probably means that you are speeding up too suddenly. It is important that you be comfortable and feel in control with one tempo before increasing it. Take your time.

Since you don't want to spend the rest of your life having sex in only one position, it's time to try different ones. Again, a caveat—go slowly. Having good control in one position does not necessarily ensure good control in others. Most men find the female superior position, the one you have used in the last two exercises, the easiest one in which to maintain ejaculatory control. Side-by-side positions are next best for most men, while the well-known missionary position —man on top—is the most difficult.

EXERCISE 16–5: USING DIFFERENT POSITIONS FOR INTERCOURSE

Step A: The best new position to start with is probably the side-by-side or lateral position. It is a favorite of Masters and Johnson and many of their clients. Perhaps the best way to assume the position is to start with your lover on top, with your penis in her vagina. She then rolls to one side until she is lying on her side on the bed, while you roll up on one side so that you are facing her. Your penis may or may not remain inside of her. If not, you can have a good laugh while figuring out how to get it back in. Once you get on your sides, you will have to do some shifting of arms and legs and whatnot to get comfortable.

Remember that the first times you try a new position there may be some awkwardness, minor discomfort, and a loss of control. Take it slow, stay focused on your arousal level, and make changes early.

If this or any other new position presents difficulties, follow the suggestions in Exercise 16–4, gradually building up to abandoned movement.

Step B: Feel free to try any other positions that you like. Since good control will probably be most difficult to maintain when you are on top, you may want to experiment with other positions first.

The next exercise is very valuable and can be lots of fun. You are going to be asked to ejaculate as quickly as possible in intercourse. This may sound quite strange to you, given that you've spent so much time and energy learning how to control your ejaculations. The point is that good control means control in any direction. You should be able to come fast or slow. At this stage, coming quickly will increase your knowledge of what makes for quick ejaculations. It will also be good preparation for the time when you come quickly without intending it, and such things happen to almost all men once in a while. You now have many new skills for dealing with a partner and also some new feelings of confidence in yourself. Use them in this exercise. All is not lost if you come quickly. It only means that you decided to ejaculate sooner rather than later. The exercise need be done only once or twice.

EXERCISE 16–6: AN INTENTIONAL QUICKIE

Try to ejaculate as fast as possible in intercourse, even faster then you did before starting your training program. If you succeed in doing this, be aware of a tendency to want to apologize, but don't act on it. Express your appreciation to your partner and see if she would like you to do something for her. You should be pleased that you are now in control of your ejaculatory process.

If you are unable to come fast, you may decide to forget the exercise and rest on your laurels, content that you have achieved your goals. Or you may want to try it again to see if it isn't possible to have a quick ejaculation. After all, you might want to have a quickie some day, and you can view this exercise as preparation for that eventuality.

Whether you have done the partner exercises or followed the principles given at the beginning of the chapter, by now you have attained good ejaculatory control and are enjoying your sexuality in a more confident, relaxed, and carefree way. You will have noticed that results come gradually and that it takes a while for the effects of the training to really sink in and become automatic. This process will continue for months. All you need do to facilitate the process is to stay aware of your arousal level and make adjustments when needed.

You want to remember that there is absolutely no way to avoid losing control some of the time. Whether because you haven't had sex for a long time, are extremely excited, are tense or angry, or perhaps because of some other reason, there will be quick ejaculations once in a while. As time goes on, they will decrease in frequency, but they will probably never completely disappear. This is simply part of normal male functioning. There is nothing you can do about it and there's no need to get concerned about it.

When you realize that you have not made an adjustment in time and are going to ejaculate, don't fight it. Let it happen and enjoy it. No need for apologies; you can do something for her later if she wants. And no need to assume that all your training has been in vain. It hasn't. Just go a bit more slowly the next time, stay focused, and make your adjustments earlier than usual.

We hope you'll keep in mind the discussion in Chapter 9 on the effects of tension. If you get extremely upset about anything, you may start to lose some of your ejaculatory control. So be especially aware and careful in sex during tense times. Anything you can do to relieve or mitigate the tension will of course be extremely helpful.

If for any reason you notice yourself slipping back into your old, quick ways, take some time and figure out what is causing you to lose control. A brief refresher course with some of the exercises in this and the previous chapter may be very useful.

Now that you can last a long time, we hope you won't assume that every sexual encounter must be a long one. Compulsively lasting a long time is not much better than compulsively coming quickly. You have options and we hope you'll use them. Long-lasting sex can be a wonderful experience, and so can a quickie.

17

Erection Problems, or Why the Damn Thing Won't Act Like It Should

While every sex problem is accompanied by discomfort and concern, nothing equals the devastation wrought by the lack of an erection at the right time. Nothing except perhaps the loss of his job can make a man feel more worthless and hopeless. Impotence, the term traditionally used to signify the inability to get erections, also means a lack of power, strength, and vigor—the negation of all that we consider masculine. Men have securely tied their self-respect to the upward mobility of their penises and, when their penises do not rise to the occasion, they no longer feel like men.

Sam Julty, who interviewed a number of men with erection problems, described their situation like this:

The man without the erection sees himself as being less than a man, as an unworthy, as a fraud. It is as if the flag of his manhood must remain furled for lack of a mast. Thus the terror, the shame, the withdrawal spurred by the dysfunction far exceed the reaction to almost any other medical condition. . . .

Here, in more personal terms, is what a client we saw recently said when asked what he wanted to gain from therapy:

> I want to feel like a whole man again. If I could just function normally at least some of the time when I'm with a woman, that would do it. I know I can use my hand or tongue to satisfy them, and that's fine some of the time, but I'm not going to feel good about myself until I can get a good hard-on and use it. I feel so useless when that thing just hangs limp between my legs.

Women are often baffled by the agony a man goes through when he fails to get or keep an erection, but they have no parallel experience with which to compare it. The lack of erection, except in the relatively few cases caused by medical problems, signifies a lack of readiness for sex—the man is tired, bored, angry, anxious, or is in some other way preventing his sexual feelings from influencing his penis. But men have not had the permission women have to say that something is getting in their way or that they'd rather not have sex now.

A woman can participate in intercourse (which most of us learned was *the* sexual act) without being aroused or even interested. If she fails to lubricate sufficiently, saliva or artificial lubrication can be brought to the rescue. She might not have an orgasm, of course, which would be construed by some as a failure of sorts, but at least she can go through with the act and give her partner pleasure. A man is in a somewhat different position. Because of the incorrect but deeply embedded belief that sex demands a rigid penis, there is nothing that can be brought to the rescue. And his "failure" is so obvious. There is his limp organ, dangling in full view. There is no way to fake an erection and, though not impossible, it is quite difficult to have intercourse without at least a partial erection.

So a man without an erection can't have intercourse, which he usually translates as meaning that he can't have sex, and feels that he has failed as a man and a human being. Of course his partner may be sympathetic and offer support and understanding. But he may be so consumed with self-loathing that he can't accept what she offers. Many men withdraw from their partners after such "failures" and engage in an orgy of self-flagellation. The result is usually a miserable experience for them and their partners.

Erection problems are as old as recorded history and so are the agony and self-torture of men who experience them. Even today, however, there is no agreed-upon definition of what constitutes an erectile problem. Almost all men have had at least a few experiences when they wanted an erection and didn't get one or when they lost an erection at some embarrassing point. This is not really a problem. But what about the man who usually does not get or maintain an erection in sexual encounters? Or the man who does fine with one partner but not with others? Or the man who complains that his erections aren't as hard as they used to be?

Our belief is that if it bothers you, it's a problem. But the solution may not lie where you think.

Too many men with erection difficulties think that all they need is some procedure or device to get it up and keep it up. After all, the job of a penis is to get hard, so perhaps the doctor has a pill or shot to get this misguided penis back on the right track. Unfortunately, the situation is usually a bit more complex.

The real problem usually lies not in the man's functioning but in his ideas of how he should function. Far too many men uncritically accept the superhuman standards and myths about men and penises and then get concerned when they discover they are merely human. Erection problems are almost always due to one or more of the following: unrealistic expectations; lack of arousal; absence of the proper conditions; and the undue emphasis placed on the need for an erection.

An example of unrealistic expectations is a man in his forties or fifties who complains that his erections are not as full or firm as they were twenty years ago.

If this "problem" gets the best of him and he becomes obsessed with it, he may end up without any erections at all. Fifty-year-old penises don't feel or act exactly the way twenty-year-old penises do. They can still do their jobs and provide much pleasure to the man and his partner, as long as the fantasy ideal of penises that are hard as steel and always jumping about doesn't get in the way. What needs adjusting in such cases is the standards and expectations, not the penis.

The lack of arousal causes much confusion and frustration. Most men think they should have erections even if they aren't really turned-on. While penises can get hard in the absence of arousal, such occurrences are rare and unpredictable. If you aren't interested in sex, your penis will usually remain soft. That's not a problem, but many men succeed in turning it into one by trying to force erections when there is no arousal.

The lack of proper conditions leads to many erection problems, but many men do not understand the importance of meeting their conditions and wonder what is wrong with them for not having erections even under the most adverse circumstances.

Sam came to therapy because he had not had an erection with a woman he had been seeing for three months. He was totally befuddled by his problem. He claimed that Greta was the best thing that ever happened to him. She was European, which he liked, and very experienced sexually. She was lots of fun, a wonderful companion, and he feared losing her unless he could perform. After some probing by the therapist, it turned out that Greta had some other interesting qualities. She had a quick and violent temper, and had several times thrown dishes and other objects at Sam. She continually berated American men in general and Sam in particular for their sexual ineptness. She frequently compared Sam to her last lover, with Sam coming out on the short end. She demanded erections and intercourse, threatening to leave if they were not forthcoming. Although he hardly recognized it when he first came to therapy, Sam was seething with resentment toward her. He trembled as he talked about her callousness toward him. Yet he continued to call himself impotent and wanted to know what was wrong with him.

That Sam could ask such a question demonstrates the power of our sexual mythology. He believed that, no matter what the circumstances, no matter how angry he was, and no matter how fearful he was of his partner's critical outbursts, he should have an erection with her. A more realistic question, but one that didn't occur to him, would have been: how could anyone get an erection in that situation?

If you have a lot of negative feelings toward your partner, if you feel guilty about having sex with her, if you aren't turned-on by her, if you are preoccupied with other matters, if sex with her is a tense experience —if any of these things are true, what makes you think you should have an erection? The answer, of course, is our sexual conditioning, the nonsense we discussed in Chapters 3 and 4.

One aspect of our learning important to consider here is the inordinate emphasis placed on erect penises. We men have so much at stake in getting an erection—not only the success or failure of the particular sexual event, but our entire identity as men. Because so much is at stake, the absence of an erection is greeted with the same degree of calmness as would be the announcement that someone in the neighborhood had the bubonic plague. When a man doesn't get an erection, invariably because the situation isn't right in the first place, he panics. He loses his ability to think clearly and flings himself into an ocean of self-doubt and fear.

A vicious cycle often is set in motion, all because of a penis that refused to get hard on one occasion. The man wonders what is wrong with him, if he is over the hill. He may think that this proves he's not as good as the other guys or perhaps that he's a closet homosexual. In his panic, he distances himself from his partner, thereby ensuring that the event will end badly and that his concerns will grow.

If this panic is not immediately resolved (in ways we will discuss shortly), the stage is set for real trouble. The next sexual encounter is looked forward to with both anticipation and apprehension. If it goes well, the man's worries are over. If it goes badly, his worst fears will be confirmed. The next encounter becomes too important. The stakes are much too high. Too much pressure is being generated. The man's penis is confronted with conditions under which it cannot operate. The more the man peers at his penis, wondering what is wrong with it and whether it will embarrass him again, the more it wilts.

The man is doing everything possible to ensure that this experience will end at least as badly as the first one. He's not doing it purposely, but he doesn't know what else to do. A second bad experience will only make things worse the next time around. And pretty soon the man realizes that he almost never gets erections with a partner. Because he ignored his conditions and put too much pressure on his penis, it now refuses to function at all.

What could he have done differently? What can you do when you don't get an erection when you think you should? Several things.

First, remember that every man sometimes experiences a lack of an erection. It's just one of those things that all men must learn to live with. If you can avoid worrying yourself to death about what it means, things will probably work out fine the next time.

Second, realize that all is not lost. You and your partner can have an enjoyable experience even without an erection. Women are much less concerned with the erectability of penises than are men, and your partner can probably take your soft penis in stride as long as you don't make a catastrophe of it. Resist the temptation to withdraw in shame and anger. You may want to tell her what you are feeling. You may remember that many of the women in the Zilbergeld and Stanton study requested this type of expression. Whether you tell her or not, however, the important thing is to stay with her and do whatever the two of you enjoy.

It's paradoxical but true that if you ignore your lack of erection (that is, don't make a federal case of it), it may not be lacking for long. This won't happen every time, and it rarely happens if you are only pretending to be unconcerned about what your penis is doing, but it happens often if you can leave it alone and not pester it.

A third thing you can do when you don't get an erection is avoid the tendency of launching into an internal dialogue about what the matter is with you. Instead, think whether your conditions are being met, if you are aroused, and if you are getting the kind of stimulation you want. If something is lacking—a certain kind of stimulation, some of your conditions—do what is necessary to get it. If you are not aroused, the best thing is probably to call it a day and wait until you are more in the mood.

Last, if you find yourself thinking that you have to prove yourself the next time, remember that such pressure is self-defeating. You now have many ways of dealing with it, such as having sex only when aroused, meeting your conditions, talking to your partner about your feelings, and clarifying her expectations and desires. You might also want to set a rule for yourself not to use your penis in the next sexual encounter. Any of these methods, used singly or in combination, should reduce your anxiety. The important thing is that you give yourself the opportunity to enjoy yourself and your partner rather than setting yourself a test that can be passed only if your penis behaves in certain ways. Penises respond to pleasure but are only too ready to fail any tests you set for them.

What we have said here, of course, is only a summary of what we discussed in earlier chapters. You are human and operate according to laws governing human sexual behavior. Treat yourself and your penis with respect by having sex only when you are aroused and your conditions are met, and things will usually work out fine. Once in a while they won't, but that's just the nature of the beast.

If you have had erection problems for some time and are wondering specifically what to do, the next two chapters are for you. You have already done most of what is necessary, perhaps without realizing it. The exercises and suggestions in the following chapters will help you put your skills to the best use.

Before going on to them, however, we want to discuss briefly some of the appliances and medications sometimes used to treat erection problems. All sorts of nostrums and remedies have been developed for the improvement of a man's sex life, and particularly for dealing with penises that refuse to do what they're supposed to do. If you have been considering any of these scientific wonders, it will pay you to read on.

Although the search for an aphrodisiac is as old as recorded history, none has ever been found. James Woods, a research pharmacologist and expert on the subject, had this to say:

> In reality, there are no known drugs that specifically increase libido or sexual performance, and every chemical taken for this purpose, without medical advice . . . poses the danger of drug interaction or overdose to the user.

That goes for all the common folk potions as well as the sophisticated products of modern chemistry. The well-known Spanish fly is not only not very effective but is also dangerous. It causes acute irritation of the intestinal and urinary tracts, which sometimes leads to a feeling of sexual excitement, but has also led to continued and painful erection (priapism) which sometimes requires surgical treatment. Deaths have also been attributed to its use.

Some massage oils are advertised as having aphrodisiac properties. This is false advertising. Massage oil may be nice; it can lubricate and give you a good, warm feeling, but that's as far as it goes. If that turns you on, that's fine, but the oil itself, no matter what "secret herbs" it contains, is not going to change your sexual desire or functioning.

As for the bands to be tied around the base of your penis, don't use them. You may keep the erection but there is a possibility of causing damage. The penis is a very sensitive and vulnerable organ, best left untampered with.

Testosterone injections and penile implants are prescribed by some physicians. Testosterone therapy is fashionable in some medical circles and the implants show indications of becoming the next fad.

Testosterone is an androgen, or male sex hormone, produced in the testicles. It was once thought that production of this hormone decreased abruptly with aging, and that this decline was responsible for decreased sexual interest and performance. Injections of testosterone were therefore recommended as appropriate therapy. Current thinking is that production of the hormone does not suddenly decline at any age, except in rare cases. In cases where there is a hormone deficiency, injections are often very helpful. But such cases are not common.

When no hormone deficiency has been established, results are much less certain. Even when positive, they are often transitory. We have seen many men who had either received no benefit from testosterone shots or who had experienced some change, only to have it fade away soon after the treatment ended. Because of possible side effects (mentioned below), testosterone injections cannot be administered indefinitely.

Some physicians recommend testosterone almost routinely for men over forty who complain of erection problems or decreased sexual desire. Other doctors are more cautious, using it only when a deficiency of the hormone is proved. Before considering this type of treatment, you should know that it is suspected of having a very dangerous side effect. In his book, *Male Sexual Health*, Phillip Roen, a well-known urologist, explains:

We know that hidden in the depths of the prostate there may be a latent group of cancer cells which ordinarily would not produce any trouble but which can do so when they are stimulated by testosterone injections. This kind of treatment therefore seems to me to carry too high a risk to be justified.

Sometimes testosterone therapy is a desperate last resort on the part of the doctor, who has no idea of what to do if it fails. This can lead to problems for the patient.

Ollie, a man in his early fifties, saw a urologist at a well-known medical center for his erection problems. He was given Afrodex pills (a combination of testosterone and yohimbine, a natural substance thought by some to possess aphrodisiac qualities). When no progress was forthcoming, the urologist began a course of testosterone injections, telling Ollie that if they didn't work, nothing would. The shots didn't work and Ollie was seriously depressed for several months because he believed there was no help for him. After a while, he inquired about other possibilities and someone referred him to us. Six weeks after his first session, he was having enjoyable sex.

We wonder how many men have accepted a sexless life because the testosterone shots failed to help and their doctors said there was nothing else.

The best advice we can give regarding testosterone is don't even consider it unless your doctor says you have a hormone deficiency. If such a deficiency exists and your doctor recommends injections, talk to him about the possible side effects before making a decision. Better yet, try the exercises in the next two chapters first. You'll probably find that you don't need any injections.

Two types of penile implants have been developed in recent years. The first consists of one or two silicone rods surgically implanted in the penis. The result is a permanent state of semi-erection, firm enough to insert in the vagina for intercourse but usually not so obtrusive as to cause embarrassment in nonsexual situations. The surgery itself is fairly simple and the risk is low. The implant does not impair penile sensation or the capacity for orgasm and ejaculation.

The newer device is much more complex. It is a hydraulic model, involving inflatable cylinders in the penis, a reservoir of fluid placed under the abdominal muscles, and a pumping mechanism in the scrotum. When a man with such an implant desires an erection, he pumps the bulb in his scrotum, causing the fluid in the reservoir to inflate the cylinders in the penis. He may then engage in whatever sexual activity he desires. Orgasm and ejaculation are not interfered with by the implant. To return his penis to its normal state, the man activates the bulb that deflates the cylinders.

The hydraulic model has both advantages and disadvantages compared to the simple implant. The penis looks and feels more normal than the semi-rigid one produced by the earlier procedure. The erection can be full and firm rather than semi-firm and there is no problem about concealing the erection. On the negative side, it is a much more complex device (meaning that there is more that can go wrong) and much less is known about it. Only a few of the hydraulic models are in use and not enough time has elapsed to have good follow-up information. It is therefore impossible at this time to give a fair appraisal of their usefulness.

Both kinds of implants were originally designed as a last resort. They were to be used for men with severe physical impairment, so severe that the implant was the only way they could ever hope to have an erection again. As so often happens, however, once a procedure exists, it gets used on all sorts of people. Some implants have been done on men who did not have physical impairment.

We have talked to a number of urologists who have either done the surgery or were in some other way involved and the consensus is that the implants often work out well for men for whom it really is the only hope, i.e., those with organic impairment. For those without such impairment, however, and those who have not tried other alternatives, there is often trouble. They complain about the implant, they want adjustments made and none that are made satisfy them, they want them removed, or they just don't ever use them. In other words, the implant only provides new things to complain about.

Implants are tempting to many men. Surgery seems so much simpler than thinking about conditions and how relaxed you are, considering whether or not you want sex, talking to your partner—all these silly human things. Just have an operation and—barring equipment failure—you're all set. This logic appeals to many men who are accustomed to technological solutions for all problems.

There is another side, however. Surgery, no matter how simple, always carries a risk. The risk varies according to age, physical condition, type of anesthetic, and other factors. Surgery is also expensive, usually more expensive than short-term therapy and certainly more expensive than this book.

Another consideration is what it means to replace your own functioning with a mechanical device. In some cases, of course, it may be absolutely necessary. If your heart, lungs, or kidneys don't work, having yourself hooked up to a machine may be the only way to preserve your life. If your penis won't work, even after trying the exercises in this book and going to a good sex therapist, an implant may be the only recourse left. But it should be considered only after you have exhausted the other alternatives.

If you are in a hurry to get an implant, we suggest you carefully consider why. What problems do you think it will solve for you? Why are you so unwilling to try the book or see a therapist? It's a terrible mistake to think of the implant as a panacea. It will give you an erection and nothing else. It will not increase your desire or sexual skills, it will not help you find a partner, nor will it necessarily circumvent the need for talking about sex. Your partner, after all, may wonder how come you always have an erection or why you're always pushing buttons. If you are engaging in magical thinking about the wonders that an implant will produce for you, you are probably headed for a huge disappointment.

18

Resolving Erection Problems I

Successfully dealing with erection problems requires that the following criteria be met:

1. Having sex only when you feel aroused, and only the kinds of sex that you want;
2. Meeting all your conditions for good sex;
3. Recognizing when you are tense, and getting more relaxed;
4. Getting the kinds of stimulation you like and focusing on this stimulation.

In short, you need to be able to take charge of a sexual situation so that you are enjoying rather than performing.

Each of the four criteria above is composed of a number of separate skills. Having sex only when you want to, for example, requires you to be able to say no to sex when you are not in the mood, to get the type of sexual activity you like, to be able to stop in the middle of a sexual encounter if you realize that you are no longer in the mood, and to initiate sex when you want it. Being able to communicate clearly with your partner is, of course, necessary for the application of these skills.

If you have done the conditions, assertiveness, relaxation, talking, and focusing exercises presented earlier in the book and feel reasonably confident of your ability to apply what you have learned, your erection difficulties are probably all but resolved. The suggestions and exercises in this and the next chapter can help extend your learning and increase your confidence, but you may not need them. Some of the men we've worked with resolved their erection problems without doing any of the exercises in these two chapters. We want to be clear that these exercises are useful only as a supplement to, and not as a substitute for, the conditions, assertiveness, and other exercises given earlier.

Now is a good time to take stock of where you are and what you need to do. Read this and the next chapter without doing the exercises to get an idea of which exercises might be useful and which exercises given earlier in the book require further work. Pay particular attention to the section in the next chapter called Partner Sex without Exercises. If you think you can carry out the suggestions given there without doing any more exercises, feel free to do what you want. If, on the other hand, you feel you need more confidence or better development of certain skills, do what is necessary to achieve these ends.

The guidelines for doing exercises on pages 172–173 apply to all the exercises in this and the next chapter. An additional suggestion for men with erection problems is not to do more than one exercise a day. You want to give your penis the best possible conditions in which to respond, and having sex more than once a day may not be conducive for reaching this goal.

The masturbation exercises require the ability to focus, an ability developed by Exercise 10–1. If you need more time with that exercise, now is the time to get it.

The first masturbation exercise is simple and will help you to understand that a lost erection can often be regained when conditions are right and the stimulation good. Men often forget this and get anxious when their erection goes down. It is useful to remember that it is common for the strength of an erection to fluctuate during a sexual experience. Your penis may be very firm and full one moment, softer the next, and then either regain its firmness or become completely flaccid. If it does get soft, try not to panic. If your conditions are met, if you are reasonably relaxed, and if you are getting the kind of stimulation you like, the chances are good that your erection will return.

EXERCISE 18–1: LOSING AND REGAINING ERECTION
Time Required: 15 to 20 minutes

Masturbate with lubricant and focus inside your penis. When you have an erection, stop. Take your hand away from your penis, stop focusing, and think about something nonsexual. Let your erection go completely down, which may take from a few seconds to a few minutes. When your penis is soft, resume masturbating and focusing. Most of the time your penis will get hard again, in which case you should again stop and let it get soft. Two stops are sufficient in a 15- to 20-minute session.

If your erection does not return in a few minutes after the resumption of stimulation, consider if there is anything you should do to get into a more relaxed, sexier frame of mind (for example, recalling a good sexual experience or looking at some stimulating pictures or literature). If the changes you make result in an erection, just continue the exercise. If not, call it quits for then and return to the exercise some other time. Whatever you do, don't try to force an erection. It won't work.

Do this exercise two to four times, or until you are reasonably confident that an erection can often be regained by the proper atmosphere and stimulation.

POSSIBLE PROBLEM

You *never* regain your erection after letting it go down. (If you usually get it back but not always, that's not a problem). Be sure you are feeling sexy before you resume stimulation, that you are comfortable, and that all your conditions are met.

You may have found that you did not always regain your erection. If you didn't have this experience in this exercise, you probably will in one of the later ones.

This is simply one of those difficult facts of life that all men need to accept. The only reason it's difficult is that our sex education didn't leave room for it.

All you can do about erections is meet your conditions. Sometimes, even when conditions are met and everything seems perfect, you still won't get or maintain an erection. Penises sometimes decide to take brief vacations at the oddest moments. See if you can accept this as a fact that you can do nothing about (assuming, of course, that your conditions are fulfilled). The more you accept this idea, the better you'll feel about yourself and the less pressure you'll put on your penis. The less pressure your penis feels, the more likely it will respond in the future.

The next three exercises involve the use of structured fantasy. Before doing them, read the discussion of the role of fantasy in exercises on page 273–276.

EXERCISE 18–2: MASTURBATION WITH FANTASY OF SEX WITH A PARTNER
Time Required: 20 to 25 minutes

Step A: Masturbate with lubricant while fantasizing a sexual experience with a partner. Start the fantasy with the first touch or kiss and slowly go through all the activities that might occur in this imagined sexual event. A typical sequence might go like this: kissing, hugging, removing clothes, caressing while nude, playing with her breasts, playing with her genitals, her touching your penis, oral sex, inserting your penis into her vagina, being in the vagina with no movement, slow movement, and movement that gradually becomes rapid. (We are not implying that a real sexual encounter should include all these activities or that there is a special order in which the activities should occur. The important thing is that you fantasize all the possible sexual activities you might actually encounter.)

Be aware of your anxiety level and, should it rise, visualize yourself doing something to make yourself more comfortable. At the same time, actually do something to make yourself more relaxed. When the anxiety decreases, resume sexual activity in the fantasy and resume masturbation. Here is an example of how this might go:

You are masturbating and enjoying your fantasy until the scene where she touches your penis. At that point your anxiety goes up. Stop masturbating and do some-

thing to get comfortable, e.g., taking a few deep
breaths. At the same time, visualize yourself doing
something to relax with your partner. You might see
yourself telling her you want to stop and just hold her
for a while; or you might do something for her; or
perhaps you could see yourself talking to her about
your feelings. When you feel more relaxed, resume
masturbating and see yourself continue or resume sexual activity in the fantasy. If your anxiety rises at the
same point as before, do Step B.

If you are doing the exercise slowly and carefully, as you
should, the allotted time will probably not be sufficient to get
through the entire fantasy. That is fine. Next time you can
start the fantasy at a later scene, e.g., where you are already
undressed and caressing each other. Regardless of how many
sessions it takes, make sure you cover all possible aspects of a
sexual experience while doing this exercise.

Most men experience some difficulty with one or more of the
fantasized scenes. Perhaps your anxiety increases when you
imagine her touching your penis or when you imagine starting intercourse. Since what gives you trouble in fantasy will
probably do the same in reality, you want to devote special
attention to the difficult scenes. When you run into an anxiety-
producing scene that does not get easier after a few repetitions,
use Step B.

Step B: Instead of masturbating to a fantasy of a whole
sexual encounter, fantasize only the scene that causes you
trouble. It is essential that you be relaxed before beginning.
Get into a sexual mood, then slowly begin masturbating and
gently ease yourself into the difficult scene. Here is an example.

If your difficult scene involved your partner's playing
with your penis, first imagine her hand just lightly
brushing your penis. When that feels comfortable,
see her holding your penis for a second or two. Then
holding it a bit longer. Then stroking it for just a moment. Gradually increase the amount of time you can
visualize her stroking your penis until you can fantasize it for as long as you like without an increase in
anxiety. If you do get tense at any point, stop and get
more comfortable, then resume that fantasy at a point
preceding the one that caused the increase in anxiety.

Repeat this process as many times as necessary until you
can go through the entire scene without any increase in anx-

lety. When this is accomplished, return to Step A and incorporate this scene into the larger fantasy. You may then find that another scene gives you trouble, necessitating a return to Step B. Continue this procedure until you can go through the entire fantasy in Step A feeling very comfortable.

POSSIBLE PROBLEMS

1. You have difficulty staying with the fantasy, finding yourself drifting to other thoughts and fantasies. When this happens, simply bring your attention back to the scene you were imagining. You will need to do this a number of times each session.

2. You forget about your relaxation level. It is crucial that you be aware of how relaxed you are so you can stop and get more comfortable when you need to. If this is a problem for you, try keeping most of your attention on your relaxation level even though this may result in less distinct fantasy images.

If you have a tape recorder, we encourage you to record the fantasy and play it while you masturbate. Since you won't have to put any effort into developing the fantasy, you can listen to it while keeping your attention on how relaxed or tense you are.

3. You try to do too much in one session. It's important that you really get into your fantasy and slowly go through it, which means that this exercise will take at least a few sessions to complete. You will probably need to stop a number of times to get relaxed, and also need to do Step B at least a few times. Speed is not important. Carrying out the exercise exactly as suggested is.

We generally like to cover in fantasy most or all of the disappointing or anxiety-producing events that may occur in reality, e.g., not getting or maintaining an erection. This helps you think of how you can deal with such a situation, making its actuality less threatening. The next exercise deals with not getting or maintaining an erection, a situation that may have caused you much grief in the past. You need to learn to handle it in a way that makes the sexual experience a good one for both you and your partner.

EXERCISE 18–3: MASTURBATING WITH FANTASY OF LOSING AND REGAINING ERECTION
Time Required: 15 to 20 minutes

While masturbating, you are to fantasize losing your erection at the point at which this usually occurred in partner activities in the past. If your main problem is not getting an erection when with a partner, fantasize that situation instead. It is important that the fantasy be reasonably vivid and detailed. What is going on the moment that you lose your erection? What are you doing and what is she doing? As you picture yourself losing your erection, stop masturbating. You may experience the awful feelings you usually have in such situations (hopelessness, anger, and so forth). Imagine yourself doing something to get more comfortable, e.g., asking her to give you a light massage, holding her, talking to her. Get into the fantasy of the relaxing activity and allow yourself to relax. When you are more comfortable, think of what would be needed for you to get aroused again, perhaps a certain kind of stimulation or telling your lover what you are feeling. Then imagine yourself doing it. As you imagine these scenes, resume masturbating. Picture in as much detail as possible getting the things you need to become more aroused. Then visualize yourself regaining your erection and having a good time.

Do this exercise as many times as needed to develop some confidence that you could actually carry out what you fantasized with a partner. For many men, four to six repetitions are sufficient, but others will want to do more.

You probably felt good about regaining your erection in the fantasy in this exercise. But since that won't always happen in reality, we go to a fantasy of a situation that may be quite threatening to you—failing to get or regain an erection regardless of how relaxed and aroused you feel. This situation frightens most men, particularly those who have experienced it and not handled it well. It is important to confront the situation, otherwise your sex life is going to be overcrowded, with the fear of not regaining an erection taking up a lot of space. That fear can be put to rest if you prove to yourself that you can have a marvelous time in bed without an erection. We hope that your reading of Chapter 13 has at least raised the possibility in your mind that your partner can probably be satisfied without an erection. The following exercise is intended to help you realize that you also can have a good time without a hard penis.

EXERCISE 18–4: MASTURBATION WITH FANTASY OF NO ERECTION
Time Required: 15 to 25 minutes

Masturbate to a fantasy where you either do not get an erection, or you have one which goes soft, whichever situation has been most true for you. Stop masturbating and imagine yourself doing something to help yourself relax. When you are relaxed in the fantasy, imagine yourself getting all your conditions met and the types of stimulation you like best. And imagine that none of this brings you an erection. You may at this point experience some negative feelings, similar to those you actually experienced in such situations in the past. You may need to exert some effort to keep control of the fantasy.

Now imagine yourself accepting the fact that your penis is not going to get hard. You may want to visualize yourself telling your partner this ("I guess I'm not going to get an erection tonight," or something of this sort). Then imagine doing whatever seems right to make the experience an enjoyable one for both you and your partner. One possibility is to do something for her with your hands, mouth, or something else (but not your penis). While fantasizing about carrying out these ideas, resume masturbating and have a good time.

As you repeat the exercise, you might want to try different things that can be done after you and your partner accept the fact of your nonerection. Some of the possibilities can be non-sexual, e.g., talking, massage, holding each other, going for a walk together. Keep control of the fantasies and do not let them wander to include such nonproductive alternatives as sulking, fighting, or stomping out of the room. You may have done such things in the past but you're in a different place now, with many more satisfying alternatives to choose from. If you have difficulty keeping control of the fantasy, we suggest you record it and play it back while you are masturbating.

Remember that whatever you do in the fantasy, it does not result in an erection. See how many alternatives you can discover for an enjoyable experience in this situation.

Do this exercise as many times as necessary to give you a feeling of confidence that you could carry it out in reality.

You may have had some trouble when you saw yourself without an erection despite all your fantasy attempts to get one. Repeating the exercise a number of times will help. Having good sex is not dependent upon having an erection and you should be well on your way toward accepting that fact.

19

Resolving Erection Problems II

This chapter presents two approaches to partner sex for men with erection problems, both of which have been used very successfully. The first approach involves a list of principles to be followed in partner sex and requires no partner exercises. It does require you to meet the four criteria listed at the beginning of Chapter 18. This program has been successfully used by men without steady partners, by men with partners who would not cooperate in treatment, and by men who had cooperative partners but who didn't want to do partner exercises.

The second program requires a partner who is willing to work with you on a series of exercises. It follows an outline developed by Masters and Johnson, but with several of our own variations.

Read both approaches and pick the one that feels right for you. If you do not have a partner, of course, you have to go with the first one. Otherwise, either method can work. The first one is a bit more difficult for most men, so if you have trouble with it, you can always do some exercises with your partner.

Partner Sex
without Exercises

If you have done the exercises given earlier in the book, you are ready to carry out our suggestions for sex with a partner. You have already seen most of the suggestions, in the section on sex with a new partner on pages 212–214. You should follow them whether you are in a new or an old relationship. Here we offer some elaboration and a few new ideas.

If you are in a relationship and have broken off physical contact because of your sexual problem, it is important to reestablish that contact as soon as possible. Start holding hands, hugging, snuggling, taking baths or showers together, doing light body-rubs, or anything else that is mutually agreeable. You need to feel comfortable being physical with your partner, and engaging in these activities is one of the best ways to get there. Of course, you should stop and get more comfortable if at any time you get tense.

Use your list of conditions and systematically go about meeting them. Work out any unfinished business with your partner that is getting in the way, talk to her about how you can satisfy her if you don't have an erection, use transition activities to help you relax—do these or anything else that will fulfill all your conditions. And don't even consider doing anything sexual until they all are met.

While engaged in any type of physical activity with your partner, most of your attention should be on the pleasurable sensations you're feeling. But you should also be aware of how tense or relaxed you are. Whenever you are tense, even if during nonsexual contact with your lover, do something to get more comfortable.

Plan not to have intercourse the first few times you have sex with her and stick to the plan no matter what comes up. It's a bad pun but we're serious. You may get an erection but you shouldn't use it in intercourse. A mistake commonly made by men who've had erection problems is to attempt frantically to "stick it in" as soon as they have an erection. Such frenzied efforts usually end with the erection disappearing. Let your lover play with your penis and give her plenty of directions so she'll do it just the way you like. If an ejaculation happens, that's nice, and if it doesn't, that's also nice. Enjoy the feelings and don't attempt any "sticking it in."

When engaging in sexual activities other than intercourse, see if you can't have a good time. Some men are so busy thinking about intercourse that they don't enjoy anything else that happens. Focusing on the sensations in your penis as it's being stimulated will help keep your mind where it belongs. When you do get around to intercourse, keep focusing in your penis.

It's a good idea deliberately to lose your erection with your partner. You can ask her to stop stimulating you and do something else until your erection has gone away. Then, if you feel like it, ask her to resume stimulation. If your erection doesn't return soon, don't try to push it. Do something else that feels good. You may feel bad because you want to reward her efforts with an erection. She's playing with you because it feels good to you and good to her. That usually is sufficient reward for anyone. You don't owe her an erection, just as she doesn't owe you an orgasm when you stimulate her.

Since you are at some point going to be asking your penis to go into her body, it is helpful if she and it become better acquainted. Have her touch, pat, hold, and caress it when it's soft. Some men find this difficult to do ("I only want her to touch it when it's hard"), but it's well worth practicing. You'll feel much more comfortable if you can let her touch your penis regardless of what shape it's in. Have her do a little at a time, gradually increasing the amount of touching as you feel more comfortable (most women, by the way, like this type of activity).

Another way of developing diplomatic relations between your penis and your lover is to gently rub it on her body. Whether it's hard or soft, you can rub it almost everywhere on her. When you are comfortable doing this, rub it in her pubic hair, between her thighs, on her vaginal lips, and perhaps put it in her vagina just a little way. Of course you should stop and get comfortable if you get tense. Go slowly, keep your attention on your penis, and allow it and you to get to know your partner better.

The business about helping your penis and your partner to get better acquainted strikes some men as silly, but we assure you that the techniques we've suggested are powerful ones. Besides, they can be lots of fun. You really can play fun games while in bed without feeling that you have to achieve some goal or put on a performance.

Remember to go no further than you are comfortable with. Respect your anxious feelings by not doing anything to increase their strength. If that means that you don't have intercourse the first three, five, or ten times you are sexual with your partner, that's fine. Enjoy what you do with her, and, sooner or later, you will be ready for intercourse.

If you don't get an erection after a few times with a partner, she may wonder what is going on. She may even wonder the first time it happens. Many women take a lack of erection as a sign that the man is not attracted to them or that they are not doing the right things to arouse him, just as many men take a lack of orgasm on the part of their partners to indicate some deficiency in the men's attractiveness or lovemaking skills.

Obviously this is a potentially explosive situation and needs to be defused as quickly as possible. You need to let your partner know that she is attractive and desirable to you (assuming that this is true) and that your lack of erection is not her fault. Here are two possible ways:

Mary, I don't exactly understand what's going on but I can tell I'm not going to get an erection. I like you and am really turned-on to you. I've been looking forward to tonight all week and you've been doing everything I could want and I'm turned-on like crazy. I think it's because I like you and want to be a good lover for you. I'm just trying too hard and whenever I do that my penis goes on vacation. I'd like to leave it alone for a while. But I'd also like to touch you some more.

Ginny, I better level with you. I've had problems getting an erection for some time. I've been getting some help with it and I thought things would be different with you because I feel close to you and I really want you. But I can see that I'm still very nervous and that's getting in the way of getting hard. I'm sure I won't get an erection tonight, but I'd love to do whatever you want me to.

What you say may be quite different from either of these examples. Just make sure your partner understands that you are not blaming her. It's also a good idea not to apologize. You haven't done anything wrong or anything to be ashamed of. Apologies in such situations often lead to self-flagellation and other forms of destructive behavior. Just tell her what is happening, in as direct and honest a way as you can. No one has the right to expect more than that.

Regardless of what anyone has a right to expect, however, we want to acknowledge that there are some women who will be put off by your lack of erection, regardless of what you tell them about it. Because of their own insecurities about their attractiveness or sexual competence, or for some other reason, they may not be able to deal with a man who has a problem. Such women are probably few, but should you find yourself with one, you need to realize that you don't have many choices. Since her unwillingness to accept you the way you are is only going to make you feel bad about yourself and put more pressure on your penis, the situation can only get worse. Unless she can become more accepting of your situation, the only reasonable choice you have is to leave. Not a happy prospect, perhaps, but staying with her (assuming she is willing) will probably only add to your sexual woes.

Better to find a woman who is more interested in a man than in a rigid penis. With a more supportive attitude, you'll probably soon have erections.

To avoid unnecessary disappointments, remember that you won't always get erections when you think you should, you will lose erections sometimes and not be able to regain them, and at times your erections may not be as full or hard as you would like. As long as you are following all the suggestions we gave, you are doing all you can to maximize the chances for having good sex.

If you can't seem to get past a certain point, however, or if a problem keeps recurring, you can do something about it. First, figure out as precisely as possible what the problem is. For example, "I get erections without any trouble but often lose them when she goes to insert it." If you don't lose your erection when *you* insert it, you could decide to insert it yourself all the time, thus easily solving the difficulty. If you would like the option of her inserting it, one way of dealing with this is to use a scene of her doing that in Step B of Exercise 18–2.

Another option is to create an exercise of your own. An appropriate exercise might go like this. She sits on top of you and stimulates you to erection. She then rubs your penis in her pubic hair, then on the lips of her vagina. All this is done slowly and you move from one step to the next as you are comfortable and feel ready. She can then insert your penis just a little. Gradually, and not necessarily in one session, she can insert your penis deeper and deeper until it is all the way in.

Reading the partner exercises that follow will give you some ideas of the kinds of exercises you can use to deal with any problems that arise. You may not want to tell your partner that what you want to do is an exercise, and there's no reason you should. You can just say that you'd like to try such and such. As long as you proceed slowly enough to keep your anxiety level down, you should be able to handle any difficulties that come up.

That's really all there is to it. This program has worked for hundreds of men and it can work for you. You already have most of the skills and only need practice in applying them. Keep referring back to this section and make sure you are following our suggestions to the letter. When you have developed more confidence, you can be more flexible and do pretty much what you want as long as you are not totally disregarding your conditions. That is a certain invitation to trouble for anyone, no matter how much experience and confidence he has.

Partner Exercises

Before starting these exercises both you and your partner should read and discuss them. Talk about your feelings about the program and work out any conflicts. You both should understand that these exercises constitute a training program and will not be needed forever. Since how long they are needed is mainly determined by how often they are done, work out an agreement about frequency. Your partner should understand that you are in total control while the exercises are being done; she is not to push you faster or further than you want to go. You need to assure her that you are willing to satisfy her with your hands or mouth when she desires, but that no demands can be made on your penis.

It is common for disagreements to arise in the course of doing the exercises. To get the maximum benefit from the program, work out the disagreements as soon as they occur.

Do not restrict your physical contact with your partner to these exercises. Allow plenty of time for mutually satisfying expressions of physical affection, and be sure to have some physical contact before starting each exercise.

The basic principle to be followed in all the exercises is that you should engage in the suggested activities only up to the point where anxiety arises. When you become anxious, stop what you are doing and do something that will allow you to become comfortable. Then, if you desire, you can resume the previous activity, remembering to stop again if the tenseness returns.

The following suggestions apply to the exercises:

1. If possible, do exercises two to four times a week, no more than one exercise per day.

2. You probably will do best if you don't masturbate while engaged in this program. There are two exceptions to this rule. You may want to masturbate if you and your partner are not able to get together several times a week. Masturbating is then fine and it will help if you use the focusing technique or one of the exercises in Chapter 18. The other situation in which masturbation is acceptable is if you feel the need to gain more confidence with one or more of the masturbation exercises. If so, take a break from the partner work, returning to it when you have accomplished what you wanted with the masturbation exercises. It's best not to alternate between masturbation and partner exercises on a daily basis. That may be just too much sex.

3. Both you and your partner should read and discuss an exercise before doing it.

4. Make sure you are relaxed and your conditions are met before starting an exercise.

5. Don't try to rush through the program. That will only add pressure. It will take as long as it needs to and there is little you can do to speed up the process. Take it slowly and see if you can enjoy what you are doing.

6. At some point you will get an erection and be tempted to have intercourse. Resist the temptation. Don't attempt insertion until it is suggested in the exercises and never attempt it in a hurried or pressured manner.

Since most of the exercises parallel some of the masturbation exercises in the last chapter and/or the ideas in that chapter and the first part of this chapter, we keep our explanations here to a minimum.

EXERCISE 19-1: PARTNER PLAYING
WITH YOUR SOFT PENIS
Time Required: 15 minutes

After making sure that you are both in a comfortable position (you may want to try the position recommended by Masters and Johnson, illustrated on page 283, let your partner play with your soft penis. Try not to get an erection since you want the experience of being touched and played with when soft. If you do get an erection, stop for a while until your penis gets soft, then have your partner resume.

Your partner can explore, caress, stroke, and play with your penis in any way she likes. Don't let her do anything that is painful or uncomfortable but, aside from that, keep your hands to yourself and your attention in your penis. Be aware of what it feels like to be touched. You may be aware of some pressure to get an erection. Just let the feeling be there and continue to focus on the sensations in your penis.

Do this exercise three or four times, or until you are quite comfortable with her touching you when you are soft.

POSSIBLE PROBLEM

You find yourself trying to get an erection. That's natural since men were taught that they should be hard when a woman touched them. If they weren't hard to begin with, they certainly should get that way within a few seconds after she started her ministrations. Be aware of the pressure if it is there but don't act on it. Talking to your partner about these feelings can be valuable. Remember that the goal is to keep your penis soft. Having an erection interferes with the purpose of the exercise.

EXERCISE 19-2: PARTNER STIMULATION
OF PENIS WITH FOCUSING
Time Required: 15 to 20 minutes

Assume a position that is comfortable for you and your partner and have her stimulate your penis in ways that you like. Pay attention to the sensations in your penis and give her instructions on how to touch it. Suggest different strokes, pressures, and rhythms and see how they feel. If she has any trouble following your instructions, be more specific or show her how to do it. Be sure to tell her when she's doing it the way you like. Give your directions in ways that encourage her to follow them. Do not criticize her under any circumstance. Just tell her what you want as clearly as you can and show your appreciation for what she's doing.

Whether or not you get an erection is not the point. The goals are to give you practice in focusing and giving directions. If you are aroused, your conditions are met, and you are getting the kind of stimulation you want, you probably will get an erection some of the time. It's fine if you ejaculate.

Do the exercise three to five times, or until you feel confident that you usually do respond in a satisfying manner with the proper stimulation.

POSSIBLE PROBLEM

You never get an erection in this exercise, even after doing it a number of times. Check that your conditions are met, that you are aroused and comfortable before starting the exercise, and that you are getting precisely the kind of stimulation you want. If everything checks out and there's still no change, you might want to try the next exercise, particularly if you like oral stimulation.

If you responded in the masturbation exercises but not with your partner, there is obviously something in the relationship that is getting in your way. Ask yourself what it would take for you to be able to have an erection with your partner. What issues, attitudes, or behaviors would have to be resolved or changed? See if you can work them out. If not, you may have no alternative to seeking professional help.

If you responded to neither the masturbation exercises nor the partner exercises, you should definitely see a competent sex therapist.

If you are like most of the men we have worked with, you are now convinced that things are not as bad as you had imagined. In fact, you may be thinking that things are going well and be in a hurry to get to intercourse. We hope you are willing to put that off for a bit.

The next exercise is optional. Many men have enjoyed it and found it valuable. However, not all women are willing to do it, so you and your partner will have to discuss it carefully. If she is not willing to do it, don't push her. It's not a necessary exercise. Perhaps, as your sex life becomes more satisfying, she will be willing to try oral sex.

EXERCISE 19-3: ORAL STIMULATION
OF PENIS WITH FOCUSING
Time Required: 15 to 20 minutes

This exercise is identical to the preceding one in all respects except that your partner now stimulates your penis with her mouth rather than her hand. Use whatever position is comfortable for the two of you but resist the temptation to stimulate her orally at the same time. Just focus and give directions.

By now you should be confident of getting erections most of the time when you have the proper conditions and stimulation. You now need to learn that it's really OK to lose your erection with your partner. Most of the time you will be able to regain it. And when you can't you can still have a good time.

EXERCISE 19–4: LOSING AND REGAINING ERECTIONS
Time Required: 20 to 25 minutes

Have your partner stimulate your penis with her hand or mouth. Keep your attention in your penis and give directions as needed. When you have an erection, tell her to stop and allow your erection to go down. You can do anything you want to accomplish this—have a chat, give her a back-rub, or whatever. Take as much time as you need for your penis to become flaccid. Then have her resume stimulation. When your penis gets hard again, repeat the above procedure. Two repetitions are sufficient for one session.

You will not always regain your erection and, in fact, you will not always get one to begin with. When this happens, let her know that it's not going to get hard ("I guess it's tired today; I'd like you to stop"). Then ask yourself what you'd like to do with your partner. Perhaps you'd like a back-rub, some cuddling or talking, or to do something for her. Whatever it is, let her know and see if you can do it. It is quite important that you master this little procedure. You can be sure your penis will not always respond; you need to let your partner know when this is true and be able to have a good time without an erection.

Do this exercise at least four times or until you are confident that your erection will usually return with proper stimulation and that, when it doesn't, you can still have a pleasurable experience.

POSSIBLE PROBLEMS

1. Your erection doesn't go down in a reasonable length of time. This really isn't much of a problem but it does increase the amount of time it takes to do the exercise. Check to see if what you're doing while waiting for it to get soft is arousing. If

so, do something else. You might even have to leave the room and take a walk around the house. That usually does the trick.

2. Your erection, once lost, never returns in a reasonable length of time. Consider whether your conditions are being fully met and whether you are aroused and relaxed when stimulation is resumed. The problem often lies in anxiety about getting the erection back. If that is the case, try to remember that you don't have to do anything to make your penis hard. It gets hard of its own accord. You only need to remove the obstacles that hinder this from happening. Talking to your partner about any concerns you have about regaining the erection can be helpful.

You're probably thinking that it's about time for intercourse. We agree. The next two exercises employ our usual step-by-step approach, moving slowly from insertion to intercourse with full movement. You can, of course, explore insertion and intercourse without following our method, but be sure you do so in a gradual, easy manner, stopping to get more comfortable when you need to. Frantic or pressured activities will only hinder your progress.

EXERCISE 19-5: PENIS IN VAGINA
WITH MINIMUM MOVEMENT
Time Required: 20 to 25 minutes

Before beginning this exercise you should make sure your partner's vagina is well lubricated. You may need to use an artificial lubricant such as KY jelly or Albolene. Discuss this with her.

Lie on your back and have your partner sit on your thighs, as in Figure 11. She should stimulate your penis while you give instructions and focus. When you have an erection, rub your penis in her pubic hair. As you feel comfortable doing that, rub it against the lips of her vagina (she will have to shift position for you to do this). When that is comfortable, have her put your penis very slowly into her vagina. You need not insert it all the way in one session. Let your comfort be your guide. Gradually, your penis should be inserted until it is completely inside her. Then be still for a few minutes. Focus in your penis and be aware of how it feels inside of her. Then ask her to move slowly, just enough to provide some stimulation for your penis. Give her directions on how much to move. Feel free to ask her to stop moving or to get off if that is what you want.

Continue intercourse with minimal movement for about ten minutes. You can ejaculate if you want to when time is up.

It is essential that you be in full control over how much movement there is. Your partner should understand that she is not to move for her own enjoyment at this time.

Repeat this exercise as many times as needed for you to feel comfortable with insertion and slight movement. Then, with you still in complete control, increase the pace—which is the goal of the next exercise.

EXERCISE 19–6: PENIS IN VAGINA WITH MOVEMENT
Time Required: 15 to 20 minutes

The position and format are the same as in the preceding exercise. Here you want to increase the amount of movement you can comfortably handle.

With your penis inside her, give her directions to slowly increase the pace. As you become comfortable with a given pace, increase it. You can move too, if you desire.

Take as many sessions as you need to get to the point where you are comfortable with any amount of movement.

POSSIBLE PROBLEMS
You lose your erection during intercourse. This happens occasionally to most men, but there are some things you can try if you feel it's a problem. Check to see that you are relaxed; if your penis is still in her vagina you can leave it there and try to get the stimulation that you want—moving in certain ways or having your lover squeeze her pelvic muscles may do the trick. Or you can take your penis out and get the type of stimulation you want, resuming intercourse when you are hard.

If you find that you usually lose your erection at a particular point—for example, when your partner is thrusting very quickly—you can do two additional things. First, using the instructions given in Step B of Exercise 18–2, masturbate to a fantasy of your partner moving quickly in intercourse. When you can handle it comfortably in that exercise, you'll be better prepared to handle it in reality. Then, with your partner, slowly approach the problem activity. Start with a pace that is very comfortable for you, gradually building up the speed as you are comfortable with the slower movements. Stay focused and, should you become anxious or start to lose your erection, stop and relax, then resume at a slower pace, gradually increasing the speed again. Done consistently, this procedure will allow you to tolerate and enjoy more and more movement.

When you are comfortable with uninhibited movement in the female superior position, you can try other positions. You don't need a formal exercise for this. Try any positions you want, remembering that the first experience with a new position may be a bit awkward and uncomfortable. The first few times you try a new position, go slowly, as in Exercise 19–5, then gradually work up to a pace which you and your partner enjoy.

There is one last exercise to be done. The chances are extremely good that sooner or later you will again lose your erection during a sexual experience. By going through this under instruction, you can learn some useful ways of dealing with the situation and preclude the possibility of its upsetting you when it happens spontaneously. This exercise extends the understanding you developed in Exercise 19–4.

EXERCISE 19–7: LOSING YOUR ERECTION
Time Required: 20 to 30 minutes

You are to reenact your old erection problem and handle it differently than you did in the past. If your problem was that you did not get an erection while hugging and kissing your partner, then hug and kiss her and see to it that you don't get an erection. If your problem was losing your erection during insertion, attempt insertion while trying to make your erection go away. Whatever the old problem, see to it that you get your penis soft.

There are many ways of accomplishing this. Worrying whether it will stay hard, if the kids are listening, or how tired you'll be in the morning are all good methods. If none of these work, try pacing around the room for a while.

Now deal with the situation in a way that is enjoyable for you and your partner. Stick with your partner and find some things to do that satisfy both of you. These activities can be sexual or nonsexual.

Repeat this exercise as many times as required for you to feel comfortable about losing your erection and dealing with the situation after that. For some men, one or two repetitions are sufficient. Others can benefit from more.

Once you can handle this exercise with equanimity, you know you are in good shape. By fulfilling your conditions, you are ensuring that your penis will be hard most of the time you want it that way. And when it doesn't come up to expectations or when you lose your erection in the middle of things, you no longer have to worry about it. You are now prepared to have a good time no matter what your penis does.

As time goes on and your sexual confidence develops even further, you will not need to be as careful about your conditions. Just don't forget about them altogether. If you should ever find yourself getting back into the old rut, if you begin to get tense in sex (which can happen, for example, when you're with a new partner) or find that sex isn't as satisfying as it is now, start being more careful about meeting your conditions and stopping when you get tense, and it probably won't be too long before things are well again.

20

Male Sexuality and the Aging Process

There is no special age at which one becomes old. We start aging and the inexorable march to the grave the minute we are born. This chapter is not only for men who are over sixty or who think they are old. It is intended for all men because all of us are aging and will someday consider ourselves old, and also because younger men suffer from the same affliction as older men—the inability to live up to the sexual standards that they have accepted.

Sex, we have been led to believe, is for the young and healthy. We glorify youth and health, forgetting that both are gradually lost. We segregate the aged and make jokes about them, such as the one that follows, conveniently forgetting that someday we will be on the short end of these same jokes.

An elderly man was hoping for some solace from the minister speaking on the radio. At one point the minister said that if the members of the radio audience would put one hand on the radio and the other hand on the ailing part of the body, he would pray for healing. The old man put his left hand on the radio and reached for his penis with the right. At which point, his younger wife laughed. "He said that he was going to heal the sick, not raise the dead."

Ours is not a good country in which to grow old. Aging is regarded not as a natural and inevitable process, full of possibilities and challenges as well as limitations, but rather as a dread disease to be fought and staved off as long as possible by all the resources of modern technology. The result is those who think they are old or who reach a certain birthday or who notice some wrinkles often feel unattractive, unwanted, and useless. And they are, at least according to the standards that many people in this society subscribe to.

In discussing a subject like aging it is useful to have a reference point, a time of life to which aging or being old can be compared. Although, as we have said, the aging process begins at the moment of birth, this is not the reference point that most people use. Rather, it is the period of life in which most of us reach the peak of our physical abilities—adolescence and early adulthood, which we arbitrarily define as the years between thirteen and twenty-five, give or take a few years—that people use as a standard when they talk about youth and age.

In conformity with this idea, we begin our discussion of aging with a look at adolescence. During the teenage years and for a few years thereafter, males —with few exceptions—are in better physical condition than they will ever be again. It is a time of seemingly boundless energy, enthusiasm, and exuberance. You can play football all day, boogie half the night, masturbate during breaks, sleep for four hours, and still be up in time for class or work in the morning. It is not like this for long and it will never be the same.

Never again will we run as fast, climb as high, move around as strongly and briskly. And few of us will ever again feel so strong and healthy. For in these years most of us hardly know the meaning of ulcers, high blood pressure, arthritis, coronaries, chronic constipation, and the many other discomforts and diseases that the adult body is heir to. Even if we smoke, drink, eat too much, and sleep too little, our young bodies are resilient enough not to be too badly scarred.

Adolescence is a time of great physical and emotional upheaval. Adult size and strength are attained, along with full adult sexual capacity. Hormonal changes cause an increase of sexual feeling. Sex, sex, sex—most teenaged boys are obsessed with it. Masturbation usually begins during this period, as well as the first sexual experiences with partners.

Boys experience and deal with their budding sexuality in different ways. Some find it more of a curse than a blessing. Some stick to masturbation while others quickly turn to partner sex. Some are so concerned with other activities or so repressed that they seem to be almost unaffected by sex. Despite these differences, there seems to be sufficient uniformity of experience to justify talking about an adolescent model of sexuality.

Adolescent sexuality, when not repressed or sublimated, is obsessive. Nothing else matters as much as sex—thinking about it, fantasizing about it, learning about it, doing it, talking about it. We would prefer, at least at times, to concentrate on our schoolwork or other activities, but fantasies and warm tinglings and erections continue to intrude. We are unable to control our sexual feelings. It is not enough that we get turned-on by almost every female we see on the streets and in magazines and movies, but many of us also feel the stirrings of flesh and fantasy when we look at our sisters, cousins, and mothers of friends. Where, we wonder, will all this lead? Are there any limits?

In his hilarious and deeply moving account "Being a Boy," Julius Lester tells of his experience:

No wonder boys talked about nothing but sex. That thing was always there. Everytime we went to the john, there it was, twitching around like a fat little worm on a fishing hook. When we took baths, it floated in the water like a lazy fish and God forbid we should touch it! It sprang to life like lightning leaping from a cloud. I wished I could cut it off, or at least keep it tucked between my legs. . . . But I was helpless. It was there, with a life and mind of its own, having no other function than to embarrass me.

Which brings us to the adolescent penis, a penis that for many of us knew only one position—rigid. As one man said, "I had a hard-on from the day I was fourteen until I graduated from college." Whether we were pleased or embarrassed by its erect state, we were always aware of its presence.

Refractory periods were something many adolescent penises had not heard about. A few seconds or minutes after ejaculation, there it was again, as hard as if nothing at all had happened. And boy, was it hard! It felt like it was made of steel and would burst apart if something wasn't done to appease it. But there seemed to be no way. No matter how many sexual experiences we had, whether alone or with partners, the insatiable appetites of our penis seemed unaffected.

The ejaculations were marvelously strong, just like explosions. Many of us tried to see how far we could ejaculate, often in competition with our friends. It was something to see, our vigorous bodies sometimes pushing the ejaculate halfway across the room.

The process of sex was quick and explosive. Once we got started—and it took little enough to get us going—there was an awesome rush toward ejaculation. We were out of control; passion (or something we took for passion) pushed us and we exploded in orgasm.

That is adolescent sexuality, something many men look back upon as the good old days. It may not have felt very good at the time, given our anxieties about our pimples, girls, whether anyone would notice our erections, and other teenage concerns, but it did serve as our first experience with adult sexuality. It became a standard against which later experiences would be compared.

It is also a standard that would be reinforced by

many sources because, as you may have noticed, adolescent sexuality is very similar to the fantasy model of sex discussed in Chapters 3 and 4. In its obsession with sex, the functioning of the penis, and the uncontrolled nature of sex, adolescent sexuality is the closest most men will ever get to fantasyland sexuality. Our first experience of adult sexuality is therefore similar to the dominant model in our culture that is held up as a standard for the rest of our lives.

And that is quite unfortunate because adolescence is soon over, with the larger portion of life still to come. Every day and every year take us further and further away from the only models of sex we know. Which means that we are but poorly equipped to deal with the changes that aging brings.

We go along after our adolescent years, often unaware that time is passing and we are aging, until one day it suddenly hits us. It may be when we develop an illness or condition that we had considered something that only happened to middle-aged or old folks —such as ulcers, back trouble, heart problems—or perhaps when we notice that we have developed a pot belly, or that we can't run as fast or play tennis as well as when we were younger. Or it may be something sexual: when we notice that our erections aren't as full or firm, that our orgasms aren't as powerful, or that we are having sex less often. Whatever the exact stimulus, it is frequently a moving experience.

At one point in my mid-twenties, I realized that my erections were not as firm as when I was in high school. In those days they seemed hard as rock. Now they were hard but not quite rocklike. I couldn't believe that I was over the hill at the tender age of twenty-six. At this rate, I was certain, I wouldn't be able to get an erection at all by the time I was thirty. With some difficulty, I talked about it with my doctor. He assured me that nothing was wrong, that I was simply experiencing the effects of aging, and that I would probably be able to get it up long past thirty, although it might never again be as hard as when I was seventeen. This discussion had repercussions for many months. I often thought about it and tried to make sense of it. I realized that I had always believed that I would be young until one special day, like my seventieth birthday, I would suddenly become old. It was quite a shock to recognize that I was already experiencing the aging process. It was a process that went on continuously, whether one was twenty, forty, or sixty. I had a strong sense of the fact that I, too, was aging and that I, too, would someday die. And I realized that there really were no special days when anything happened. What seemed like special days were those on which I took the time to become aware of how much had changed since the last special day on which I looked.

Men react to aging in many different ways. Some retire from physical activity in their twenties and never again do anything more strenuous than walking to their cars. Others retire for months or years at a time, then suffer attacks of energy and play five sets of tennis or shovel snow for several hours, often causing themselves severe injury in the process. Still others continue regular physical activity—be it walking, jogging, swimming, or something else—for many years, not moving as fast in their sixties as in their thirties, but moving nonetheless. And some of these men continue their activities well into the years where they "should be too old to do them" and become local celebrities.

Sexual changes are similar. Things slow down for all men as the years go by, but the changes occur at different ages and with different consequences. Some men retire from sexual activity quite early in life, engaging in it only rarely thereafter. Others move along well until some illness intervenes and then they, too, retire. For others, reaching a certain age spells the end of sex. It is as if they had heard that there is no sex after, say, sixty, so they fulfill the prophecy upon reaching their sixtieth birthday. Still others just keep on going. They don't function exactly as they did in their twenties and thirties, but they keep on enjoying sex in their sixties, seventies, and beyond.

We now list and discuss some of the more common sexual changes that occur in men as they get older. Most of them also accompany illness (whether temporary like a cold or flu, or chronic) and some types of injuries. These changes do not necessarily happen at the same time for a given individual; they occur at different times for different men; and not all men experience all of them.

1. *It takes longer to achieve erection.* Since sex is no longer like a new toy, and since the hormones are no longer racing through your body the way they did when you were in high school, your penis is slower to jump up from its naps. Just thinking about sex or kissing your lover may no longer be enough. Direct penile stimulation may be required to achieve erection even in the late twenties or early thirties.

This bothers many men. They remember "the way it used to be" and feel embarrassed that it isn't that way anymore. Some of them come to therapy wanting to get an erection "the normal way," meaning without direct stimulation. Sometimes something can be done, especially if the man is bored with his partner or is having sex under less than appropriate conditions. But most often he needs to accept the fact that there isn't any normal way to get an erection, that it is perfectly acceptable to get one through penile stimulation from his partner.

The problem many men have in accepting this is the idea that a man should produce his own turn-on and not need anything from a woman. For some men, needing stimulation (or information or anything else) from a woman means that they are weak and dependent on their partners. Such is the influence of our sexual mythology. Here, as elsewhere, we need to realize that the mythology is just that and not very useful as a guide for human behavior. After all, why should we value a spontaneous erection more highly than one attained through the tender, loving care of a partner?

2. *Erections may not be as full or as hard.* This phenomenon is noticed by some men in their twenties and thirties, and by many who are older. Some men play a numbers game, offering information that their erections are only 60 or 80 or some other percent as

hard as they used to be. This is understandable, given the "hard as a rock" model we learned, but has unfortunate consequences because it can lead to worrying about what isn't instead of enjoying what is.

3. *It takes longer to achieve an erection after ejaculation* or, in more technical terminology, longer refractory periods are experienced. Masters and Johnson found that many men in their fifties and sixties could not get an erection, regardless of how much stimulation was applied, for twelve to twenty-four hours after their last ejaculation.

Another related discovery by Masters and Johnson is that some older men who lose their erections without ejaculating may be unable to regain them during the same sexual experience no matter how much stimulation is applied. They may have to wait several hours or longer before again having erections. This phenomenon seems restricted to men over the age of sixty and is by no means universal even within that group.

4. *It takes longer to ejaculate.* Ejaculatory control, a problem for many younger men, often comes automatically with aging. This is not usually experienced as a problem. In fact, many regard it as a gift, particularly those who were quick on the trigger when younger.

Not only does orgasm take longer to reach, but many men past forty find that they have no desire to ejaculate every time they have sex. They can maintain an erection for relatively long periods of time and need not end each experience with an ejaculation. Few men see this as a big problem, but many are surprised and a bit discomforted by it. Sex without orgasm is a new idea for them that takes some getting used to. A few men have great difficulty with this, feeling that somehow they are failing by not having an orgasm. All that is needed is acceptance of the fact that we have stated several times: orgasm is not necessary for a good sexual experience.

Not ejaculating every time he has sex can have positive results for the older man, since the lack of ejaculation means he can have more frequent erections (refractory periods are usually shorter when there is no ejaculation).

5. *Ejaculation is less powerful.* As the male ages, particularly past sixty, the ejaculatory process becomes less efficient. The sense of ejaculatory inevitability may vanish altogether and the orgasm may feel less intense. The ejaculate may seem to seep out rather than being expelled under pressure. This does not mean that orgasm is not pleasurable, but only that it may feel somewhat different than it did before.

6. *Sex is engaged in less frequently.* On the average, frequency of sexual activity declines with advancing age. There are many reasons for this decline—boredom with sex, decreased desire, the belief that sex is not for the old, physical infirmities—some of which we discuss later in the chapter.

Despite the general decline in activity, however, there are important exceptions. Some men have as much or almost as much sex in their seventies as in their twenties. And one study reported that about 15 percent of the people over sixty-five in the population studied said they were having more sex than ever before.

7. *Automatic functioning may no longer be possible.* In order to have good sex, an older man may have to consider factors he could safely ignore when younger. He no longer can function automatically; he has to set the stage carefully for a good experience. Arousal, conditions, and proper stimulation become crucial.

Whitney, a man in his late sixties who was having trouble getting erections, had some difficulty understanding why he had to pay attention to things he had never before considered. But, since he wanted to get remarried, he was open to exploration. A surprising discovery was that time of day made a great deal of difference. He almost never got an erection late at night but, after meeting some of his other conditions, he found that a good time for him was immediately following his afternoon nap. He later was able to expand his "good periods" to include

early morning and evening, but the afternoon remained the best time for him.

Four of the age-related changes mentioned have to
do with erections. This is quite disturbing to many
men who can barely conceive of sexual relations without an erection. God forbid the silly thing shouldn't
get hard! For reasons we have discussed throughout
the book, men forget that they have fingers and mouths
and lots of sensitive skin elsewhere, and also that a
penis doesn't have to be hard to be enjoyably stimulated. Older men, as well as many younger ones,
would probably have more sex and enjoy it more if
only they could let go of the idea that there can be no
sex without an erection.

Why do so many older men retire from sexual activity or develop sexual problems? It is easy to jump
to the conclusion that the answer is obvious: the aging
process destroys both interest and the ability to function. We suggest that this is only rarely the case. Aging
may make things different but it doesn't destroy them.
A man of ninety is probably not going to run a four-
minute mile, no matter how much he trains. But if he
wants to and is willing to get himself in condition,
there's no reason why he can't enjoy jogging.

Although, as we have seen, aging does have some
effect on erections, Masters and Johnson found that the
male "does not lose his facility for erection at any
time." And we have worked successfully with dozens
of men in their sixties and seventies who came to
therapy complaining that they hadn't had erections
or sexual interest in years. It is clear that something
other than biological mechanisms is what causes older
men to give up on sex. It is to these other mechanisms, psychological and social, that we now turn.

We have already said that our society defines
sexuality as something that belongs to the young and
healthy. To most people, sex in the aged seems somehow inappropriate and is a source of discomfort.
Many of us can't even conceive of a man and a wom-

an in their sixties or seventies in bed. It strikes us, as one young man put it, as "gross and disgusting." An elderly man interested in sex is a "dirty old man," while a younger man with precisely the same interests is admired and praised.

Older men realize that they don't fit the picture of people who are supposed to be interested in sex. They learned the adolescent and fantasy models of sex just like everyone else, and they know how poorly they fit the models. Often they are confused because, contrary to what they have learned, they find that the feelings are still there, they are interested. And many feel guilty for having sexual feelings when they know they "shouldn't" have them.

For some, the easiest way of reconciling the differences between what they were taught and what they feel is to capitulate to society's view and suppress their own feelings. If this sounds strange to you, perhaps you can think of some examples from your own life where you felt a certain way or wanted to do a certain thing but then, realizing that your feelings or desires were contrary to your image of yourself (as a "nice boy," "grown man," "mature and responsible adult"), you pushed away the feelings or decided not to engage in the activity. In a similar way, older men often decide, consciously or not, that sex is not for them.

And they have plenty of help in making such decisions. That they are asexual is reinforced by the attitudes of those close to them. Adult children, for example, often view their parents' normal sexual urges as embarrassing and put obstacles in the way. A not very subtle example was given by a man in his seventies.

He was still interested in women and sex but, for financial reasons, lived with his daughter. She was repulsed by his "carrying on" and frequently criticized him for "acting like a child" and "running around with loose women." She also refused to take messages for him if his women friends called when he was out.

Relatives, friends, and physicians are often shocked and do all they can to remind the man that he is acting with impropriety. As for hospitals and other institutions in which many of the aged spend a fair portion of their time, probably the less said the better. Most such places make no provision for sexual expression of any kind (even for their permanent residents) and anyone caught masturbating or having sex with a partner is subjected to inhuman degrees of embarrassment and humiliation.

The message gets through—sex is not for you.

The elderly are often treated very delicately, as if they were in danger of falling apart, especially if they have had any serious medical problems. Sometimes, the heavy emphasis by the doctor and concerned friends and relatives on taking good care of oneself and not doing anything that might cause harm are taken to mean that the man shouldn't do anything. Since sex is a something, many think it is healthful to stay away from it or at least not do it too vigorously. Sometimes the man, sometimes his partner, and sometimes both conspire to deny or limit his sexuality, or at least to keep it from being very interesting. All with the purpose of preventing the poor fellow from doing himself harm.

Thus far we have been talking about general ways in which the social definition of the role of older man is inconsistent with active sexuality. There are also other problems. Older men realize that they can't live up to the rules laid down in the fantasy model of sex. Of course, they never could; but now they can't even equal the poor imitation they used to do. The results of this kind of comparison with the fantasy model are often tragic, extending far beyond the area of sex.

After giving a talk about friendships in old age to a group of men and women over sixty-five, I had the opportunity to chat with some members of the audience. One man who had a hearing problem and a hip injury that necessitated using a cane when he walked said that he missed female companionship since the death of his wife, but that nothing could be done about it. When I asked what prevented him from befriending some of the women in his apart-

ment building, he replied: "Are you kidding? Look at
me. I can hardly hear and I don't walk so good. They
don't want me. They want a man, someone who is
strong and can take care of them. They don't want
an old cripple!" What is particularly interesting about
this story is that my invitation to speak had come
from the women. They outnumbered the men five
to one and were desperate for some male attention
and company. Not only that, but two of the women
had told me that they were interested in this particular man but found him unapproachable. He was
so locked into his idea of what a man should be
and what he thought women wanted that he couldn't
see what was happening right in front of him.

There is no question but that many men feel very
bad and apologetic for being old or for not being as
healthy as a twenty-year-old. In the country of the
young and healthy, being old is in itself something many
people feel guilty about, as is being ill. Feeling bad
about oneself is, of course, hardly conducive to good
sex or good anything.

Still another problem for many older men is a restrictive view of sex. Having learned about sex when the
Victorian influence was much stronger than it is today,
their ideas about sex are frequently unnecessarily
narrow. Many believe that masturbation is totally
inappropriate for adults and so deny themselves
this form of gratification, or engage in it with a great
deal of guilt. Still more are convinced that sex equals
intercourse and refuse to have much to do with manual or oral stimulation. Which means, of course, that
they view an erect penis as the main actor on the
sexual stage. This is a heavy enough burden for men
who are young and healthy; it is impossibly difficult
for many who are old and in less than perfect health.
They get so concerned about the erectility of their
penises that they sometimes bring about what they
most fear—erection problems. Because they fear failure to get an erection or have already experienced this
problem, they stay away from sex.

It is important to recognize that these fears often

occur in a context of low self-esteem. The man knows he is growing old, that he cannot do all the things he used to do, and that society does not see much use for old men, and he may feel bad about all these things. His image of himself is deflated; he feels like something less than a man, less impressive than he would like. And perhaps he has heard that old men are usually impotent.

Feeling bad about himself and fearful of being unable to be an adequate lover, an older man may simply give up on sex, claiming to be too old or too sick for such things. Or he may attempt sexual activity but, because of his fears, develop problems. This makes him even more worried, even more concerned if he still "has it in him." A cycle of failure and anxiety ensues, leaving him feeling worse about himself each time. After a while he may come to the probably erroneous conclusion, perhaps with the aid of his partner, friends, or doctor, that his age or physical condition is the cause of his problem and that nothing can be done about it.

There is one other reason for retirement from sexual activity. Contrary to popular belief that all men love sex and can't get enough of it, there are men who experience sex as a burden and engage in it only through a sense of duty or in order to avoid hurting their partners' feelings. This is usually not true at the beginning of a relationship. The newness and mystery of the partner and the relationship generate a passion that is often expressed in sex. But as the novelty decreases, the man realizes that sex just isn't what he thought it would be. There are more important things that require his attention (usually his job or career) and sex is just more work without a lot of rewards.

Many women will recognize the pattern—the man who can't get enough sex at the beginning of the relationship but not long after seems to lose all interest in the subject. Some women, as well as some sex experts, put the blame on man's presumed nonmonogamous nature or on the woman for not being seductive enough. We think differently. It is usually the man's unrealistic expectations of what sex can provide and his limited idea of how he should be in sex that cause the trouble.

Once a man starts feeling that sex is something to be endured rather than enjoyed, he's not far from sexual retirement. In his novel *Go to the Widow-Maker*, James Jones gives a realistic picture of sex as obligation.

> *Grant didn't know if he could. In silence he finished his drink. Finally both pity and a terribly painful sense of how embarrassing it would be for her if he didn't, plus a vague moral obligation which he knew was ridiculous, plus the fact that she was a female, all came to his aid. . . . Gracelessly, flat on his back, he groped at her crotch a little to aid him. . . . He rolled over onto her, stuck it in her, and pumped away until he came.*

With this type of sex, it's no wonder that a man would rather stay late at work or watch TV. Who needs anything as dull and listless? But he needs a respectable reason for leaving the field. The demands of his career, illness, or old age provide it. His partner can't complain because it's not that he doesn't want to, it's just that his job or condition or age won't allow it.

While we can understand why anyone who is disappointed with sex should want to discontinue their participation in it, the fact is that it doesn't have to be this way. Sex can be fun. But, because of a rigid adherence to the fantasy model of sex that they learned while very young, many men see no alternative and decide that sex just isn't worth the trouble.

One of the saddest consequences of giving up on sex is that often this means that all forms of physical affection are dispensed with. Because of the fear that the partner will want more than snuggling or the fear of being unable "to finish what I start," many men discontinue all forms of affectionate expression—handholding, cuddling, kissing, everything. And this at a time when such expressions could convey so much caring, support, and affection. Thus the elderly who have given up on sex often become even more isolated and discontent.

While not denying that sexual functioning does change with age, we have said that there is no age at which a man should give up sex or at which sex becomes unseemly or unenjoyable. Sexual expression can be a part of your life for as long as you live. There are no biological or medical reasons for sexual retirement, there are only a lot of cultural myths that cause lots of older people lots of misery.

While we don't mean to say that you should have sex—that decision being yours to make—we do say that there are many enjoyable ways of having sex, some of which may be new to you. If you are interested, the relevant chapters in this book can be valuable. All the suggestions and exercises have been used with men of all ages. Of course you may have to fight some prejudices of your own and those of others, but it may not be as difficult as you think. Societal attitudes about aging have started to change in recent years and while there is still plenty of room for improvement, we think and hope that it won't be too long before being called a dirty old man will be taken as a compliment.

If you have little desire and/or a persistent inability to get an erection, and you are on medication of any sort, it's a good idea to talk to your doctor about this. A number of prescription drugs are known to have, or are suspected of having, negative sexual side effects. If a doctor has told you not to have sex because of a medical condition, find out more about what that means. Sex is not a dangerous activity and there is usually no reason for refraining from it for long, even after major illness or surgery. If you're well enough to take a walk, you're probably well enough to have sex. If your doctor doesn't agree, get a second opinion. If your doctor thinks that men your age shouldn't be interested in sex, find yourself another doctor.

If you decide that sex isn't for you, that's fine, but we would ask you to consider if you're getting as much physical contact as you like. If not, we hope that reading this book has at least raised the possibility that you might be able to get more without having sex or doing anything else you don't want to do.

We close with two stories, one of a woman who is a

relative of a close friend and one of a former client. Their stories are close to our hearts and cheer us when we contemplate our own old age.

Auntie Grace, as she is known to all her friends, is now eighty-four and still carrying on. She has always liked men and sex, and survived three husbands and many lovers. Her older sister, with whom she has lived for the past decade, is scandalized by her activities. A few years ago, as Auntie Grace was leaving for a date, her sister started on her usual lecture about how a woman of her age shouldn't act this way and what would the neighbors think. Just before walking out the door, Grace turned and said: "Don't worry, I won't come home pregnant." When last heard from, Grace was getting involved with the younger set. She had just returned from a vacation where she had met a "nice, young doctor" who was only seventy-one.

Norton came for sex therapy when he was seventy-six. He had enjoyed a good sexual relationship with his wife for over forty years but then had had a few erection failures and assumed that he was over the hill. For almost ten years since then, he hadn't tried to have sex. He and his wife still engaged in some physical contact but not as much as before, because he didn't want to lead her on. After reading an article about sex and aging in a popular magazine, he decided to see if anything could be done. He had all the usual, narrow ideas about sex, as did his wife. Intercourse had always been the culmination of their sexual activity and they could barely think of anything that could be done without an erection. But they had a very close and warm relationship and were able to support one another in looking at new models of sex. It took only a few weeks for them to resume satisfying sexual activity. Here is what he said in his last therapy session. "I guess it's never too late to teach an old dog some new tricks. Hell, I haven't had so much fun in a long time. And to think of all the time we wasted because I was so fired up with concern about that old pecker. He comes around pretty good now, but like you said, not every time. But that's all right, I don't need him every time. I just like to be playing around with

Emmy, and she loves it. I haven't seen so much fire in her eyes for twenty years or more. And when she plays with me, it's just like I was back in high school again. Wow, I just want to eat her up. It's really good to be back with her again like this. And I don't intend to stop, ever."

21

Male Sexuality and Medical Conditions

You should be warned that we are entering one of the most confused and least understood areas of sexuality. There is vast disagreement over if, how, and why various diseases and injuries affect sexual functioning and enjoyment, what kinds of sexual expression are possible for those afflicted with the various conditions, and what the patient should be told. Many physicians are no better informed in this area than lay people and, in fact, have themselves been the source of much misinformation and harmful advice. Our intention is to give you sufficient information so that you can start being a better consumer of medical services and find out for yourself what is possible and enjoyable for you.

The diseases and injuries thought to influence sexual functioning are too numerous to be discussed or even listed here. Some of the more common ones are alcoholism, some types of cancer, diabetes, epilepsy, hypertension, multiple sclerosis, and spinal cord injuries or lesions. Sexual functioning can also be seriously affected by what the doctor does for you. Radical prostate surgery, for example, often leads to erection problems. Some types of back operations may also result in sexual problems. Decreased sexual interest and/or impaired sexual functioning is produced in many people by the medications so liberally dispensed in our society. Some of the most widely prescribed drugs—including Valium, the most popular medication these days—have been implicated in sexual problems.

It is not surprising that so many diseases and conditions influence sexuality. Almost anything that affects the way you feel physically or the way you view yourself can have sexual consequences. As a simple example, you might consider what happens to your sexual desire and functioning when you have a bad cold, a severe headache or stomach ache, or the flu. And these, of course, are simple and transient conditions. More severe and chronic conditions involve not only more extensive physical disability and discomfort, but also one's view of oneself as a person (e.g., "I'm a cripple," "I'm a sick man, not as good as other men").

Even given this, however, it is clear that men are affected differently by the same physical problem. There is hardly any physical disability that prevents all men who have it from enjoying sex. Some diabetics, for example, have erection problems. But many do not. And many men who developed a sexual problem after getting a certain disease or sustaining an injury have been able to overcome the problem and have good sex. We will return to this point later.

It is easy to get depressed reading the medical literature about the sexual effects of many physical disabilities. It is full of gloom and doom, citing statistics showing higher frequencies of sexual problems for men with these disabilities than for those without, and spinning many interesting-sounding theories about the supposed mechanisms causing the sex problems.

The depressing conclusions in the literature have been picked up by physicians and the popular culture, and the "knowledge" has a wide circulation. We "know" that diabetics have erection problems, that men with spinal cord injuries can't have sex, that sexual problems caused by long-term alcoholism are irreversible, and so forth, just as we "know" that older men aren't interested in sex and, even if they are, can't function satisfactorily. This "knowledge," no matter how erroneous it is, has consequences.

It has consequences for the same reasons that the idea that older men don't function well in sex has consequences. The man with a physical disability becomes frightened. Will he be able to have sex or won't he? His fears may be so strong as to discourage him from even trying to have sex. Or he may try but, because of his worries, bring about the failure he is worried about. When statistics are being compiled, this man may well be included among those who are having sexual problems—which is fair because it is a fact. But then things will become confused because it will be said that his physical condition caused the problem. But did it?

Almost everything we said in the last chapter about the sexual situation of older men is true of most disabled men. The sexual model most of us learned has no room for sick or crippled participants. Where is the encouragement for a man with epilepsy or multiple sclerosis or a colostomy or a spinal cord injury to think of himself as sexual? And everyone "knows" that men who have had coronaries shouldn't have sex or at least should make sure that it's not very exciting.

Like men who feel bad about being old, sick and disabled men may feel bad about their condition. They may not like the way they are—"only half a man," as a man with a colostomy called himself—and may wonder why anyone would want to make love or do anything else with them. They often have special requirements in sex ("special" meaning anything not part of the fantasy model of sex) and feel guilty about them, just as many healthy men feel guilty about their special requirements. Sometimes they can barely stand to think of their requirements, let alone communicate them to a partner.

Paul, a man in his forties with multiple sclerosis, decided to seek therapy after twelve years of no sexual activity. He claimed that his penis was dead but after a while he found that he could get erections with prolonged penile stimulation. But he was greatly bothered by his condition. Since he was confined to a wheelchair and had only limited strength in his arms, it took some doing to get into a bed. How would a woman feel, he wondered, having to wait the five minutes it took him to make the transition? He felt embarrassed and helpless as he contemplated the possibility. He was also bothered by the vigorous and lengthy stimulation he required to get an erection. He bitterly complained about his rotten luck and wistfully talked about how easy sex would be if he could just hop into bed and get an erection without any help from a partner.

Men who have only recently had surgery or found that they have a serious illness have another issue to contend with. In addition to the discomfort and physical limitations they have to endure, there is the psychological shock of learning that one really is mortal, a realization that is often accompanied by feelings of despair and depression. All these responses add to the man's feelings of inadequacy. He feels bad about himself, he's worried about his condition and his future, and he's not sure what he can or should do. This is quite a bundle of woes to bring to bed, and it can't help but affect what happens there.

There is also an excellent chance that the medical authorities in charge of a sick or disabled man's treatment will add to his sexual worries. We wish this weren't true, but it is a fact that most doctors know very little about sex and don't feel comfortable discussing it with their patients. The situation is beginning to change—most medical schools have instituted required sex courses in the last decade and doctors are now being encouraged to attend workshops and seminars on sex—but it is still very far from ideal or even good. Almost every man with a serious illness or disability whom we have treated—and there have been scores—had been told by at least one doctor that he would not be able to have "normal sexual relations." Such words of good cheer served to increase his fears and, sure enough, he developed sexual problems.

We want you to be very clear about what we are

saying before going further. We are not implying that illness and injury have no sexual consequences. They certainly do. Nor are we saying that there are no cases where sickness or injury or surgery has caused serious and perhaps even irreversible damage to the organs or nerves involved in sexual functioning. There are such cases. But we *are* saying that the number of such cases has been seriously exaggerated. The fear of being unable to function and all the other worries attendant upon being physically impaired cause the majority of sexual problems for sick and disabled men, not the condition itself. No matter what kind of impairment you have, some kind of enjoyable sex life is possible for you.

To understand why there have been such exaggerations and such confusion in this field, we need to look at how a doctor typically decides that a man is too ill or crippled to be capable of functioning sexually. Doctors view the complaints presented to them—whether a fever, an erratic heartbeat, an erection problem—as symptoms of some underlying disease process. Their job is to determine what that process is and recommend appropriate treatment. Doctors are, of course, trained to think in terms of physical disease or injury such as nerve degeneration or spinal cord lesion rather than in terms of psychological factors such as the ones we discussed above.

Once a physical cause has been found—nerve damage, for example—the options are often limited. The cause should be treated, but this can't always be done. There's not a lot to do about nerve damage, cerebral palsy, or multiple sclerosis, but one can try to get the alcoholic to stop drinking and the diabetic to maintain better control. But if this doesn't help, it is often assumed that nothing can be done. And it sounds so convincing. Not only can the physician supply you with a scientific-sounding explanation of why you have the problem, but he can also cite statistics demonstrating that many men with your condition have the same sexual problem.

The real problem, however, lies elsewhere. Medical

deduction works well in many areas but very poorly when dealing with sex problems. The deduction game the doctor plays—we know that disease X damages nervous tissue; this patient has the disease and can't get erections; therefore the disease has damaged the nerves that govern erection—is simply the wrong game. The premises are too loose and inexact. Disease may damage nerve tissue but not in all patients; we don't know how much damage is necessary to impair or destroy a given function, and it is difficult to determine how much damage has been done; further, even if some nerves have been damaged or destroyed, others may be able to take over some of their work. Such deductions are also wrong because they ignore the many nonphysical factors that can cause sex problems. The following example will help you understand how easy it can be to make a wrong diagnosis when physical illness is involved.

I found that I was diabetic when I was twenty-one. A few years later, the first time I had sex with Allie, I didn't get an erection. I got very worried about this and didn't get an erection on numerous successive occasions. I started wondering what was wrong with me. Since there was no such thing as sex therapy in those days, I didn't consider getting professional help. But apparently I did all the right things. I spent lots of time with Allie in and out of bed and we had plenty of physical contact. My impotence lasted five weeks. Then, all of a sudden, all was well and remained well.

Looking back, it's easy to see what caused my problem. Allie was the first woman I had been with who was sexually assertive. She knew what she wanted and made no bones about it. I was scared. My sexual confidence was precarious and I didn't know if I could satisfy her. My fear was what caused my erection problem. It took several weeks for me to become accustomed to this situation and feel more comfortable with her. When that happened, my erections returned.

But I have sometimes wondered what might have happened had I gone to a doctor for help. Given what I have heard from many doctors, from what other diabetics have told me about what their doctors did, and from what I have read in the medical literature, there is a good chance it would have gone like this. The doctor would have taken a medical history and focused on the diabetes. He would have checked my blood and urine. If I were not well controlled, he would have helped me with that, hoping that resumption of good control would solve the problem. If it didn't, or if I already was under good control, he might have said that the impotence was caused by the diabetes and that nothing could be done. (If this sounds extreme, you should know that it happens all the time.) I would have freaked out—my sexual career over at twenty-four!—and been unable even to think about sex without trembling, which would have ensured that my problem would go on forever. I have many times thought that someone up there must like me, for I didn't know at that time that diabetes was thought to cause erection problems and I didn't consult anyone who might have told me.

It is tragic that standard practice should be such that this man can rightly claim that ignorance is what saved him. We have seen numerous men who sat around for one to twelve years, worrying themselves into total impotence because their doctors had told them that their "organically caused" impotence was incurable.

The medical deduction game is also called into question by the successful results that some sex therapists have had with men who were told by doctors that they were too impaired to have sex. The results obtained by us and other therapists with almost every condition said to lead to irreversible sex problems indicates that there is more hope for the physically disabled than had previously been believed.

Are we saying, then, that regardless of your physical condition you have the capacity to function sexually as you once did or as a man in very good health can? In truth, we aren't sure. Some men have been able to do so. For others, however, it wasn't the way it used to be. But the way it used to be isn't the only way to be sexual. You may have to learn some new ways of sexual expression, ways that deviate widely from the adolescent and fantasy models of sex but that can still be enjoyable.

> Paul, the man with multiple sclerosis mentioned earlier in the chapter, finally got around to having sex with a partner. He was uncomfortable at first because of his problems getting from his wheelchair into the bed and the vigorous stimulation he needed to get an erection. But he learned some things as time went on. He could ask his partner to help him get into bed, a practice which both shortened the amount of time it took and also kept them in close contact. He later realized that it wasn't necessary to have sex in bed; it was much easier for him to roll onto the floor. He also learned some things about his penis. While he continued to need more stimulation than most men, he found some new ways of having his penis stimulated that shortened the amount of time required to get an erection. He also found that he could sometimes have a very good time satisfying his partner and rubbing against her without an erection. Paul is not totally happy. He still wishes he didn't have multiple sclerosis and that he could have sex the way he did before he got the disease. But he's much more content than when we first saw him. He's no longer afraid to go out with women and he no longer backs away from sex. When he has sex, he usually enjoys it. Not too bad for a man who had been told by several doctors, and who himself believed, that nothing could be done for him.

So what does all of this mean for you? Simply that if you haven't been having sex or have been experiencing sexual problems because of what you have been told or think is a physical disability, you have some choices. You can decide that nothing should or can be done. If you are content with this decision, well and good.

Another possibility is to proclaim that you would do something about sex if only things were different, if only you didn't have a disability, if only other people had a different attitude toward your disability, and so on. The "if only" game is common and often very comforting to those who play it. It places responsibility for the problem on people or factors over which the player has no control, thus relieving him of any responsibility for changing his situation. The man in a wheelchair thinks that he would get his sex life together if only he could walk; the older man, if only he were thirty years younger; the man with a colostomy, if only he could control his elimination functions.

The "if only" game is also played by many who are not technically disabled. It's easy to see why when you realize that we are all deficient and disabled compared to the unattainable sexual standards we learned. Many young and healthy men say they would have more sex, or better sex, or deal with their sexual problems, if only they had bigger penises, if only they could prolong intercourse for an hour, if only they knew more about turning women on, if only their sexual upbringing hadn't been so restricted and oppressive.

We are reminded of a high school friend.

Billy wouldn't go out with girls and his friends tried to help. If only he knew what to talk about, he said, he would go out. So we suggested some topics and had some practice conversations. He finally felt confident that he had something to say, but strangely he still wouldn't get a date. Now he said that he didn't know how to dance. How, given this deficiency, could he ask a girl out? So one of our girl friends taught him to dance. But he still stayed home. If only he had a car, all would be well. One of us promised him a ride when he got a date, but Billy still wouldn't go out. It turned out that none of the several hundred girls in our school was his type. If only he could meet the right girl. Billy never did have a date in high school.

Many years later Billy told one of us that the problem really had nothing to do with talking, dancing, rides, or any of his other "if onlys." The reason he hadn't gone out in high school was simply that he was scared silly of being alone with a girl. She might not like him and make him feel like two cents. Or he might not like her and not know how to deal with that situation. Or worst of all, they might like each other and then what should he do? Billy discovered on his own that all the reasons why he wouldn't go out were only cover-ups for his tremendous fear, a fear, incidentally, that was only a bit more powerful than that felt by most of his friends.

There is no question but that sex, like most human interactions, can be frightening. Possibilities abound for rejection, humiliation, and hurt. This is true for all men, but those with medical problems, because they depart so much from the model of men we all aspire to, are much more vulnerable. "Who wants a man with a weak heart?" "What will she think when she finds out how long it takes for me to have an erection?" "How can I tell her that I sometimes have epileptic fits or insulin reactions?"

Questions like these plague many men. And there are no simple answers. There is always the possibility that you will be rejected and hurt. It is silly to assume that it can be otherwise. You will be rejected not only for the reasons that all men sometimes get rejected but also because of your physical condition. Some women don't want to have sex with a man with heart disease, cerebral palsy, a colostomy, or whatever you have.

So you can sit around for the rest of your life contemplating how wonderful everything would be if only you weren't who you are. A fascinating pastime, perhaps, but always a losing one, for you will never be other than who you are and you will therefore never get any of the benefits that you think would accrue to the person you wish you were. Sex as you are may well carry risks of disappointment and rejection but, since you'll never be anyone else, it might be in your interests to consider if the risks are worth taking.

Which brings us to the third choice you can make. You can decide that, whatever the risks, you are interested in a more enjoyable sex life and that you are willing to find out what is possible for you. This may be a difficult decision. No one can guarantee you'll get precisely what you hope for. Even if you put a lot of time and effort into it, you may not end up performing the way you want. And your ideas about what is acceptable sexual expression will probably have to undergo some revision.

We're not saying it will be easy and we don't want to offer any false hope. But our experience has been that an enjoyable sex life is possible for almost all men, regardless of the type of physical impairment they have, providing that they are willing to work on it and be reasonably flexible about what acceptable sexuality is. You probably won't end up acting like the men in the fantasy model of sex, but then neither does anyone else.

If you choose to go on, do the exercises in the book that are relevant to you and feel free to make any adjustments required by your physical condition. The suggestions and exercises here are exactly the same as we use in therapy with disabled men. You will have to make some changes in some of them to make them better fit with your situation but that shouldn't be difficult.

It is preferable that you have the cooperation of a doctor who knows you and your condition, and who knows about and is comfortable dealing with sexual issues. If you don't have such a doctor now, we strongly suggest you find one. A local medical school or university with a sex program should be able to give you an appropriate referral. But it is up to you to make sure that you get the kind of medical care that you want. Be a wise consumer. Let the doctor know what your interests and concerns are, ask about his experience and training in the field of sex, and ask all the questions you have. Try not to expect him to perform magic. If you believe that he is not qualified to help you, or that he is uncomfortable discussing what you are concerned about, find someone else. You are as responsible for good medical care as your doctor. Do your part and you'll find a good doctor who can do his.

If a doctor has ever told you that you should not have sex, get some clarification. If the advice remains the same, get another opinion, preferably from a doctor experienced in dealing with sex.

If you are taking medication of any sort, check with your doctor regarding possible sexual side effects. As we mentioned earlier, many prescribed drugs do affect sexual desire and functioning. Switching medications or changing dosages can sometimes help, but this should never be done without a doctor's supervision.

Surgery is another issue that requires your attention. If your doctor recommends surgery, you should talk to him about why and what the potential benefits and side effects are. Ask specifically how it will affect your sexual functioning. If the chances of negative sexual side effects are present, ask if there is another treatment available or another kind of surgery. Some doctors don't give much thought to the sexual lives of their patients and suggest radical procedures when more conservative ones would do as well and not affect sexual functioning. This is sometimes seen in prostate surgery, where the radical approach through the perineum often destroys the nerves that control erection while the other methods of reaching the prostate do not.

Before having any type of surgery, we strongly recommend that you get a second opinion from another reputable doctor. Discuss the options and side effects with both doctors and form your own opinion. Being a wise consumer will help you get the best possible treatment for yourself.

If the suggestions and exercises in the book don't produce the desired results after being given a reasonable chance, that doesn't necessarily mean that you should give up on sex or decide to get a penile implant. Before making any such rash decisions, we suggest you consult a competent sex therapist.

22

The Uses of Sex and Sex Problems

People have sex for a variety of reasons. Even in one sexual experience, the motivations of the participants are usually numerous and complex. Among the more common motives for, or uses of, sex are physical release; giving or getting comfort, affection, or love; proving one's popularity, masculinity (or femininity), or sexual prowess; and expressing tenderness or hostility.

The point is simple but important—sex has many uses. What feels like a desire for sex can be something quite different, as Erich Fromm pointed out in *Man for Himself* many years ago:

> *Intense sexual desire . . . can be caused not by physiological but by psychic needs. A . . . person who has an intense need to prove his worth to himself, to show others how irresistible he is, or to dominate others by "making" them sexually, will easily feel intense sexual desires, and a painful tension if the desires are not satisfied. He will be prone to think that the intensity of his desires is due to the demands of his body, while actually these demands are determined by his psychic needs.*

We are not implying that sex should be engaged in only for certain "right" or "correct" reasons. Human sexuality is flexible and can satisfactorily serve many needs. While we have frequently said that sex is for fun, this formulation is obviously too narrow, as the following example indicates.

Peter had sex with a woman he barely knew and wasn't particularly attracted to, the day after his father's funeral. When asked what led him to have sex with her, he replied: "I really wasn't that turned-on and had some difficulty getting hard. But I needed to feel close to someone. Feeling her body and feeling mine respond helped me feel that I was alive. As a purely sexual experience it wasn't much but it was important in another way. It gave me some comfort and a feeling of aliveness that I really needed."

Peter certainly didn't have fun with his partner but got warmth and comfort during a very bad time in his life. He had no regrets about the experience and remembers it as being important.

But it would be a different story if Peter always had to have sex to feel alive. A possible outcome would be that his penis would refuse to function, which it almost did on that occasion. Another possible result is that he would have problems with his partners. He was clearly using the woman. He was too wrapped up in his own feelings to pay any attention to hers. Given the circumstances, it is understandable. But as a consistent pattern, it might not be either understandable or acceptable to his partners.

While sex can be used to meet a number of needs, it has its limits. Sex is not appropriate for meeting all human needs and there are needs, which while they can be satisfied in sex, are best fulfilled in other ways. When sex is consistently used in pursuit of goals for which it is not appropriate, disappointment and problems may develop. In this chapter we discuss a few ill-advised uses to which sex is put by men and what can be done about them.

Then we deal with the functions sometimes performed by sexual problems. If you have had difficulty in changing your sexual behavior by following the ideas and exercises in this book, the reason may lie in the functions that your present situation serves.

The purpose of this chapter, then, is to help you better differentiate among your various needs and desires so that you satisfy them in the most appropriate and enjoyable ways.

Sex as Proof
of Masculinity

In Chapter 2 we mentioned the tremendous pressure felt by men to continually offer proof that they are indeed worthy of being called men. The types of proof required vary and can be almost anything that we and our peers accept as masculine—making a lot of money, talking tough, having an important job, being good at mechanical tasks, being athletic, and so on.

And, of course, sex. Sex has long been a major way of asserting one's manhood. In earlier times, manhood could be demonstrated by siring children, especially sons. While this notion still retains power for some men, it has been largely replaced by a different kind of sexual demonstration—enthusiastic interest in sex and engaging in it frequently and well. In many circles, men who show little interest in sex—who do not leer at every woman who goes by or talk about their sexual escapades—are regarded suspiciously by other men.

Many of us have known or at least heard of a man who ran around having sex with a different woman every night, and more than a few of us have envied him not only because of all the fun we assumed he was having but also because of the admiration he inspired in us. Anyone having that much sex must be quite a man. Surely he must possess all the manly attributes we feel we are lacking—confidence, aggressiveness, unlimited libido, a way with women, and the techniques of a great lover.

Sexual prowess as validation of one's masculinity is an equation that most of us implicitly accept and, while only a few of us would choose to be Don Juans, it does affect our thinking and behavior. Even if we don't go so far as to have sex every day to prove what real men we are, we are tempted to live up to at least some of the canons of the male mythology, whether or not we are capable of such feats or whether we are really interested in them. But we try anyway, just to reassure ourselves of our manhood.

Otto had been in a bad relationship for several years. As it grew increasingly bitter and disappointing, his partner made a lot of angry comments about his sexual abilities and told him that he wasn't man enough for her. After they separated, Otto was in a bad way. He half believed that his partner was right, that he was no good in bed and couldn't satisfy a woman. He felt like "not quite a man" and set out to do something about this. Three or four nights a week for over a year he picked up a different woman at one of San Francisco's "body bars" and attempted to have sex. He was not interested in any of his partners. He just wanted to prove that he was a man. He was rarely turned-on and, to make matters worse, drank a lot to try to still the tremendous anxiety he felt when with these women. A perfect set-up for failure. For over a year, with over one hundred different women, he did not get one erection or have one good experience. And yet he must have looked to all the world as the great stud on the prowl.

Inside, however, he was hurting terribly and finally decided to get professional help. He soon solved his problem, but only after he started paying attention to what he wanted and stopped trying to prove himself. He learned that he valued companionship and intimacy more than casual sex, and stopped going out altogether for several weeks. He then met a woman he liked and formed a friendship with her. As they got close and comfortable, they started having sex. There were a few minor problems at first, but they were soon worked out.

Otto is unusual only in the large number of unsatisfactory experiences he underwent in his great adventure to prove that he was really OK. By using sex inappropriately to try to prove his adequacy as a man and lover, he didn't get what he needed to have good sex.

Many men equate sexual frequency with masculinity. They have read or heard about men who have sex more frequently than themselves and wonder if they are missing something. They think that they should have greater sexual interest. This notion is easily reinforced if their partner wants sex more often than they do. These men are often shocked when they discover that they really want something other than sex.

Henry, a man in his early forties, made this announcement after being in therapy for a few weeks. "You're going to think this is crazy but I'll say it anyway. I don't think I have that much interest in sex. I've thought about it a lot the last few weeks and realized that my sexual needs have never been great. I could probably get by with three or four times a month. What I really like is a lot of touching and hugging and sleeping next to a woman, but I usually don't want to go further. I guess I'm more like a woman in this respect. The problem is that I'm a man and none of this makes sense. I wish I wanted sex more often."

Henry had tried to live up to what he thought were the masculine norms, pushing himself to have sex when he wasn't interested and when he would have preferred nonsexual physical contact. His penis had tired of the charade and stopped functioning.

Both Henry and Otto tried to force themselves to function in unfavorable situations. They violated their conditions for good sex and expected their penises not to notice. Both of these men had to learn that masculinity is not defined by wanting to fuck rather than wanting a hug or a caring relationship.

Another aspect of this issue is using sex as a means of dominating your partner. Sex is your show, done your way, with you in charge. Your partner can of course participate, but only if she follows your rules.

A woman friend told us this story. A man she was dating insisted on having sex his way, meaning that he always initiated and always got on top of her in intercourse. One day, she initiated and after arousing him, assumed the superior position. He was horrified and yelled: "Who do you think you are, fucking me? I'm supposed to be on top!" It looks comical on paper but that's not the way he meant it. He couldn't deal with her being in charge and refused to continue with the experience. Whereupon she refused to continue the relationship.

The phrase "making a woman" describes the idea well. You "make" her—make her submit to your will, do your bidding. Then you feel like a man. The example we gave is extreme in its lack of subtlety and there are many more delicate ways of playing the same game: for example, never being interested when your partner initiates, never following her instructions or her desires, and having lots of reasons why whatever she suggests is wrong.

Aside from the fact that such a game makes for a very one-sided relationship where many things cannot be explored and experienced, it usually also generates a lot of resentment from the partner. Not many women are willing to put up with it anymore.

Sex As Demonstration or Proof of Love

Sex can be a wonderful way of expressing caring and love. For many men, however, sex is the only way of expressing these feelings. We have given several examples elsewhere in the book of men who were attentive to and communicative with their partners only during sex. This often causes problems.

Most women want affection expressed in both sexual and nonsexual ways. Many of them say things like, "Just once I'd like him to show me he cares without its leading to sex." What do these women want? We can't speak for all of them, but the desires we have heard included shared activities, nonsexual touching, and verbal expressions of appreciation and affection.

You might want to ask yourself if sex is the only way you have of expressing affection. If for some reason you couldn't have sex for a month, would your partner know you cared for her? How?

Exclusive reliance on sex to express certain emotions overburdens sex; and, as we have mentioned several times, the less the burden, the better the sex.

A different twist to using sex as proof of love occurs when the man tries to get a woman to show that she cares by having sex, or engaging in some particular type of sexual activity, with him. It's as if he believed that "if she'll do even this with me, then she must care." Some nice male-female friendships have run aground on this rock, well expressed by the following example:

Janice and I had a great friendship for a year, the only good friendship I've had with a woman. We did lots of neat things together and talked about everything, including our lovers. But after a while, it got to me. I mean, I thought she really cared for me, but here she was fucking other guys and going down on them, and I wondered if she cared enough to do the same for me. So I put pressure on her and she finally gave in, but it was lousy. She wasn't into it and I guess I wasn't either. Our friendship wasn't based on physical attraction or sex and it just wasn't the right thing to do. We still see each other but it's not as good as it was.

Sometimes the man thinks that sex is a good way of determining how far his partner's interest or affection extends. At the beginning of a relationship, her willingness to have sex may be sufficient. Later, the ante may be raised. "If she'll give me a blow-job (or swallow my come or have anal sex or whatever), then she accepts and loves me." If she won't do it, this thinking goes on, then obviously something is lacking in her feelings toward the man.

What the man doesn't understand is that what his partner will or will not do may have little or no bearing on her feelings about him. She may not want to have oral sex because she learned that it was dirty or because she had a bad experience with it in the past or because she just doesn't like having a penis in her mouth. On the other side, complying with his demands may also not mean what he thinks or hopes it does. She may comply because she's afraid of losing him or because she was taught always to do a man's bidding in sex or because she thinks he knows what is best for her. None of these motives, of course, has anything to do with caring or love.

Two types of problems derive from this use of sex. First, it can be coercive. Pressuring someone to do something she really doesn't want to do in order to prove she cares is a dangerous game. She may refuse, despite all your entreaties, leaving you feeling that she doesn't love you, and with no recourse but to break up what may have been a nice relationship. Or she may give in because of fear or guilt. Such gifts have a way of being very costly. She will probably harbor a great deal of resentment over the coercion. Relationships built on such foundations rarely do well.

A second problem, common to all proofs and tests, is that there can never be sufficient proof. Even if she complies with your requests, will you feel loved for more than a few minutes? Somehow it doesn't work out this way. The ante must be raised, a new test proposed. And it goes on endlessly.

If you have been using sex as a proving ground and want to change, we offer a few suggestions. Whether you have been trying to prove your masculinity or affection, or getting your partner to demonstrate her feelings for you, the important thing is that you begin gradually to stop acting on your impulses to prove anything. These impulses will not immediately disappear. You need to acknowledge their presence and do what you can to go in another direction.

Let's assume you have been relying solely on sex to express all your good feelings toward your partner and want to expand your repertory. The next time you feel loving toward her or want sex, don't have sex. Express your feelings some other way. Give her a big hug; tell her you love her; share some of your thoughts and feelings with her; offer to give her a back-rub; suggest doing something you know she enjoys; or tell her you'd like to do something for her to express your love and would like to know what she wants.

For a while—at least a few weeks—deliberately express affection in nonsexual ways. You can have sex if you want, but first express affection nonsexually. Make sure that such expressions are not always followed by sex. Do this as an experiment and then determine how you and your partner feel about this new pattern.

You may have some negative feelings when making a change. Many men reported feeling vaguely uneasy, irritated, or frustrated. This is to be expected when you change a habit. In time, however, the uneasy feelings will decrease in intensity and be more than balanced by the positive ones that result from feedback from your body and your partner.

Sex As Sensation-Seeking or Nirvana

Most of us, because of the fairy tales we heard as children, believe somewhere in the back of our minds that there is a way of avoiding all the problems and hassles of everyday life, of walking into the sunset and living happily ever after. It's a nice fantasy, but many people are acting as if they took it seriously.

In recent years, sex has been advertised as one of the main paths to that walk in the sunset.

The rewards of sexual experience have been exaggerated almost beyond belief. It is the fantasy model all over again, and with a vengeance. *The Joy of Sex* tells us that "Sex is the one place where we today can learn to treat people as people." Later it informs us that "orgasm is the most religious moment of our lives, of which all other mystical experiences are a mere translation." If all the saints and mystics had only known! Many sex manuals read suspiciously like religious tracts. It is easy to get the impression that eternal happiness or the salvation of one's soul is what is being discussed. Sex, or the right kind of sex, it seems, can unite us with the cosmos, radically changing and fulfilling our lives.

This line of thought, if it can be called that, is supplemented and abetted by the attitude well expressed by Herbert Hendin as the "unquestioning belief in the unquestioned good of trying everything." There is pressure from everywhere to "search for all the gusto you can," as one advertisement put it, to experience every possible activity. Hendin calls it "a rapacious greed for experience." It matters little if the experiences are good, bad, or indifferent; the important thing is having them, being able to say that you have done it all. Sex is considered to offer a utopia of unexcelled thrills and vibrations, so it must be experienced with as many people and as many permutations as possible. Nirvana here is not so much a mind-blowing experience as the sheer aggregate of experiences.

Whichever version of heaven is being sought, nothing is too drastic or bizarre for experimentation. Sex with drugs, sex on the floor and ceiling or in the road, sex with children and animals, sex with urine and enemas—everything must be savored. The results are usually disappointing because the ideas that are peddled deal with fantasy while real sex is only human. One is forced either to drop out of the game or to up the ante by trying something even farther out.

But raising the ante never quite does it. As Gregory Curtis says in his fine article on sex manuals, "The New Facts of Life," "No matter who one is with or what is happening, real sex seems always to be some place else with someone else." Many people don't understand that what they experience can never equal what they think they ought to feel. They assume they should have mystical orgasms, and blame themselves for not doing so. They think they haven't yet found the right activity or partner or that they are too uptight to let themselves experience the ultimate joy. And the search continues.

It is tragic that such notions require comment, but the need is a reflection of the degree to which they have been accepted. Literally millions of people peer through countless sex manuals and magazines looking for the secrets that will send them into orbit.

The first thing that needs to be said is that sex simply does not have the power that has been attributed to it. No matter how good it is, sex does not have the power to radically alter your life. You still have to contend with work, taxes, the children's allowances, and all the interesting and annoying nonsexual aspects of your relationship, like who left the top off the toothpaste, how you should spend your weekends, and who should walk the dog. Sex researchers John Gagnon and William Simon put sex in perspective when they say that "it is by its very nature a dependent variable. It is something that is more caused than causing, and only through its ties with other human experience is it given its meaning."

A second point is that even if there are not problems, sex is only rarely of the earthshaking variety. Frequently it is merely pleasurable and pleasant in a quiet, lazy way. And sometimes it's just a physical release, enjoyable in a small way but maybe not worth missing Johnny Carson for.

As for sensation-seeking, it is often a very disheartening and disillusioning experience. Nothing lives up to its billing, so newer activities must be found. In the process, people often violate themselves by doing things quite inconsistent with their feelings and values.

We recall a man who for four years tried to force himself to have sex with another man. He had been heterosexual all his life but thought that his inability or unwillingness (he was never sure which it was) to have sex with a man represented a deficiency on his part. Loving a man sexually was an important experience he didn't want to miss. When we asked why he just didn't go and do it, he said: "I'm not ready yet. I'm too uptight because of my upbringing. I know that everyone is inherently bisexual but my training was so strict that the thought of actually doing it with another man almost nauseates me. But I'm working on it." We don't know the outcome of this story but we wonder if the agony and self-torture this man went through was worth it.

Another problem with the frenzied scramble to experience all things is that it sometimes leads to an inability to experience anything. You can become so obsessed with the wonders you will someday experience that you don't pay any attention to what's happening now. And even if it doesn't go to this extreme, bizarre experimentation tends to cheapen almost everything and rob you of the joy of experiencing the simple things of life. A hug or even the conventional type of intercourse can seem very dull and not worthwhile if you've been spending the last few months doing it in the road with donkeys and whips.

Real sex is not and never has been a magical solution. It cannot bring intimacy if there is no closeness or affection to begin with. It cannot bring joy if you violate your needs and values.

We are not saying that experimentation is wrong. It can be fun and a nice, sharing experience. But not when it becomes a consuming, labored goal and when expectations run far ahead of what reality can deliver.

If you think your expectations have gotten out of hand, you might want to ask yourself some questions. Whose expectations are you trying to fulfill? Why are they so important to you? See if you can attend to what is happening in your next sexual experiences and then determine what, if anything, was lacking. What

would you have to do to make up any deficiencies
you noticed? Are you willing to pay the prices involved? Talking about these issues with a friend, partner, or therapist can be valuable.

Impersonal Sex

We define impersonal sex as sex with minimal emotional involvement. The bodies make contact but the
people do not. There is little curiosity, warmth, caring,
closeness, or feeling of any kind. While the correlation
between impersonal sex and casual sex is probably
quite high, the two terms are not synonymous. A
one-time experience with someone you just met sometimes does include personal sharing and involvement.
On the other hand, a long-term relationship is no
guarantee against impersonal sex.

Impersonal sex flourishes today. It is the hallmark
of prostitution which, contrary to the hopes and expectations of many philosophers of sexual freedom, is
doing a thriving business. It is also characteristic of
the activities of millions of people—singles and mar-
rieds alike—who would never even dream of paying
for sex.

There are a number of reasons for the popularity
of impersonal sex. Often it is not a goal in itself but
rather a by-product of striving for other goals. When
the goal of sex is to prove something—be it one's
masculinity, sexual prowess, popularity, or liberation
—impersonal contact is the likely result. The proof assumes such importance that the partner, and even
one's own feelings and satisfaction, are lost sight of.

Impersonal sex is also a goal in its own right. It
is tempting as a release from loneliness and sexual
tension. It offers at least a semblance of human contact
without the problems that real contact entails. Many
people these days seem to have sex rather than shaking hands or talking. In some ways sex is easier, because talking and shaking hands can be risky. They
invite contact and sharing. Whether the relationship

is long-standing or just beginning, it is difficult to know how much of oneself to reveal and how much involvement and commitment to allow. It often seems safer to hop into bed where, one can hope, the bodies will do their part and it won't be necessary to deal with silly and annoying things like communication and vulnerability.

There is a great deal of talk about intimacy these days, but it is well to remember that intimacy is always difficult and there are powerful forces arrayed against it. In a world where constant happiness is considered a reasonable expectation and where there is much pressure to experience everything, the complexity, responsibility, and pain of intimacy or personal sharing seem somehow out of date and not worth the trouble.

For some, sexual activity itself has become the main defense against involvement. You may be able to recall some examples from your life where you initiated sex not because you wanted sex but because it provided an escape from an otherwise uncomfortable situation. Sex often seems easier and safer than deciding what you really want to do or working out a disagreement, and it therefore can be more of a running away from something else than an activity engaged in because it is attractive in its own right. We agree in large part with Herbert Hendin's claim that the sexual revolution "has become a revolution against intimacy."

All of us have impersonal sex at times. Even in the most caring of relationships, there are times when you are so wrapped up in your own thoughts and concerns that you really aren't there when sex is happening. Sex at such times often feels rather blah, but an occasional occurrence isn't something to be concerned about.

But there are people for whom impersonal sex is the norm.

Aldo was forty years old when he came for therapy because of erection problems he had experienced for about a year. He exuded sex, something noticed even by our receptionist to whom he had only said hello.

He worked in a bar that catered to young singles and it was a rare night when he was not picked up. He had sex with almost every woman he met and almost never saw them again. It was easy to believe his claim that he was a fantastic lover (at least for those women who didn't want their sex cluttered up by feelings). Satisfying his partners was always his main goal and his only criterion for a good sexual experience.

Involvement of any sort was anathema to Aldo. He rarely thought about whether or not he liked his partners. It was sufficient that he was attracted to their bodies. The worst fate he could imagine was having feelings for a woman and being with her more than a few times. Everything had been going fine for him until his penis stopped performing. Now he was frequently embarrassed in bed. Everything he did, said, or implied with women in one or another revolved around the moment when he would enter them and give them the greatest sexual experience of their lives. Without an erection, he was lost.

Until he began to have problems with his erections, Aldo was a good example of automatic functioning. He could perform without regard for conditions, arousal, feelings, or anything else. But then, as so often happens, the whole system broke down.

It may sound as if Aldo was exploiting women. We don't see it this way and we don't believe that impersonal sex is always, or even usually, a case of men using women. Women are as implicated as men (Aldo, in fact, rarely initiated contact or gave invitations; the women came after him and he never promised more than sex) and usually both partners are using each other in the same way. They have sex and nothing else, then part, and it is often quite embarrassing if by chance they run into each other again.

The only important question you need to answer is whether impersonal sex works for you. If you are satisfied, fine. We know, however, that many men are not happy with it. They do it but are not content and wish for something better. The human contact it provides is illusory and the sexual release it affords is often less satisfying than what could have been derived from masturbation. Many men who have tried this kind of sex find that they often don't function well. Others can perform but get little from their experiences. Aldo didn't want to feel anything, but other men do.

One man, very much like Aldo in many ways, loved to talk about all his sexual adventures. When the therapist interrupted his rambling account of his latest exploit by asking if he enjoyed it, the man's tearful reply was, "No. I feel dead inside."

If you want to change to a more personal type of sexual expression, you need to consider the prices you will have to pay. You will, at the least, have to deal with some feelings you have kept hidden, you will feel uncomfortable some of the time, you will have to take risks, and you may well be hurt, rejected, and disappointed. The costs must be paid.

If you think you are willing to pay the fare, begin by getting to know some women and, for a while at least, stop having so much sex. Do things that are pleasurable and talk about what you want, as long as it's not sex. When difficulties and complications arise, acknowledge at least to yourself the temptation to run. But try to stick it out and work out the problems. The process is not easy and can't be accomplished overnight. It takes a long time and you may want to get some professional help along the way.

It should be obvious by now that we believe that sex is only sex and consequently has a limited area of applicability and utility. This really isn't a problem except when sex gets used for purposes for which it isn't appropriate. There are many better ways of dealing with most issues than having sex. Even when sex is relevant, it still may not be the best course to follow. As an example, we return to our story of Peter, the young man who had sex the day after his father's funeral.

After recounting the experience presented earlier in the chapter, Peter was asked if there were any ways other than sex that could have been used to make him feel alive and comforted. He couldn't think of any but agreed to take a fantasy trip back to the day after the funeral. The therapist gave instructions to help Peter reexperience his feelings on that day and then asked Peter what he would want if he could have anything at all (the only thing he could not ask for was that his father be brought back to life). Peter got deeply involved in the fantasy and imagined himself being held by a woman (a cross between his mother and Marti, a woman he knew only slightly but was very attracted to) while he "cried my guts out." He actually cried for some time, and then became calm.

Peter said he felt better and was glad he agreed to do the fantasy. In fact, although he felt sad, he said, he felt better about everything than he had since he heard of his father's death. He added that doing what he had done in the fantasy was obviously a better way of dealing with his feelings about his father's death than having sex. He was then asked what he thought he would do if he had that day to live over again. His reply is instructive.

"This sounds contradictory, but I think I'd have sex. Sitting here it would be easy to say that I'd have Mom or Marti hold me, but out there isn't the same as in here. I know how to have sex. It was easy for me to approach Ann [the woman he had slept with], make some moves and notice her response, and just go ahead. I can see now that it didn't meet my needs half as well as the fantasy I went through with you. But I don't know how to ask someone to hold me. How can I ask someone to let me sit in their lap and cry my guts out? My mother is finally starting to treat me like an adult and here I'd go crying like a child. And Marti, I like her and want to get something going with her. Crying on her lap doesn't exactly seem like the best way to start a relationship. It's funny, as I'm talking something is telling me that I'm full of shit, that both Mom and Marti would understand and would even have a special kind of respect for me, for the fact that I could feel the sadness and cry. But, boy, when I think about actually doing it, it still seems hard."

The fact that Peter, a very intelligent and sensitive man, resorted to sex when other alternatives might have better met his needs is a good indication of how sexualized our lives have become. The chains that bind us are, to use a metaphor from elsewhere, as hard as steel. But they can be slipped out of or broken and, as we get free, we are probably going to feel better about sex and the rest of our lives.

The Uses of Sex Problems

If you have done the exercises in this book carefully but have not achieved the results you wanted, or if you thought you wanted to make some changes but couldn't find the time, energy, or privacy, you have three choices. The first is to conclude that nothing can be done for you at this time and call it quits, at least for now. The second is to decide that you can't get the help you need from a book and consider seeing a good sex therapist. Before you do that, however, you might want to consider the third possibility, that your sexual problem may be serving a positive function for you.

Nearly everyone thinks of bad sex or a sexual difficulty as a problem that should be solved. However, and we realize this may sound very strange at first, a sex problem may be a solution to another problem. Of course the sexual difficulty is in itself a problem. It makes you feel bad and creates misery, but it may also protect you against something which might be far worse. Most often the person is not aware of the protective or positive function performed by his problem and is shocked when he discovers it. Here is an example that may help to make this concept clearer.

Harry, a young psychiatrist, came to see us because of persistent erection problems with a woman he had dated for a year. It was immediately clear that Harry was afraid of being overwhelmed by his partner. She had already talked about living together and marriage, neither of which appealed to him at all. But he couldn't tell her about his feelings. He couldn't

say no to her or anyone else. When asked what
changes would occur in his life if he could get erections, he said: "There would be no reason for not
living together and she would move in." He was
shocked by what he said but after thinking about it
for a few minutes realized that it was true. When
asked if such an occurrence would be good or bad,
he said, "Disastrous." It was explained to Harry
that there was no sex problem as such. His lack of
erection was more of a solution than a problem; it
was the only way he could keep his partner from
moving in with him (since she wanted to make sure
they were sexually compatible before deciding to live
together). Since Harry was very intelligent and efficient, once he saw what the problem was it wasn't
necessary to tell him much more. He was simply told
that when he found another way of dealing with
her desire to get closer than he wanted, his penis
would behave differently and that he should call
if he wanted another appointment. He never did
call but we received a note from him about a month
later which said only, "Now that I'm saying no with
my mouth, my penis is saying yes. Thank you." A few
months later we ran into him and a brief conversation revealed that he continued to be more assertive
with his lover and that his sex life was fine.

We have worked with many men whose sexual problem was the only thing standing between them and
marriage or some other situation that they did not
want but could not deal with in a direct way. Sometimes the sex problem is used to hide other problems
that would be even more difficult to deal with: for
example, the possibility that the relationship is no longer much fun and should either be radically altered or
abandoned. The sex problem is a way of denying the
larger problem and keeping hope alive. The man acts as
if he were thinking, "If only I could have erections, all
our problems would be over and we'd have a good
relationship." So he can hope that a solution to his sex
problem will someday be found (while at the same
time unconsciously subverting any solution) and all
will be well.

Sometimes the sex problem is a way of expressing
negative feelings that cannot be communicated more

directly. Negative feelings are part of every relationship, but it often happens that these feelings are not dealt with openly and are left to seethe in someone's insides until they are expressed in some inappropriate way. Sex can provide a means of giving vent to the feelings, though the person who is doing the expressing is usually unaware of what he is doing.

Not getting an erection can be a way of saying, "See, you don't turn me on anymore," or "I know you'd like to fuck but I'm not going to do that for you." Coming before your partner wants you to or never being interested in sex when she is can also express hostility.

The sexual problem allows the man to avoid taking responsibility for his feelings. He can't take responsibility because he isn't aware of his motives. He honestly believes that he wants to resolve the sexual problem so that he can satisfy his partner and himself. But somehow he just can't seem to find the time, space, or whatever to solve his problem. That's a good clue that the problem is serving a protective function.

Marc, a man in his twenties with arousal problems that had not responded to almost two years of treatment with four different therapists, was at the end of his rope when he came to see us. He claimed he had a very loving relationship with his wife and there was no reason not to solve the problem. Things just somehow hadn't worked out with the other therapists. We convinced him to do a variation of Exercise 22-1 with us and he fought us all the way. Nothing, he swore, would be bad about solving his problem. We told him that we didn't think we could help him, given that four therapists whom we respected had already failed, but, since he had already paid for the session, we could chat a bit longer. We asked if he had ever felt angry with his wife. His response told us we were on to something. She had had an affair shortly after they were married and he was furious about it. But he had never let her know how he felt. When asked what prevented him from telling her his feelings, he replied: "I can't stand it when she gets angry. That's what she'll do. She'll listen a while, then start crying, which bugs the shit out of me, then start yelling and screaming at me, throwing up to me all

the bad stuff I did to her then, blaming me for pushing her into the affair. I hate it when she gets like
that."

Marc's lack of sexual interest allowed him to get
back at his wife without having to be honest about his
feelings or dealing with hers. It protected him from
dealing with anger, something quite difficult for him,
but at the same time was wrecking their relationship.
Marc decided to return for more sessions but we never
worked directly on sex. All we did was help him express
his own angry feelings and get more comfortable dealing with his wife's expression of hers. They had the
worst fight of their marriage about two months after he
first came to therapy. They didn't speak to each other
for a few days after that, then gradually they started
talking about the affair and their feelings for each
other. Not surprisingly, the sex problem vanished and
the relationship became sounder than it had been since
before their marriage.

We want to be clear about what we are saying because we know that these ideas can be easily misunderstood. A sex problem may be protecting you from
something that you consider far worse. This is not to
say that you enjoy your problem, that you don't want to
resolve it, or that you are fully aware of what is going
on. Contradictions flourish in human beings and it is
possible both to want something so much that it hurts
and at the same time to fight tooth and nail against
getting it. Discovering why you are resisting resolving
the problem is a good first step in coming to grips with
this type of contradiction.

The following exercise—adapted from one developed by John Enright, one of the most creative and
effective therapists it has ever been our pleasure to
learn from—will help you discover the obstacles in
your path.

It is not an easy exercise to do. Your mind may re-
coil from taking it seriously, since it asks you to look
at feelings or issues that are not pleasant and that you
have so far kept out of your awareness. It may help if
you remember that doing the exercise does not commit

you to any further action. You may decide, after determining what is in your way, that the price of removing it is too great and you'd rather leave things just as they are. But then you can at least stop worrying about your sex problem and get on with your life.

It's best not to read the exercise until you are ready to do it.

EXERCISE 22–1: WHAT WOULD BE BAD ABOUT RESOLVING MY SEX PROBLEM
Time Required: 1½ hours

Take your pen or tape recorder in hand and address yourself to whatever version of the question makes the most sense to you.

1. What would be bad (potentially harmful, negative, destructive) about resolving the problem?
2. What does having the problem do *for* me (in a positive sense)?
3. How would my life be more difficult or complex if I overcame the problem?

You may find that you can think only of positive outcomes, like how good you'd feel without the problem. Let yourself go through all the positive results, then for each one ask how it might make your life more difficult or lead to negative consequences.

Spend no more than 45 minutes on this part. If absolutely nothing comes to you, guess. If that doesn't help, put the exercise aside and come back to it a few hours or days later.

When you have completed this part, put it aside for a day or two. Then reread it and see if you have anything to add. For each item on your list, consider the following:

1. Is the negative outcome you expect a likely probability? If you don't know, can you find out? (E.g., "Is it probable that Susan will push for a more involved relationship than I want if the problem is resolved?")

2. What price would you have to pay to deal with it? (E.g., "I'd have to tell her straight out that I don't want to have a closer relationship with her at this point. That would be very hard for me to say.") Picture yourself paying the price in as much detail as possible. Back off if you get very anxious, get yourself comfortable, then start again. You might want to go over some of the relevant sections in this book for assistance. Keep dealing with the fantasy of paying the price until you can actually imagine yourself carrying it out.

3. Now ask yourself if you are willing to pay the price to solve your sex problem. (E.g., "Am I willing to tell Susan I'm not willing to have a closer relationship in order to solve my sex problem?") Take the first answer that comes to you and put it in the form of a statement. (E.g., "I am willing to tell Susan that I'm not interested. . . .") If the statement rings true to you, you'll know what you have to do. If it doesn't quite sound right, play around with it, changing a word here and there until you arrive at something that feels right.

Just because you know what you need to do is no assurance that you'll feel confident of doing it immediately. Get whatever assistance that you think you need, from this book or elsewhere.

If you concluded that you are not willing to pay the price, you might want to check your thinking to see if a more acceptable price would do the trick. Or you may decide to accept your situation as it is for now.

If you find that you do not implement your decision within a reasonable period of time, it's probably safe to assume that your obstacles have not been fully dealt with and need more attention. Doing the exercise again may help. If not, consider enlisting the aid of a competent therapist.

23

Sex and Liberation

Saying that we live in an age of transition is a cliché but is true nonetheless. The values that once gave structure and meaning to life have been falling apart for at least the last hundred years, leaving us to play or cry, as the case may be, in the ruins. The decline of religious values has had a great influence, but it can be persuasively argued that traditional sex roles, now in a state of grand disarray, played at least as large a part in supplying order and meaning to life.

The crumbling of the old order has both good and bad aspects. We have argued throughout this book that most of the problems men have with sex are a result of the traditional male role. Forced to bury the expressive, tender side of themselves and to relate in restrictive, stereotyped ways, men have not been well prepared to have real sex with real women. And it goes much further than sex. Our social scripting has not prepared us for meaningful relationships with other men, women, or children, for self-knowledge and expression, or almost anything else. In short, conventional sex roles are both impractical and destructive. They are based on fantasies and illusions, on a world long since past, and probably contribute as much as any other factor to our lives of noisy desperation.

We are accustomed to hearing this kind of talk—

from women. For at least the last seventy years many women have been questioning their role and trying to change it. This movement has gathered new momentum and influence in the last fifteen years. Women have taken the initiative in examining the whole institution of sex roles and they have wrought changes that affect men as well as women.

The fact that women have taken the initiative and are bringing about vast changes in the way all of us understand and act is itself a powerful indication of how far the traditional roles have deteriorated. Men have taken a very passive position, mainly confined to watching the women from the sidelines.

The position of men seems similar to that of many women prior to 1965. Although a great deal of dissatisfaction was felt by women in the past, they tended to blame themselves rather than questioning their role. Thus, women who were frustrated and unhappy about being home all day with the children questioned their ability as mothers rather than the idea that all women should be content sitting at home. There is no doubt that many men are today dissatisfied with their lot. We have mentioned that large numbers of men are not content with the sexual part of their lives, but the discontent extends far beyond sex. Men are unhappy about their work and their inability to be successful according to standard definitions. Many of those who have attained success realize how little happiness it brings. But most have been inclined to fault themselves rather than the standards and unrealistic expectations society has imposed.

Change is here to stay and its rate will probably accelerate whether or not men decide to play a more active role. Sex roles and other traditional institutions and values are crumbling precisely because they aren't working. While anything like a men's movement is clearly several years in the future, some men have started to question the established order as it affects them. More and more men are asking if there isn't a better way. They wonder if it's necessary for men to suffer from such a disproportionate number of diseases,

to die so much younger than women, to have so many
problems expressing themselves and relating to others.
They admire the audacity of women in seeking to
change their lives, the way women are struggling with
issues that men are afraid to face, and they envy the
closeness among women. In short, such men think that
change may be necessary and positive.

But there is another side to the picture, one that has
to be understood lest the opportunity for constructive
change be lost in a sea of confusion and chaos. Sex
roles and other societal institutions, no matter how
harmful they are in some ways, perform useful and
necessary functions. They provide the framework in
which one can live a meaningful life; they supply the
guidelines for thought, feeling, and action, and the
standards by which to measure oneself. These guidelines ensure a predictable and orderly world, thereby
giving a sense of security. These are not minor matters.

When institutions and values lose their influence,
predictability and security are diminished. Nothing can
be taken for granted. Issues that before had been ritualized and therefore made trivial now become subjects
for thought, debate, and anxiety, with no clear guides
for behavior.

A woman told us this story about a man she knows.
He had always performed small courtesies for wom-
en. One day a woman for whom he had opened a
door in a large department store loudly lambasted
him ("Don't you think I can open my own door, you
pig?"), which was quite different from the smiles and
thank-you's he was used to. He was embarrassed and
gave serious thought to the matter. He decided that
the new order was here and he would have to conform to it—no more courtesies. Things went fine
until one day when he was roundly criticized for not
offering his seat to a woman on a bus. He thought
about this for some time and came to a conclusion:
"There's no way of doing things right. If I act the
way I was brought up to act, that's wrong. If I don't
act that way, that isn't right either. I'm going back
to being the same old asshole I've always been and
I don't care if it's right or not."

Friends who work in restaurants have told us how often they overhear disagreements and arguments between couples, about who should pay the bill. When opening doors and giving up seats and paying for dates become subjects of debate and dissension, where it is no longer clear what is expected or who should do what, you know the old order is in trouble. And so are we all.

The world becomes a strange and frightening place when nothing can be assumed or predicted. A man used to know that sex would happen, if at all, when he wanted it to happen, because God knows women didn't initiate. A man could therefore be secure in the knowledge that nothing would happen until he was good and ready. But now he has no assurance whatever that his date or partner won't make sexual advances when *she* feels like it.

Despite fashionable talk about how wonderful change is and how nice it is not to know what is going to occur, we believe that uncertainty is difficult. Human beings do like variety and some degree of uncertainty—there is no doubt about that—but they like them best in a context of stability and security, and that is precisely what is lacking today.

Not only is there an absence of external stability and order, but the internal guidelines aren't working so well either. You can't depend on anyone else to follow certain rules and you also aren't sure which ones you should follow. The issue, of course, is freedom, one of the most difficult subjects we humans have to contend with.

To apply freedom to sex means that instead of relying on rules such as "A man always wants sex" or "A man should always be in charge of sex," you need to assess situations as they occur and determine for each what you want to do. If you realize that you don't want sex right now, then you need to ask if you are willing to act on your feelings, even while knowing that there are people, including perhaps your partner, who believe in the rule that says men always want sex. If you decide to act on your feeling of not wanting sex now, you have to let your partner know. If you are serious about being free, you will have to be honest and say that *you* aren't in the mood rather than relying on some external support (like a new rule that says men don't like sex on Tuesdays). You will, in short, have to put yourself on the line, and that's rarely easy.

You will also have to accept responsibility for your decision. It is conceivable that your partner will not want to be with a man who sometimes isn't in the mood for sex. Accepting responsibility in this case means that you don't blame her or yourself but instead accept the fact that the two of you have a difference of opinion as to what men should be like, a difference that may or may not be capable of resolution.

Of course this is all difficult and that is why, despite all the flag-waving and speech-making about freedom and liberation, few people actually are willing to accept even a small portion of freedom. What is much more common, and we see it all around us today, is freeing oneself from one set of rules and immediately flinging oneself into the arms of another set, different but no less demeaning and no more tolerant of individual preference. The current notion demanding that one experience all things, whether one likes them or not, is no better than the Victorian idea demanding that so many things not be experienced. Neither has much to do with being free. The extreme form of the current fad of androgyny, which demands that men express both "masculine" and "feminine" qualities, is no more liberating than the system against which it is a reaction—that men express only "masculine" qualities. The range of acceptable behavior is broadened, but the coercion remains the same.

Freedom is not free. It has many prices but, then, so does everything else. While it is a fact that there is no way of going for free, if you are careful and have a little luck you can have a say about what prices you will pay. And that is no small thing.

Since we live in an age of confusion and turmoil, we all must consider our situations and determine how we want to relate to the changing scene around us.

You can decide to try to live by the old rules, but

you should be aware that this is not without problems. For many people, the old system didn't work well and exacted a horrendous toll. Are you willing to keep paying it? It is also true that the old rules are no longer as widely accepted and there will be those people who consider you strange just because you stick to them.

Another choice is to find a new set of rules and values to adhere to. As we have said, there is no shortage of such systems and all of them have advantages and disadvantages. Perhaps the chief advantage of all of them is that they offer the security of having a set of rules. The greatest disadvantage is that they are all narrow and restrictive in their own ways.

The third alternative is to accept to some degree the burden of freedom, adopting external rules to cover situations that are unimportant or where the rules make sense. This still leaves large areas where you will have to exercise your own judgment and be responsible for it. It seems that more and more people are at least willing to try this approach. It is difficult and there are many dropouts, but there are also many who are encouraged by their progress and plan to continue.

If this is your choice—and obviously it is our bias—this is a good time for making it. While there are always sanctions for behaving differently than others expect or want, there is probably more tolerance for individual differences today than at any previous time in history. Not only have restrictive laws and policies been abandoned at an unprecedented rate, but there also seems to be a greater individual desire for understanding and accepting behavior that does not fit the standards.

It is also a good time because everyone is having to deal in one way or another with all the changes that are occurring. We are all in the same boat in this sense, which can be a fine basis for understanding and support. For all the differences between men and women, and despite the angry charges and countercharges of the last few years, it has become increasingly clear that it's difficult to be either a man or a woman and that both share many of the same dilemmas and aspirations.

As we have repeatedly maintained, sex is not the

most important part of life. But it is a part and as good
a representative as any other of the larger context of
our lives. The hopes and fears and problems that affect us elsewhere usually also show up in sex. In our
attempt to assist you in enhancing your sexuality, we
have stressed two factors: the need for determining your
own feelings and desires and acting on them, and the
need for understanding and communicating with
others. Both qualities are needed in sex and the rest
of life. Insofar as we evaluate our situation and make
our own decisions, we are free. Insofar as we understand, consider, and communicate with others, we link
ourselves with the rest of humanity. Sex is far from
everything, but it can be a beginning.

And for all that, it won't be easy. We will bumble
and fall and there will be many misunderstandings,
conflicts and frustrations with those for whom we care
the most. It can't be otherwise since we are struggling
to reach new levels of consciousness and relating while
still being mired in the old ways. Old ways die hard
and new understanding takes time. An example we
have witnessed many times lately is the man who encourages his partner's independence and assertiveness
and then feels angry and betrayed when she becomes
assertive with him. An example from the other side is
the woman who encourages her lover to be more expressive and tender and then gets angry when he isn't
more macho in protecting her from other men or
doesn't "take her" sexually. Such occurrences are and
will be common, and it's going to take a lot of goodwill
and trust and courage to try to deal with them.

We close with a passage from the gentle poet Rainer
Maria Rilke, who not only foresaw many of the
changes we are experiencing today but also predicted
an outcome more realistic and lovelier than any we
know. May his words comfort you as they have comforted us.

*This advance [of women] will (at first much against
the will of the outstripped men) change the love-
experience, which is now full of error, will alter it
from the ground up, reshape it into a relation that*

is meant to be of one human being to another, no longer of man to woman. And this more human love (that will fulfill itself, infinitely considerate and gentle, and kind and clear in binding and releasing) will resemble that which we are preparing with struggle and toil, the love that consists in this, that two solitudes protect and border and salute each other.

Chapter References

Although it is not possible to list all the sources that have been of value in working with men and writing this book, we use this section to list those works that are of particular interest for further reading, and also to document quotations and other information taken directly from other sources.

CHAPTER 1

While the literature on men is not comparable either in quality or quantity to that on women, there are several valuable sources. Two good collections of readings are D. David and R. Brannon, *The Forty-Nine Percent Majority* (Addison-Wesley, 1976), and J. Petras, *Sex:Male/Gender:Masculine* (Alfred, 1975). Several recent surveys of the masculine condition can be recommended: W. Farrell, *The Liberated Man* (Random House, 1974); M. Fasteau, *The Male Machine* (McGraw-Hill, 1974); and H. Goldberg, *The Hazards of Being Male* (Nash, 1976). None of these, however, has improved on the fine work published over a decade ago by Myron Brenton, *The American Male* (Fawcett, 1966).

Page 2:
Some of my early work with men is described in my article, "Group Treatment of Sexual Dysfunction in Men Without Partners," *Journal of Sex & Marital Therapy* 1 (1975): 204–214.

Page 3:
H. Hendin, *The Age of Sensation* (Norton, 1975), p. 2.
"Your Pursuit of Happiness," *Psychology Today* (August 1976), p. 31.

CHAPTER 2

The two workers who have done the most to emphasize and explore the role of learning in human sexuality are John Gagnon and William Simon. Their book, *Sexual Conduct* (Aldine, 1973), is excellent though difficult. A simpler presentation of their views is given in Gagnon's *Human Sexualities* (Scott, Foresman, 1977), the best textbook in the field.

Page 13:
The influence of early learning on the sexuality of adult monkeys was explored in a brilliant series of studies by Harry Harlow, *Learning to Love* (Ballantine, 1971). An interesting study reporting on the initial sexual behavior of monkeys reared in more normal circumstances than Harlow's animals is J. Erwin and G. Mitchell, "Initial Heterosexual Behavior of Adolescent Rhesus Monkeys," *Archives of Sexual Behavior* 4 (1975): 97–104.

Page 13:
Gagnon, *Human Sexualities*, p. 118.

Page 16:
N. Mailer, *The Armies of the Night* (Signet, 1968), p. 36.
J. Lester, "Being a Boy," *Ms.* (July 1973), p. 112.

Page 17:
B. Cosby, "The Regular Way," *Playboy* (December 1968), pp. 288–289.

CHAPTER 3

The fantasy model of sex as described in Chapters 3 and 4 is our own creation. After listening to what hundreds of men said they did and thought about sex, we simply listed the more common beliefs. The original list was changed several times as we checked it against what new clients, students, friends, and other men said. At the same time, we went in search of sources that taught and reinforced these beliefs and were quite astonished to find that they were everywhere.

Some parts of the model have been discussed by writers dealing with one or more of its sources. Among the more valuable works are: J. Atkins, *Sex in Literature* (Grove, 1970); E. and P. Kronhausen, *Pornography and the Law* (Ballantine, 1959), Part 3; G. Legman, *Rationale of the Dirty Joke* (Grove, 1968); S. Marcus, *The Other Victorians* (Basic Books, 1966). A good source of sexual humor is the collection of *Party Jokes* published each year by Playboy Press. The articles entitled "Sex in the Cinema," appearing yearly in *Playboy*, are valuable guides to what the movies are doing to sex.

Two valuable resources for research on sex in literature are

Robert Reisner's *Show Me the Good Parts* (Citadel, 1964) and
Norman Kiell's *Varieties of Sexual Experiences* (International
Universities Press, 1976). Unfortunately, we discovered these
two books only after the manuscript was completed.
Page 24:
M. Goldstein and H. Kant, *Pornography and Sexual Deviance*
(University of California Press, 1973), p. 148.
Pages 24–25:
H. Robbins, *The Betsy* (Pocket Books, 1971), pp. 101–103.
Page 27:
J. Elbert, *The Crazy Ladies* (Signet, 1969), p. 81.
M. Puzo, *The Godfather* (Fawcett, 1969), p. 28.
Page 28:
H. Miller, *Sexus* (Grove, 1965), p. 287.
S. Marcus, *The Other Victorians* (Basic Books, 1966), p. 212.
"Penile Survey Results," *Penthouse Forum* (March 1976), p.
26.
Page 29:
For an account of some of the manipulations used to make
photographed penises appear larger than what they are, see
Ed McCormack's fine article, "Maximum Tumescence in Re-
pose," *Rolling Stone* (October 9, 1975), pp. 56–71.
Page 31:
N. Mailer, *An American Dream* (Dell, 1965), pp. 49 and 51.
D. H. Lawrence, *Lady Chatterley's Lover* (Bantam, 1968), p.
268.
Page 33:
J. Baldwin, *Another Country* (Dell, 1962), pp. 152–153.
H. Miller, *Sexus,* p. 287.
Page 34:
The original description of orgasm experienced as the earth
moving, at least in respectable literature, is found in Ernest
Hemingway's *For Whom the Bell Tolls* (Scribner's, 1940), p.
160. The earth moved for Robert, but his lover Maria ap-
parently got even more out of sex since she died each time.

CHAPTER 4

We did not think it necessary to illustrate every myth with
literary quotations, although there is no shortage of such
quotations. To add them would only have increased the length
of an already long chapter.

Page 42:
H. Miller, *Black Spring* (Grove, 1963), p. 85.
From the Broadway musical *Chicago,* book by Fred Ebb and
Bob Fosse, music by John Kander, lyrics by Fred Ebb.

Page 56:
H. Robbins, *The Inheritors* (Pocket Books, 1969), p. 363.
J. Elbert, *Crazy Ladies*, p. 256.
Page 57:
D. Danziger, *The Devil in Miss Jones* (Grove, 1973), p. 32.
J. and L. Bird, *Sexual Loving* (Doubleday, 1976), pp. 143–144.
Page 58:
N. Mailer, *American Dream*, p. 49.
M. Spillane, *The Last Cop Out* (Signet, 1973), p. 162.
Page 59:
D. H. Lawrence, *Lady Chatterley's Lover*, p. 187.
Page 60:
P. Benchley, *The Deep* (Bantam, 1976), p. 61.
Page 63:
A. Ellis, *Sex and the Liberated Man* (Lyle Stuart, 1976), p. 35.
Emphasis in original.
Page 64:
G. and C. Greene, *S–M: The Last Taboo* (Grove, 1974).
W. Masters and V. Johnson, *Human Sexual Response* (Little, Brown, 1966).
Page 65:
G. Sheehy, *Passages* (Dutton, 1976), pp. 312–313.
Pages 65–66:
H. Goldberg, *The Hazards of Being Male* (Nash, 1976), pp. 42–43.
Page 67:
R. Keyes, *Is There Life After High School?* (Little, Brown, 1976), p. 153.

CHAPTER 6

The concept of conditions has been useful in working with a variety of situations and problems. There are always requirements or conditions which, if met, make it easier for a person to accomplish his goals, whether these involve good sex, meeting others and establishing relationships, doing well in school or at work, or stopping some undesirable behavior such as smoking or drinking.

We were pleasantly surprised to find that even animals other than man have conditions for sex. A fascinating account of this matter is given in H. Hediger's "Environmental Factors Influencing the Reproduction of Zoo Animals," in F. Beach (ed.), *Sex and Behavior* (Wiley, 1965), pp. 319–354. What he calls environmental factors are conditions.

Page 96:
L. Barbach, *For Yourself* (Doubleday, 1975), pp. 43–44.
Page 105:
R. Alberti and M. Emmons, *Your Perfect Right* (Impact, 1974).

H. Fensterheim and J. Baer, *Don't Say Yes When You Want to Say No* (McKay, 1975).

A. Lazarus and A. Fay, *I Can If I Want To* (Morrow, 1975).

CHAPTER 7

Everyone who deals with sexual anatomy and physiology owes a great debt to the research of Masters and Johnson. Their work in this area is reported in the difficult *Human Sexual Response* (Little, Brown, 1966).

Page 111:

Our knowledge of penile activity during sleep and upon awakening is largely due to the work of Charles Fisher and Ismet Karacan. The first article on the subject was by Fisher and his associates, "Cycle of Penile Erection Synchronous with Dreaming (REM) Sleep," *Archives of General Psychiatry* 12 (1965): 29–45. More recent findings are described by Karacan and his colleagues, "Sleep-Related Penile Tumescence as a Function of Age," *American Journal of Psychiatry* 132 (1975): 932–937.

Page 121:

At least three other workers have questioned the utility of Masters and Johnson's four-stage response cycle, but so far their thinking has had little impact in the sex field. Helen Kaplan briefly discusses a biphasic model in *The New Sex Therapy* (Brunner Mazel, 1974), pp. 13–14. More detailed evaluations are offered by Bernard Apfelbaum, "A Critique and Reformulation of Some Basic Assumptions in Sex Therapy," a paper presented to the International Congress of Sexology, Montreal (October 1976), and Irving Singer, *The Goals of Human Sexuality* (Norton, 1973).

A. Kinsey *et al.*, *Sexual Behavior in the Human Female* (Saunders, 1953), p. 594.

Page 129:

Kegel reported on the sexual function of the pelvic muscles in women in "Sexual Functions of the Pubococcygeus Muscle," *Western Journal of Surgery* 60 (1952): 521–524.

CHAPTER 8

While not much has been written about nonsexual touching, there are a few good sources. Ashley Montagu's *Touching* (Perennial Library, 1971) is the best book on the subject. Other useful works are Chapter 10 of Masters and Johnson's *The Pleasure Bond* (Little, Brown, 1974); Desmond Morris's *Intimate Behavior* (Bantam, 1971); and for those interested in touching exercises, Bernard Gunther's *Sense Relaxation* (Collier, 1968), the source of the epigraph on page 131.

Pages 131–132:
Throughout his book, Montagu documents the unfortunate consequences caused by a lack of touching in both animals and humans.

Page 135:
Montagu's quote appears on page 192 of *Touching.*

Page 136:
Masters and Johnson, *The Pleasure Bond,* pp. 236–237.

Page 149:
Masters and Johnson, *The Pleasure Bond,* p. 238.

CHAPTER 9

Kenneth Pelletier's *Mind as Healer, Mind as Slayer* (Delta, 1977) offers good reviews of the role of stress in modern life, theories of stress, and some methods of dealing with tension. Fensterheim and Baer's book, *Don't Say Yes When You Want to Say No* (McKay, 1975), gives instructions for the behavioral approach to relaxation.

CHAPTER 10

Page 160:
A. Kinsey *et al., Sexual Behavior in the Human Male* (Saunders, 1948), p. 479.

Page 161:
M. Hunt, *Sexual Behavior in the 1970s* (Playboy Press, 1974), p. 66.

R. Sorenson, *Adolescent Sexuality in Contemporary America* (World Publishing, 1973), p. 144.

Page 162:
Kinsey, *Sexual Behavior in the Human Male,* p. 513.

The quotation from *What a Boy Should Know* is given in Hunt, *Sexual Behavior in the 1970s,* pp. 69–70.

A good history of attitudes toward masturbation in the last 200 years is given in Alex Comfort's *The Anxiety Makers* (Delta, 1967), which also includes descriptions and illustrations of some of the devices designed to prevent "self-abuse."

Pages 164–165:
Kinsey, *Sexual Behavior in the Human Male,* p. 514.

Page 165:
Masters and Johnson, *Human Sexual Response,* p. 201.

The Vatican proclamation on sex is quoted in the *San Francisco Monitor,* January 15, 1976, p. 2.

Page 166:
D. Reuben, *Everything You Always Wanted to Know about Sex* (Bantam, 1969), pp. 189, 190, and 213. The italics are ours.

Page 168:
Hunt, *Sexual Behavior in the 1970s*, p. 90.

CHAPTER 11

Page 177:
"What's Really Happening on Campus," *Playboy* (October 1976), p. 128.
"Your Pursuit of Happiness," *Psychology Today* (August 1976), p. 31.
Page 178:
Playboy (October 1976), p. 128.
Pages 179–180:
Statistics on age of first intercourse are found in J. Gagnon, *Human Sexualities* (Scott, Foresman, 1977), p. 184; Hunt, *Sexual Behavior in the 1970s*, p. 149; Sorenson, *Adolescent Sexuality in Contemporary America*, p. 190.
Page 181:
E. Gambrill and C. Richey, *It's Up To You* (Les Femmes, 1976). P. Zimbardo, *Shyness* (Addison-Wesley, 1977). Although it does not include material or exercises designed to help readers find partners and combat loneliness, Suzanne Gordon's *Lonely in America* (Simon & Schuster, 1976) presents a marvelous account of being alone and of "the loneliness business."

CHAPTER 12

Although there are numerous books and articles dealing with relationships, many are silly and full of romantic mythology. We seem to know far more about sex than we do about intimacy and what makes a relationship work. Some of the works that have been useful to us in thinking about relationships are: G. Bach and R. Deutsch, *Pairing* (Avon, 1971); J. Bernard, *The Future of Marriage* (Bantam, 1972); W. Lederer and D. Jackson, *The Mirages of Marriage* (Norton, 1968); S. Luthman, *Intimacy* (Nash, 1972); W. Masters and V. Johnson, *The Pleasure Bond;* and L. Rubin, *Worlds of Pain* (Basic, 1976). Rainer Maria Rilke writes briefly though beautifully about aspects of love in his *Letters to a Young Poet* (Norton, 1954).
Page 198:
Very little has been written about male involvement in contraception. Three sources can be recommended: Kristin Luker's excellent book, *Taking Chances* (University of California Press, 1975), and two articles, one by Tom Clark and one by Bernie Zilbergeld, in *The Male Role in Family Planning* (Office of Family Planning, California Department of Health, 1975).

Page 200:
Two studies reporting that male attitudes toward contraception
are influential in the effectiveness of contraception are F. Kane
et al., "Motivating Factors Affecting Contraceptive Use," *American Journal of Obstetrics and Gynecology* 110 (1971): 1050–
1054, and D. McCalister and V. Thiessen, "Prediction in
Family Planning," *American Journal of Public Health* 60
(1970): 1372–1381.

CHAPTER 13

Of the many fine works on female sexuality, the ones that
have been most valuable to us are: Lonnie Barbach, *For Your-
self;* Boston Women's Health Book Collective, *Our Bodies,
Our Selves* (Simon & Schuster, 1971); Germaine Greer, *The
Female Eunuch* (Bantam, 1971); Shere Hite, *The Hite Report*
(Macmillan, 1976); and Leah Schaefer, *Women and Sex*
(Pantheon, 1973).

Page 227:
The Zilbergeld and Stanton survey, not yet published, consisted of questionnaires returned by 426 women ranging in age
from 18 to 63 and in sexual partners from 1 to 250.

Page 241:
Kinsey and Masters and Johnson noted the great sexual similarities between men and women. Kinsey's discussion of these
similarities, in Chapter 15 of the *Female* volume, is a classic
and still worthy of attention.

Page 243:
Greer, *The Female Eunuch,* p. 36.

Page 249:
The clitoral-vaginal controversy is much more complex than
is indicated in the text. It has become difficult to discuss ra-
tionally because, first, of the Freudian premise that vaginal
orgasms are better and more mature than clitoral ones and
second, because some radical feminists have made it a political
issue. Our own thinking, which owes much to work currently
in progress by Carol Rinkleib, is that many, if not most, wom-
en can train themselves to have orgasms with intercourse if
they want to. A number of women·have done this by themselves, while others have had professional help. Whether or not
such training is worthwhile is, of course, something only the
women involved can say.

Page 250:
Hite, *The Hite Report,* p. 135.

Page 252:
E. B. Vance and N. N. Wagner, "Written Descriptions of Or-

gasm: A Study of Sex Differences," *Archives of Sexual Behavior* 5 (1976): 87–98.
Barbach, personal communication.

CHAPTER 14

Page 255:
Kinsey, *Sexual Behavior in the Human Male,* p. 580.
Page 256:
D. Reuben, *How to Get More Out of Sex* (McKay, 1974), pp. 55, 139–140.
"M," *The Sensuous Man* (Dell, 1971), pp. 39–40.
Sheehy, *Passages,* p. 313.
Page 263:
J. Semans, "Premature Ejaculation," *Southern Medical Journal* 49 (1956): 353–358.

CHAPTER 16

The partner exercise format for developing ejaculatory control differs in a number of ways from the work of Semans, cited in Chapter 14, and Masters and Johnson, *Human Sexual Inadequacy* (Little, Brown, 1970), Chapter 3, although we have liberally borrowed many of their ideas and exercises.

The approach that does not use partner exercises gradually evolved as we worked with more and more men who didn't have partners or whose partners refused to participate in treatment. Once developed, this format was frequently chosen by men who had partners but preferred to develop better ejaculatory control on their own.

CHAPTER 17

A recent novel by Romain Gary, *Your Ticket Is No Longer Valid* (Braziller, 1977), portrays well the agony felt by a man who fears that he is becoming impotent. The title itself is of course not without significance.

Page 290:
S. Julty, *Male Sexual Performance* (Grosset & Dunlap, 1975), p. 15.
Page 297:
J. Woods, "Drug Effects on Human Sexual Behavior," in N. Woods, *Human Sexuality in Health and Illness* (Mosby, 1975), p. 183.
Page 298:
P. Roen, *Male Sexual Health* (Morrow, 1974), p. 148.

CHAPTER 19

The method of resolving erection problems without doing partner exercises evolved as we worked with men who didn't have partners with whom they could do exercises. It was later also used by men who had partners but didn't want to do exercises with them. Several hundred men have learned the principles and the overwhelming majority reported that they were able to follow them when with a partner, with the result that their erection problems were either totally or largely resolved.

Masters and Johnson's partner exercise format is reported in Chapter 7 of *Human Sexual Inadequacy*. Our partner exercise approach differs from theirs in a number of ways.

CHAPTER 20

A number of very good books on aging have appeared in the last few years. Two of the best are R. Butler, *Why Survive?* (Harper & Row, 1975), and A. Comfort, *A Good Age* (Crown, 1976). Masters and Johnson's research on the sexual aspects of aging is reported in Chapter 16 of *Human Sexual Response* and Chapter 12 of *Human Sexual Inadequacy*. We have drawn on many of their findings for the discussion in this chapter. Two other good books on sex and aging are R. Butler and M. Lewis, *Sex After Sixty* (Harper & Row, 1976), and I. Rubin, *Sexual Life After Sixty* (Signet, 1965).

Pages 328–329:
J. Lester, "Being a Boy," *Ms.* (July 1973), p. 113.
Page 334:
E. Pfeiffer, "Sex and Aging," in L. Gross (ed.), *Sexual Issues in Marriage* (Spectrum, 1975), pp. 43–49.
Page 335:
Masters and Johnson, *Human Sexual Inadequacy*, p. 326.
Page 340:
J. Jones, *Go to the Widow-Maker* (Dell, 1967), pp. 42–43.

CHAPTER 21

There is not nearly as much good literature as there should be for the man with a medical condition. Although we have only seen a few parts of it, Gay Blackford's *Sex and Disability* (Van Nostrand, in press) looks as if it will do a great deal to remedy this situation. Many health organizations, such as cancer, heart, diabetes, and ostomy associations, distribute pamphlets and articles on sex. A good book for those with spinal cord injuries is T. Mooney *et al.*, *Sexual Options for Paraplegics and Quadriplegics* (Little, Brown, 1975).

Pages 353–354:
We, as well as several colleagues at the Human Sexuality Program, University of California School of Medicine, San Francisco, have worked successfully with men with many different types of disabilities—long-term alcoholism, diabetes, several types of cancer, cerebral palsy, heart disease, multiple sclerosis, ostomy, prostatectomy, and spinal cord injury.

CHAPTER 22

Page 356:
E. Fromm, *Man for Himself* (Rinehart, 1947), p. 184.
Page 365:
A. Comfort, *The Joy of Sex* (Crown, 1972), pp. 9 and 51.
H. Hendin, *The Age of Sensation* (Norton, 1975), p. 325.
Page 366:
G. Curtis, "The New Facts of Life," *Texas Monthly* (March 1976), p. 102.
J. Gagnon and W. Simon, quoted in E. Kennedy, *The New Sexuality* (Image, 1972), p. 43.
Page 369:
H. Hendin, *The Age of Sensation*, p. 336.

CHAPTER 23

Pages 385–386:
R. Rilke, *Letters to a Young Poet* (Norton, 1954), p. 59.

Index

A

abstinence, 63, 183–87

adequacy: fantasy model of sex and, 33, 34; readiness to have sex and, 46–47; sex in proof of, 360

adolescence, 110, 327–30

affection: aging process and, 340; as behavior leading to sex, 48–49; pain in intercourse and, 57; sex as proof of, 133–34, 361–64; women's view of, 230–31

Afrodex pills, 300

afterplay, 232, 250–51

Age of Sensation, The (Hendin), 3

aggression, 49, 57, 58, 95

aging: erection problems and, 292–93; male sexuality and, 7, 326–43; reaction to, 331, 332; testosterone and, 298

Albolene, 175

alcohol and alcoholism, 82, 88, 150, 345, 348

American Dream (Mailer), 31, 58

anal intercourse: in literature, 31; partner's objections to, 223; as proof of love, 363

androgen, 241, 298

androgyny, 383

anger: arousal and, 82; erection problems and, 72–73; resolution period and, 127

animal sexuality, 12, 13

Another Country (Baldwin), 33

anxiety, 150, 151; adolescent, 330; arousal and, 81, 82; expressing, 153–54; goal orientation and, 42, 43; learning about sex and, 15; penis and, 89; sexual behavior and, 39

aphrodisiacs, 297

arousal: aging process and, 334; definition of, 80; ejaculatory control and, 265–67; erection distinguished from, 111–12; erection problems and, 27; feelings and, 39; female, 252; force of will and, 83; learning and, 13–14; myths on, 54–55; nervous system and, 81–83; penis and lack of, 89; tension and, 150–52

ABOUT THE AUTHOR

Born in New Jersey, Bernie Zilbergeld graduated from Ohio University and received his Ph.D. in clinical psychology from the University of California, Berkeley, in 1973. Formerly, he headed the Men's Program and was co-director of clinical training at the Human Sexuality Program, University of California, San Francisco. There he developed many successful group and individual treatment formats for men; worked with many men who had not had any specific sexual problems but who wanted to enhance their sexual functioning and enjoyment; and organized and conducted many workshops for men to explore such topics as male sex roles and family planning. Presently, Dr. Zilbergeld is in private practice in Oakland, specializing in sex and marital therapy. He lectures frequently, and appears often in national media. His latest book, *Mind Power* (with Arnold A. Lazarus), was published in 1987, and he is currently at work on a new book about male sexuality.

We Deliver!
And So Do These Bestsellers.

Bantam
On Psychology

LWA